READY-TO-TEACH

CRAFTS ACTIVITIES

FOR THE ELEMENTARY SCHOOL

READY-TO-TEACH
CRAFTS ACTIVITIES
FOR THE ELEMENTARY SCHOOL

by **Carrie Romine**

illustrated with

drawings by **Sharon Wilson**

photographs by **Jerry Gildemeister**

PARKER PUBLISHING COMPANY, INC.   West Nyack, N.Y.

Library of Congress Cataloging in Publication Data

Romine, Carrie,
  Ready-to-teach crafts activities for the elementary
school.

   1. Creative activities and seat work. I. Title.
LB1537.R594   372.5   74-23220
ISBN 0-13-762245-7

A WORD FROM THE AUTHOR

During my many years as an art teacher I looked constantly for good books on teaching crafts to children. I often found that even the best ones required lots of advance preparation and were suitable only for certain age levels of children. Finally I decided to develop craft ideas that would be used to teach practically all ages, and were immediately "ready to teach." This book is the result, a book of workable ideas, using materials found in nearly every home.

These are projects you can teach quickly and easily to children in all elementary grades, even to kindargarteners and older pre-schoolers, including the most "unskilled." There are all kinds of useful and ornamental articles your pupils can put together with pride of accomplishment. They will produce amusing animal figures that can be taken home to serve as shelf or desk ornaments, educational games that will teach new skills as they are played, decorative baskets and colorful pencil holders, pictures and pincushions. Your boys and girls will make gifts that turn out so well everyone who receives them will be pleased. Any child can make a bookmarker, and here are a number of new and different ideas, all ready to take into your class, for bookmarkers that can be made of very inexpensive materials. There are unusual wall hangings and picture frames, flower holders and paperweights. In the very front of the book, you'll find a special section called "A Craft Teacher's Bag of Tricks" which contains many shortcuts and helpful tips that I have picked up in my years of craft teaching.

For special days like Halloween and Christmas, and for all four seasons, there are suitable, quickly started and completed projects your pupils will enjoy. You'll discover ways to help children plan their own parties, with timesaving and moneysaving party favors.

The instructions are easy to follow and to present to children. For each activity, a photograph shows you what the finished product looks like. All the materials needed are listed and you can see clearly how each article is to be put together, step by step. You'll have as much fun teaching your children to make the articles in this book as your children will have making them.

Another special section at the back of the book is a *Portfolio of Instant Tracing Patterns*. These make it easy for you to trace a "master pattern" and then duplicate copies for all your pupils, or you can have the boys and girls trace their own. These same patterns, in small size, are included among the directions, so you can see just where each one is to be used. A few patterns are not in the Portfolio because they can be drawn simply by measurement with a ruler. You'll find the Portfolio a very useful tool that makes these activities truly "ready-to-teach"!

This book is for all classroom teachers, and for everyone else who leads a group of children in developing craft skills, whether at scout camp, in Bible School, in special education classes or at home.

I gratefully acknowledge the help of many who contributed ideas for activities, including Shelly Romine, for the Santa Bank, Petra Urbansky, for Hermie the Hairy Book Marker, Nina Reed, for the Milk Carton Flower Holder, Lynn Ann Harrod, for the Praying Silhouettes, James Romine, for the Key Holder on a Wooden Square, and Zim's, Inc. for the "It" Bank.

Carrie Romine

LIST OF MATERIALS AND WHERE TO FIND THEM

All of the following materials can be found in 5 & 10¢ stores, hobby stores, and any place where craft materials are sold.

bell caps
beads
cat eyes
chenille pipe cleaners
Easter grass (in season)
Elmer's glue
moving eyes
feathers
floral tape
glitter
glitter pens
hats
jump rings
liquid glass glue
magnets
metal eyelets
white fringe
narrow ribbon

necklace chains
padlocks
paper fasteners
pearl beads
plastic bracelets
plastic greenery
Popsicle sticks or craft sticks
sequins
small Nativity scenes (at Christmas)
spray paint
styrofoam balls—eggs and circles
cotton
fake fur
feet
net
Pellon
rick-rack

These articles are found in grocery stores:

Curly Kate's pot scrubber
spring clothes pins
felt marker pens
macaroni shells and wheels
macaroni alphabet letters

If you need a large supply of materials check for a wholesale, or retail craft house in the area in which you live.

These two companies have a catalog at 50¢ each.

Zims
240 East 2nd South
Salt Lake City, Utah

or

Utah Crafts
3216 South State
Salt Lake City, Utah 84115

or

Lee Wards (no charge)
Box 206
Elgin, Illinois 60120

Builder's supply houses or lumber yards will have these materials:

picture moulding
plaster of Paris
staple gun
wooden dowels

Plastic flowers can be very expensive, and so can styrofoam. If you can find these materials cheaper or for free, your cost of crafts will be kept low.

Have you ever thought of a cemetery as a place where craft materials may be found? Here in my home town, I receive plastic flowers and flower pots, styrofoam blocks, ribbon by the yard, and lots of florist pins from our local cemetery.

If these are left at the cemetery, they are tossed out and burned. So, tell the caretaker what you need.

Flowers can be washed and dried and they look like new. Ribbon can be washed and ironed and used again.

NOTE ABOUT STORAGE OF YOUR MATERIALS

You may be concerned about where to store all of the materials that are needed for these projects. I would suggest that you go through the book and pick out all the projects you first want to have the children make. Break them down into groups for each month. Note what materials are needed for all the projects for that month. Most materials are things that are thrown away in most homes.

Each month, get all the things together that are needed for the projects. Make up lists of needed scrap materials and send them home with the children. Parents will generally be glad to help, and the lists will get them interested.

Each month, make up one of each project to show your children what it will look like when it is finished. Keep the finished article on display while the children are working on their own articles.

HELPFUL HINTS FROM A CRAFT TEACHER'S BAG OF TRICKS

*These hints will save you many hours
of work and wasted materials*

Hint No. 1: How to Make Plastic Poofs

Materials Needed: 1 cleaner bag, string or heavy thread, 1 chenille pipe cleaner, scissors

Directions for making:

STEP 1: Buy the needed amount of plastic clothes bags. If there are any bags in the closet, leave them there as they get dirty so fast and will look grey.

STEP 2: Cut bags even on the perforated end as it is easier than trying to open the perforation.

STEP 3: Fold the bag in the middle, cut in two. This makes two pieces of plastic about 15 inches long.

STEP 4: Open bag, insert hands into the bag and gather. Hold firmly in both hands.

STEP 5: Make a figure eight and bring the plastic together in both hands. This makes a circle. Keeping plastic smooth, make another figure eight. Be sure to keep plastic smooth.

STEP 6: Tie at one end, using string or heavy thread. Tie at opposite end and then tie two more pieces of thread so the circle will be in fourths.

STEP 7: Cut the chenille pipe cleaner into five pieces. Bend four pieces of pipe cleaner into a hair pin shape.

STEP 8: Put a chenille hair pin onto each tied place on the plastic bag.

STEP 9: Using sharp scissors, cut in the center of each tied place and this is the plastic poof. To make poofs fuller, brush across the hand. If some place remains bunched, pull apart and brush across hand again. These poofs are used to make the Christmas Canes and poof Easter baskets.

Step 3   fold and cut

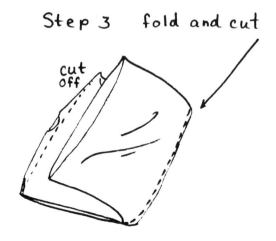

cut

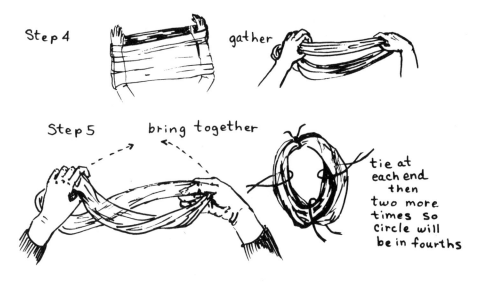

Step 4 gather

Step 5 bring together

tie at each end then two more times so circle will be in fourths

Step 9

cut in center of each tied place

Hint No. 2: How to Make a Plaster Cast

STEP 1.   Wash the plastic or rubber mold to be used in warm, soapy water; rinse with clear water. Start with a clean mold.

STEP 2:   Have a frame or support for the mold so it will sit flat.

STEP 3.   Mix the plaster and water together. A good way to measure a small mold is to fill the mold with water, then pour the water into a container and mix plaster into it, until it forms a thick cream consistency. Do not beat, as this will form bubbles.

STEP 4.   Be sure mold is wet inside before filling it with plaster. Use a small amount of mixing plaster, put in mold, and use fingers to fill up the tiny lines and details. Finish filling mold, bump mold with the plaster gently on the table to remove any air bubbles.

STEP 5.   Add a hairpin hanger, where it is needed. To make a hanger, bend both legs of the hairpin open, insert legs in plaster at top of the mold. Hairpins are painted so they do not rust. Let set until plaster hardens. To remove cast, pull the mold from the cast, smooth off any excess plaster and set aside to dry—three or four days. Smaller casts will take less time.

Hint No. 3: How to Paint a Plaster Cast

Be sure plaster cast is dry. Spray over all with white paint, back and forth.

Airplane dope is good for painting. It comes in many colors and dries fast. Use the color paint wanted. Fill in design. Be sure one color of paint is dry before using another color. One way to paint a cast is to use a metallic color spray to cover the cast; then highlight with black outlines.

Hint No. 4: How to Cut Fake Fur

Turn the fur side to the table, measure and draw pattern on cloth side. Use very sharp scissors with pointed ends; and using small snips, cut the material apart. Pull the fur apart. This leaves the fur very long.

Hint No. 5: How to Refresh Artificial Flowers

You can often buy plastic flowers cheaply because they have become grimy or faded. To clean flowers, wash in a sink full of hot, soapy water, using any good dish washing detergent. Dunk the flowers up and down until they are clean. Rinse with clear, warm water. Dry thoroughly. If the flowers are still badly faded, spray with either gold, or copper or silver paint.

Hint No. 6: How to Cut Plastic Bottles
and Bleach Jugs

Remove the labels and any glue left on the plastic. Scrape the glue with a sharp knife, wash in hot, soapy water, rinse with clear warm water and dry. Measure and draw the pattern onto the bottle or jug using a felt tip marker pen. Use a very sharp knife or scissors to cut.

Hint No. 7: How to Cut Styrofoam

Cut a pattern from paper, fasten to the foam with straight pins. Draw around pattern with a sharp pencil or felt marker pen. Use a sharp serrated edge knife, and cut with short sawing motions or use a Styrofoam cutter.

Hint No. 8: How to Use Spray Paint

Work in an open room with good ventilation (never in a closed area). Shake the can well. Hold the nozzle 10 to 12 inches from the object to be sprayed. Do not touch until dry.

CONTENTS

Chapter Five: Beautiful and Simple to Make Decorations • 64

Chapter Six: Easily Made Gifts for Family and Friends • 77

Chapter Seven: Lovely Creations for the Holidays • 90

Chapter Eight: Keepsake Jewelry and Holders • 104

Chapter Nine: Appealing Party Favors and Centerpieces • 118

Chapter Ten: Fancy Pencil Holders • 135

Chapter Eleven: Captivating Pictures • 149

Chapter Twelve: Inventing Picture Frames • 166

Chapter Thirteen: Clever Pin Cushions and Refrigerator Decorations • 176

Chapter Fourteen: Pin on Purses • 189

Chapter Fifteen: Bonus Ideas • 196

Chapter One

Kookie Animals for Play or Decoration

The children in our class love to make ridiculous-looking beasts out of odds and ends. These funny creatures can be put together quickly and easily, and they are made of materials readily available. They will look particularly cute if you make them with the plastic moving eyes which can be bought at craft stores, (see p. 4) but you can make eyes out of circles of white cloth and colored buttons if necessary.

ACTIVITY 1-1: Egg Carton Caterpillars

Materials Needed:

- 1 plastic egg carton, green
- 1 fibre egg carton
- 4 moving eyes, 1/4 inch size
- 8 chenille pipe cleaners
- glitter
- red felt scrap
- tiny hats or flowers
- scissors
- glue
- ice pick

Directions for Making:

STEP 1:   Remove the lid and hinge from the plastic egg carton. (See Fig. 1-1A.)

STEP 2:   Separate the egg cups by cutting down the center of the carton. There will be 6 cups on either side. (See Fig. 1-1B.)

STEP 3:   Set the cut side of the egg carton on top of the smooth side of the carton. Draw around the bumps. Use sharp scissors and cut to match the circles on other side.

STEP 4:   Using an ice pick or sharp pointed scissors, punch holes at the top of each bump. (See Fig 1-1C.)

STEP 5:   Measure the pipe cleaners and cut in half.

STEP 6:   Poke the pipe cleaners through both holes and bend a foot shape at both ends.

STEP 7:   Cover the round circles on top of the egg cartons with glue and add glitter. (See Fig. 1-1D.)

STEP 8:   Punch 2 holes at the front end of the carton 1 inch apart and insert pipe cleaner. (See Fig. 1-1E.) Curve the end for feelers.

STEP 9:   Glue on moving eyes.

STEP 10: To make a nose, cut 1 inch from one of the tall peaks in a fibre egg carton, Pattern C. Paint green, or roll in glue and cover with silver glitter. Let dry.

STEP 11: To make the nose stay on, cut a piece of pipe cleaner, 3 inches long. Bend in the middle. Add glue into the center of the cut-off fibre egg carton, and add the pipe cleaner inside. Let dry.

STEP 12: Punch two holes in plastic egg carton, 1/2 inch apart, halfway up the cup. Push the pipe cleaners through these holes and twist together on underside.

STEP 13: Cut a round circle from red felt, Pattern B, and glue to the end of the nose.

STEP 14: Cut 2 mouths using Pattern A. Glue one on each side of the nose.

STEP 15: Glue a tiny hat or flower to the head.

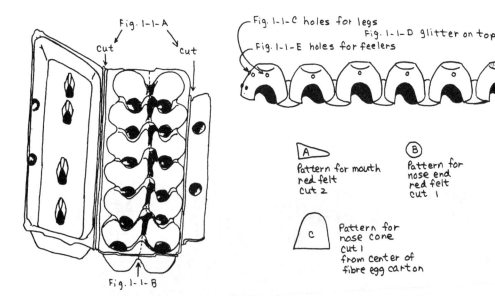

Fig. 1-1-A
cut   cut

Fig. 1-1-B

Fig. 1-1-C holes for legs
Fig. 1-1-D glitter on top
Fig. 1-1-E holes for feelers

A
Pattern for mouth
red felt
cut 2

B
Pattern for
nose end
red felt
cut 1

C
Pattern for
nose cone
cut 1
from center of
fibre egg carton

ACTIVITY 1-2: Gus and Gertrude, The Styrofoam Mice

Materials Needed:

- 1 Styrofoam egg, 3 inches long
- 1 Styrofoam egg, 2-1/2 inches long
- 4 bumps pink chenille, 3 inches long
- 4 tiny moving eyes, 3/16 inch size
- red felt scrap
- toothpaste cap
- bright colored feather
- 2 pink chenille pipe cleaners, 12 inches long
- scissors
- serrated edge knife

Directions for Making:

STEP 1:   Cut a thin slice from one side of the Styrofoam eggs. (See Fig. 1-2A.)

STEP 2:   Set the egg flat and glue the eyes and nose in place at the largest end.

STEP 3:   Cut the three inch bump of pink chinelle apart and bend each bump in the middle and insert the ends into the front end of the mice over the eyes; these are the ears.

STEP 4:   Cut a piece of chenille pipe cleaner 5 inches long. Poke one end into the large end of the egg for a tail. Curl the end up over the back of the mice. (See Fig. 1-2B.)

STEP 5:   Cut 4 pieces of pipe cleaner, 2 inches long. These are the whiskers and should be the same color as the tail.

STEP 6:   Punch one end of the 4 pieces of chenille pipe cleaners into the egg as close to the nose as possible for whiskers. (See Fig. 1-2C.)

STEP 7:   To make the girl mouse, push the stem of a small flower between the ears and tie a small ribbon bow around the tail at the end. A tiny umbrella may be added over the flower.

STEP 8:   For the boy mouse, make a tiny hat from a toothpaste cap, add a bright colored feather to one side and glue hat in between the ears. The boy mouse should be on the three inch egg, and the girl on the 2-1/2 inch egg.

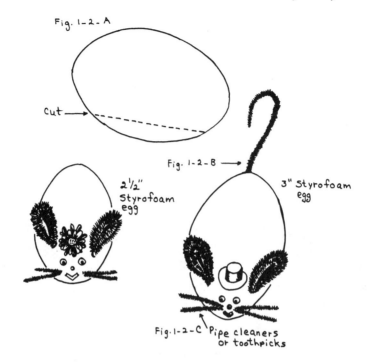

Fig. 1-2-A

cut →

Fig. 1-2-B →

2½"
Styrofoam
egg

3" Styrofoam
egg

Fig. 1-2-C Pipe cleaners
or toothpicks

ACTIVITY 1-3: Pop Bottle Pussycats

Materials Needed:

- 1 empty *7UP* or other pop bottle
- One 3 inch Styrofoam ball
- 2 green cat eyes, 1/2 inch size
- scrap of red felt
- gold Styrofoam spray paint
- black felt, 6 X 8 inches
- green ribbon, 5/8 inch X 20 inches
- 6 pointed toothpicks
- 1 large fluffy chenille stick
- baby rick rack, red, 12 inches
- scissors
- glue

Directions for Making:

STEP 1: Remove the label, wash and dry the empty pop bottle.

STEP 2: Force the 3 inch Styrofoam ball onto the top of the bottle, using a twisting motion.

STEP 3: Remove the ball, fill the rim that has been cut into the Styrofoam ball with small amount of glue and set the ball on the bottle again. Set aside to dry for one hour or more.

STEP 4: Using the gold spray paint, cover the entire bottle and ball. Let dry.

STEP 5: Cut a strip of black felt, using Pattern A. Glue a strip of baby rick rack across the top and bottom of this piece. Decorate with jewels or sequins. Glue this under the head, around the neck of the bottle. (See Fig. 1-3A).

STEP 6: Cut nose from black felt, Pattern F. Cut tongue (Pattern D) from red felt. Glue in place.

STEP 7: Glue on glass cat eyes, or use moving eyes and cut eye-lashes from black felt using Pattern E.

STEP 8: Cut legs from black felt (Pattern C). Glue onto the bottle at the bottom front.

STEP 9: Using the fluffy chenille stick, turn the bottle halfway around and glue to the bottle on the back side, at the bottom for a tail. Hold for a few minutes till glue sets.

STEP 10: Curl the tail in an arc over the head or curl around the legs in front.

STEP 11: To make a girl cat, pin a ribbon bow between the ears. For a boy, glue on a hat with a feather.

STEP 12: On each side of the cat's nose, stick 3 toothpicks for whiskers.

STEP 13: Cut the ears (Pattern B) from black felt. To make the ears stand up, fold each side of the felt in to the middle 1/8 inch. Glue and pin in place.

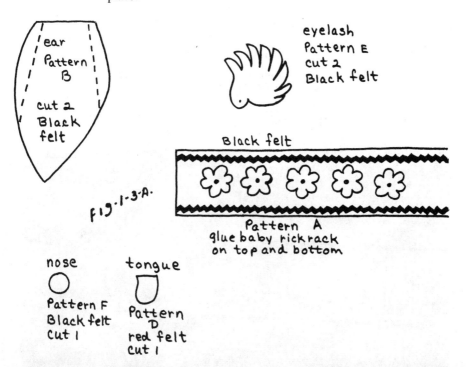

ear Pattern B cut 2 Black felt

eyelash Pattern E cut 2 Black felt

Fig. 1-3-A.

Black felt

Pattern A glue baby rickrack on top and bottom

nose Pattern F Black felt Cut 1

tongue Pattern D red felt cut 1

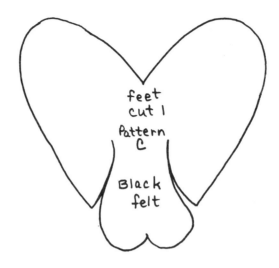

feet
cut 1
Pattern
C

Black
felt

ACTIVITY 1-4: Yarn Ball Kittens

Materials Needed:

- 1 Styrofoam ball, 3 inch diameter
- 6 feet of yarn, any color
- 2 black chenille pipe cleaners
- 2 moving eyes, 1/2 inch size
- ribbon for hair and bow tie, 1/4 or 1/2 inch size
- piece of red felt, 1 X 1 inch
- 6 toothpicks
- glue
- scissors

Directions for Making:

STEP 1:   Wind the yarn, any color, around the Styrofoam ball, using enough
          to cover the ball. Glue the end of the yarn.
STEP 2:   Glue on moving eyes.
STEP 3:   Cut a felt nose and mouth. Glue them in place.

STEP 4:   Cut one black chenille pipe cleaner into 4 two-inch pieces. Bend into a V shape.

STEP 5:   Turn with point up and stick ends into the head for ears.

STEP 6:   For feet, stick two pieces of pipe cleaner at the bottom of the ball.

STEP 7:   Leave one chenille pipe cleaner 6 inches long, insert one end into the back of the ball, down low, and curve up over back of the head. This is the tail.

STEP 8:   Tie a ribbon bow on the kitty's tail.

STEP 9:   On each side of the kitty's nose, stick 3 pointed toothpicks.

ACTIVITY 1-5: Amusing Chenille Spiders

Materials Needed:

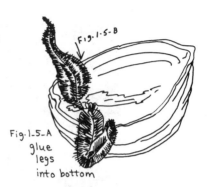

Fig. 1-5-B

Fig. 1-5-A
glue
legs
into bottom

- 1/2 large walnut shell
- 9 bumps of brown chenille, 3 inches long
- 2 moving eyes, 1/4 inch
- 1 small feather or ribbon bow
- green sequins or glitter
- 1 piece of Styrofoam, 5 X 5 X 1/2 inch
- 1 toothpaste cap or small hat
- glue
- scissors

Directions for Making:

STEP 1:   Cut the chenille into 4 three-inch bumps. There will be one extra bump.

STEP 2:   Cover the 1/2 walnut shell with glue and roll in glitter, or cover the outside with green sequins glued on. Let dry completely.

STEP 3:   Turn the shell upside down, so the hole is on top. Put a small amount of glue across the bottom of the shell.

STEP 4:   To make the legs, take each piece of the chenille with 2 bumps, bend enough in the center so it will fit down inside the shell and into the glue. Put one at the front end of the shell, one at the back end and put two in the center. (See Fig. 1-5A.)

STEP 5:   Push the chenille into the glue and hold for a minute or two until the glue sets up. Using the remaining bump, fold it in half. Put a lot of glue over the legs in the shell and push the last bump into the shell. Hold for a few minutes until the glue sets. Let dry.

STEP 6:   Make the legs bow out at the top, as they come out of the shell (see Fig. 1-5B) and fold the end into a foot.

STEP 7:   Add two small moving eyes at the wide end of the shell. Glue on a ribbon bow at the center top for a girl spider. For a boy spider, glue a toothpaste cap hat with a feather.

ACTIVITY 1-6: Ossie, The Chenille Octopus

Materials Needed:

- 3 pieces of chenille with 4 one-inch bumps, any color
- 1 Styrofoam ball, 2 inches diameter
- 2 moving eyes, 1/4 inch size
- 1 small hat
- 4 inch piece of pipe cleaner
- glue
- scissors

Directions for Making:

STEP 1:   Cut the three pieces of chenille. Be sure there are 4 one-inch bumps on each one. Lay the chenille on the table. (See Fig. 1-6A.)

STEP 2:   Between the second and third bump on each one, spread glue. (See Fig. 1-6B.)

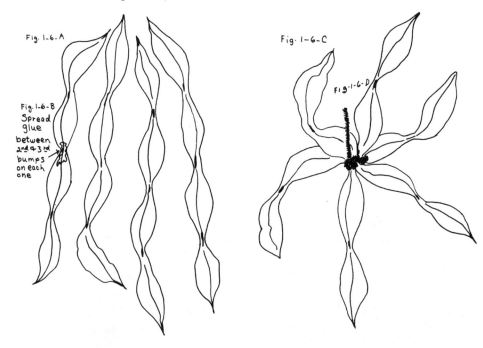

Fig. 1-6-A

Fig. 1-6-B
Spread
glue
between
2nd & 3rd
bumps
on each
one

Fig. 1-6-C

Fig. 1-6-D

STEP 3: Lay the chenille pieces one on top of the other, using the four-inch piece of pipe cleaner for a tie wire; twist it around the middle of the chenille pieces leaving one end extending up an inch and a half. (See Fig. 1-6C.)

STEP 4: Onto this pipe cleaner, force the two-inch styrofoam ball. (See Fig. 1-6D.)

STEP 5: Glue the moving eyes onto the ball. Add a small hat at the tip of one leg for the boy. For a girl add a ribbon bow or flowers on the head.

STEP 6: Twist legs in different directions.

ACTIVITY 1-7: Max, The Cotton Ball Muskrat

Materials Needed:

- 30 feet of 4 ply yarn, white
- black felt, 2 X 4 inches
- 1 inch magnet (optional)
- 2 moving eyes, 3/16 inch
- scrap of red felt for nose
- 6 inches of heavy black thread for whiskers
- patterns
- scissors
- glue
- 1 piece of black pipe cleaner, 4 inches long

Directions for Making:

STEP 1: Make a cotton ball.

STEP 2: Trace patterns and cut out.

STEP 3: Cut feet, 2 ears and 1 face from black felt.

STEP 4: Lay the feet on the table, put glue onto an inch of one end of chenille pipe cleaner. Lay it in the middle of the black felt feet. This is the tail. (See Fig. 1-7A.)

STEP 5: Cut off the piece of the yarn and add glue to the cotton ball and place on the feet, toward the back end, leaving the feet sticking out in front. (See Fig. 1-7B.)

STEP 6: Lay the face on the table; glue the eyes in place. Glue on the whiskers with the nose over them.

STEP 7: Glue the face in place on front end of cotton ball.

STEP 8: Put a line of glue on each ear, 1/4 inch long, on the small end. Squeeze together and hold until glue sets.

STEP 9: Make a hole in the cotton ball with pencil end or sharp scissors and put glue on small end of ears. Push down into the cotton ball.

STEP 10: On the bottom of the rat, add the magnet (optional). It will set on anything made of metal.

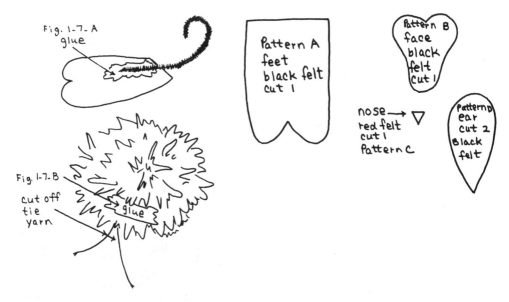

Fig. 1-7-A
glue

Pattern A
feet
black felt
cut 1

Pattern B
face
black
felt
cut 1

nose →
red felt
cut 1
Pattern C

Pattern D
ear
cut 2
Black
felt

Fig. 1-7-B
cut off
tie
yarn

glue

ACTIVITY 1-8: Priscilla and Patrick, the Cotton Ball Bunnies

Materials Needed:

- 2 cotton balls, 3 inch size
- pink felt, 2 X 4 inches
- 4 three-inch pieces pink bump chenille
- 4 moving eyes
- 2 cotton balls for tails, 3/4 inch
- 1 boy's hat or toothpaste cap and bright colored feather
- 1 girl's hat or flower
- scissors
- glue
- magnetic strip, 2 inches

Directions for Making:

STEP 1:   Make the cotton balls.

STEP 2: Trace patterns and cut out. Cut a pair of noses and two pairs of feet.

STEP 3: Lay the feet on the table, put glue on bottom of cotton balls and set in the center of the feet, letting the feet stick out a little in front of balls.

STEP 4: Glue the noses onto the front of the balls.

STEP 5: To make the ears, bend the three-inch pieces of bump chenille in half. Put glue on the ends and insert into the cotton balls, one on each side of the face. (See Fig. 1-8A.)

STEP 6: Glue a 3/4 inch cotton ball on back of large cotton ball for a tail.

STEP 7: A piece of magnetic strip one inch long may be stuck to the bottom of each rabbit so they will stick to the refrigerator or any metal surface (optional).

STEP 8: Make a tiny hat for the boy rabbit using a toothpaste cap with a feather glued to one side. A tiny flower may be glued between the ears for a girl rabbit.

nose
cut 1
for each
rabbit

pink
felt

Fig. 1-8-A make bump
chenille ears

ACTIVITY 1-9: Harry and Harriet, the Fake Fur Goons

Materials Needed:

(Harriet)

- 2 moving eyes, 3/4 inch size
- 4 straight pins
- fake fur, 6 X 8 inches
- black felt, 3 X 6 inches
- 1 paper drinking cup, Sweetheart Best Point No. C-210 or tackboard, 6 X 11 inches
- 1 sheet typing paper
- light cardboard, 4 X 4 inches
- scissors
- glue

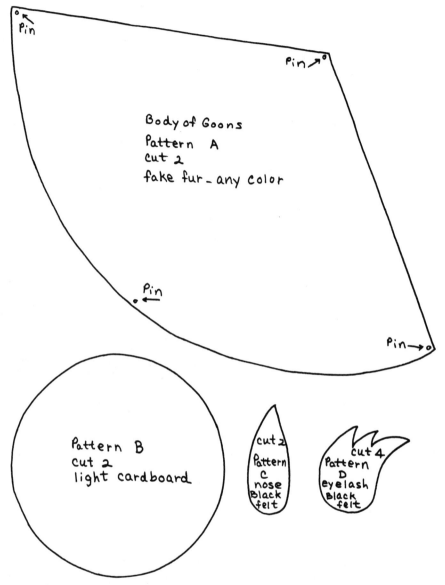

Directions for Making:

STEP 1:   Lay the piece of typing paper over the patterns in the book. Trace and cut out.

STEP 2:   Lay Pattern A on the back of the fake fur. Pin in four places indicated. Using sharp scissors, cut out. (Follow directions for cutting in Hints, No. 4.)

STEP 3:   Put glue around the cup. Smooth the fake fur on. Set aside to dry.

STEP 4:   Comb the hair smooth.

STEP 5:   Glue the eyelashes and nose in place. Add the moving eyes onto the lashes.

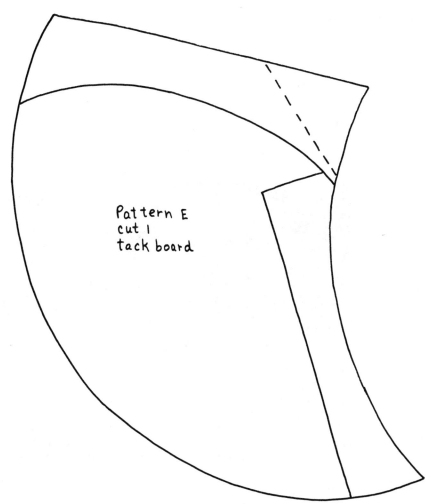

Pattern E
cut 1
tack board

STEP 6:   Tie a contrasting ribbon at the top for Harriet.

STEP 7:   (Optional) To make the goons more sturdy, cut a 4 inch circle of lightweight cardboard and glue to the bottom of the cup.

(Harry)

Materials needed for Harry are the same as for Harriet with the exception of a small hat with a feather.

Make the eyelashes from the same pattern, but turn the eyelash upside down and glue onto fur.

If the Sweetheart cups are not available, make a cone for the Fake Fur Goons as follows:

STEP 1:   Cut a piece of lightest weight tack board available 6 X 11 inches.

STEP 2:   Draw patterns from book on a piece of typing paper. Cut out pattern, draw onto the tack board and cut out.

STEP 3:   Cover the side with glue. Roll into a cone shape, hold cone until glue has set up, and finish the goon as described above.

ACTIVITY 1-10: Tommy, the Walnut-Shell Paper Weight Turtle

Materials Needed:

- 1 piece green felt, 3 X 4-1/2 inches
- 1 lid from a plastic egg carton
- 1/2 walnut shell
- multi-colored glitter
- 2 tablespoons plaster of Paris
- 1 tablespoon water
- glue
- scissors

Directions for Making:

STEP 1:   Open the walnut shell by inserting the end of a knife into the wide end of the shell and gently pry it open.

STEP 2:   Mix the plaster of Paris to thick cream consistency. Fill the open side of the walnut shell to the top rim of the shell. Set aside to harden.

STEP 3:   Draw the pattern for the turtle from the book, Pattern A. Cut out. Pin pattern to the green felt; cut out. Glue the felt turtle to the egg carton lid on the side with the writing on it. Let dry. (See Fig. 1-10A.)

STEP 4:   Cut the felt turtle from the egg carton lid.

STEP 5:   Cover the outside of the walnut shell with glue and roll in multi-colored glitter. Let dry.

STEP 6:   Glue the shell onto the middle of the felt turtle. Add the moving eyes onto the turtle head. (See Fig. 1-10B.)

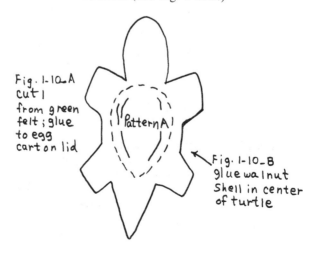

Fig. 1-10-A
cut 1
from green
felt; glue
to egg
carton lid

Pattern A

Fig. 1-10-B
glue walnut
Shell in center
of turtle

ACTIVITY 1-11: Horatio, the Turtle Memo Pad Holder

Materials Needed:

- green foam, 5 X 14 inches
- 2 moving eyes, 1/2 inch
- ribbon 1/2 X 6 inches
- green sequins
- tack board, 5 X 11 inches
- memo pad, 2-1/2 X 3-1/2 inches
- straight scissors
- pinking scissors
- glue

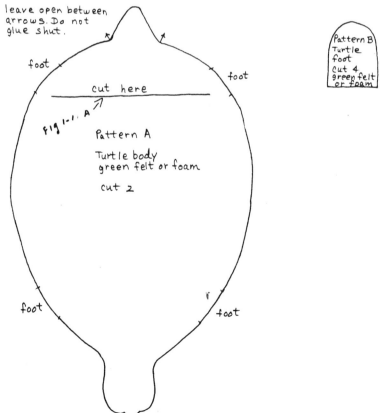

leave open between arrows. Do not glue shut.

foot

foot

cut here

Fig 1-11 A

Pattern A

Turtle body
green felt or foam

cut 2

foot

foot

Pattern B
Turtle
foot
Cut 4
green felt
or foam

Directions for Making:

STEP 1:   Lay a piece of typing paper over Pattern A, trace and cut out.
STEP 2:   Pin the pattern to the green foam; cut the body with pinking scissors; the feet, head and tail with straight scissors.
STEP 3:   Cut the line (see Fig. 1-11A) on one body to hold memo pad.
STEP 4:   Cut a piece of ribbon 6 inches long, fold in half and glue in place between the tails for a hanger.
STEP 5:   Lay the feet in place on the bottom body and glue on. Put glue around the edge of the top body, press together. Do not glue the tails as they are the pencil holder.
STEP 6:   Add the moving eyes and the memo pad in place.
STEP 7:   Cut a body from cardboard using straight scissors and Pattern A. Glue the foam body to it.
STEP 8:   Glue green sequins around the edge of the turtle on the foam side.
STEP 9:   Stick the pencil down between the 2 foam tails.
STEP 10:   Hang near the telephone.

Chapter Two

Little Coin Banks for Little Savers

Children learn the value of thrift as they work on these amusing little coin banks. The children in our special class especially like the soft but sturdy "It" bank, and describe their hopes of filling the bank as they work on it.

ACTIVITY 2-1: Him and Her "It" Banks

Materials Needed:

- 2 Junior size baby food jars
- 4 moving eyes, 3/8 inch size
- 2 pairs plastic glasses
- 1 hat for boy, 1 for girl
- 2 pieces fake fur, your color choice, 4 X 9 inches
- black felt, 5 X 10 inches
- 2 cotton balls or small red Christmas ornaments for noses
- piece of cardboard, 5 X 10 inches
- feather for hat for boy
- glue
- scissors

Directions for Making:

STEP 1:   Remove labels, wash and dry baby food jars.

STEP 2:   Set jar upside down with the metal lid to the table.

STEP 3:   Cut 4 or 5 V shaped notches in the top of the fake fur (See Fig. 2-1A.)

STEP 4:   Put glue over the bottom and sides of the jar.

STEP 5:   Wrap fur around the jar, closing the V notches at the top. Cover the bottom of the jar with fur. Hold until glue sets up. (See Fig. 2-1B.)

STEP 6:   With the seam to the back side, glue the eyes, nose and glasses on.

STEP 7:   Cut the hands and feet from felt. Cut a pair of feet from cardboard. Glue felt feet to cardboard feet. (See Fig. 2-1C.)

STEP 8:   Glue on the hands and feet. Glue a hat on top.

STEP 9:   To add money to the bank, unscrew the metal lid from the bottom; add money and return lid. Set up again.

Fig. 2-1-A

Cut notches

3"

9"

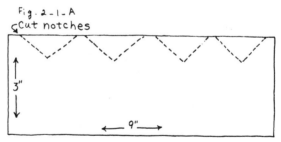

Fig. 2-1-B

feet   Cut 1
Black felt

cut 1
Cardboard

glue together

glue bank to
center -
felt side up

Fig. 2-1-C

Cut 2
Black
felt

There are many variations of this bank, such as: for a cowboy, use a cowboy hat; for a princess, add a crown made from a detergent bottle. To make a cane, use a black pipe cleaner cut in half, bending the top around your finger. Hang into the fur.

ACTIVITY 2-2: Little Bear Penny Bank

Materials Needed:

- 1 plastic wonder cup with lid
- 1 Styrofoam egg, 3 inch size
- 2 moving eyes, 1/2 inch size
- 1 black bead
- ribbon, orange, 20 inches
- scrap of red felt
- scrap of white felt, 2 X 2 inches
- 1 small hat
- sharp scissors
- glue
- brown spray paint for Styrofoam

Directions for Making:

STEP 1:   If making a brown bear, spray the plastic cup and the Styrofoam egg brown. (Be sure to use Styrofoam spray or the paint will dissolve the cup and ball.) A white bear with brown felt ears and face is a possibility—no spray needed.

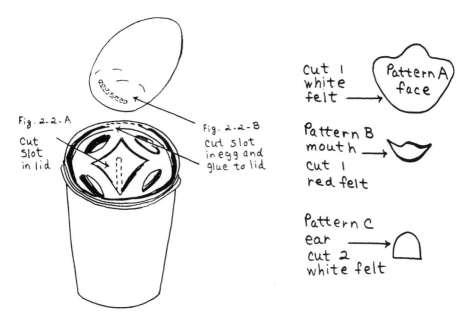

Fig. 2-2-A
Cut
Slot
in lid

Fig. 2-2-B
cut slot
in egg and
glue to lid

cut 1
white
felt ——→ Pattern A
face

Pattern B
mouth ——→
cut 1
red felt

Pattern C
ear ——→
cut 2
white felt

STEP 2:   In the lid at one side, make a slot so a penny can be inserted. (See Fig. 2-2A.- Use a sharp knife.

STEP 3:   Cut a small slice from the large end of the egg, and glue to the top of the lid. Do not cover the money slot. (See Fig. 2-2B.)

STEP 4:   Trace the patterns for the face, mouth and ears onto paper, cut out, and cut them from desired color felt.

STEP 5:   Glue in place on the egg shape. Put glue on the wide end of the ears, set on head, hold until the glue sets.

STEP 6:   Add the moving eyes and black bead nose.

STEP 7:   Glue a small hat between the ears. (The hat I used was removed from the end of a piece of pipe used by a plumber.)

STEP 8:   Wrap the ribbon around the neck and tie in a bow at the front.

ACTIVITY 2-3: Heart Banks

Materials Needed:

- 1 plastic yogurt or honey box with lid
- red spray paint
- glue
- scissors
- 1 sheet typing paper
- silver glitter

Directions for Making

STEP 1:   Remove the label from the plastic container and the glue. Wash inside and out with hot, soapy water, rinse with clear water and dry.

STEP 2:   Spray the container with red paint. Use two coats to cover the writing. Let dry.

STEP 3:   Trace and cut out the hearts from the typing paper. Cut as many as desired. Trace and cut out the cupid (Pattern A) or use a pretty Valentine cutout.

STEP 4:   Cut a slot in the lid one inch long and also one in the heart shape (Pattern B). Glue this heart shape over the slot on the lid. (See Fig. 2-3A.)

STEP 5:   Glue hearts around the container wherever they are wanted.

STEP 6:   Glue cupid or Valentine cutout at the top rim of lid opposite the money slot.

STEP 7:   (Optional) If a prettier bank is wanted, outline the hearts and cupid with glue and sprinkle on glitter.

Fig. 2-3-A
cut slot

Pattern A

Pattern B

ACTIVITY 2-4: Santa Bank

Materials Needed:

- 1 salt box
- 1 strip of red felt, 10-1/2 X 10 inches
- 1 small padlock
- 6 inches white fringe, 1-1/2 inches wide, or fake fur, white
- moving eyes, 1/2 inch size
- 1 small cotton ball
- 1 small red cotton ball or tiny Christmas ball
- 1 piece of pink felt, 3 X 2 inches
- 1 piece pellon, 1 X 10 inches
- glue
- scissors
- felt tip marker pens

Directions for Making:

STEP 1: Cut the top from a salt box. (See Fig. 2-4A.)

STEP 2: Using the red felt, glue it around the salt box. The extra felt at the top makes the hat. (See Fig. 2-4B.)

STEP 3: To make the hat, sew the ends of the red felt together. (See Fig. 2-4C.)

STEP 4: At the opposite side of the box from where the 2 ends of red felt are glued together, glue on the pink felt face.

STEP 5: Glue on features. Glue the white fringe or fake fur around the face for whiskers.

STEP 6: Cut the strip of pellon. Using a black felt marker pen, write ''Bank on Santa,'' in the middle of the strip. (See Fig. 2-4D.)

STEP 7: Add the strip of pellon to the top of the face; glue on. Be sure ''Bank on Santa,'' is over the face. (See Fig. 2-4E.)

STEP 8: At the top of the sign in the red felt, cut an oblong hole one inch long by 1/8 inch wide. (See Fig. 2-4F.)

STEP 9: Cut a hole in a piece of white pellon or felt, one inch long by 1/8 inch wide. Glue over the hole in the red felt. This piece of pellon should be 1-1/2 inches long by 1/2 inch wide. (See Fig. 2-4G.)

STEP 10: Fold the red felt at the top of the box in from both sides about 1 inch. (See Fig. 2-4H.)

STEP 11: Make a hole on either side with a punch and insert a metal eyelet. (See Fig. 2-4I.)

STEP 12: Fold the felt over again so holes match and insert a small padlock. (See Fig. 2-4J.) No money can be removed until the lock is unlocked.

Fig. 2-4-B

Fig. 2-4-A

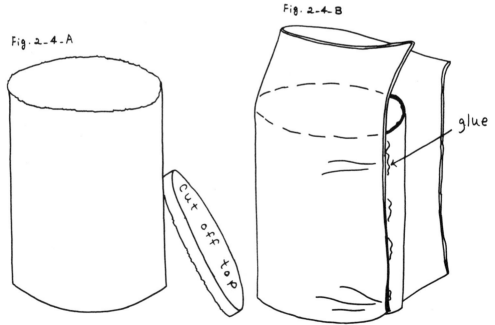

glue

Fig. 2-4-C
Sew

Fig. 2-4-E

glue → Bank on Santa

Fig. 2-4D

Bank on Santa

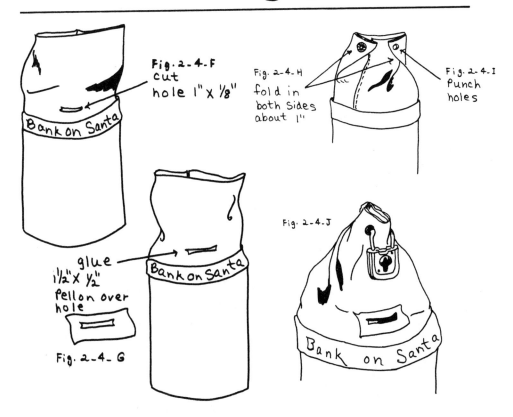

Fig. 2-4-F
cut
hole 1" x ⅛"

Bank on Santa

Fig. 2-4-H
fold in
both sides
about 1"

Fig. 2-4-I
Punch
holes

glue
1½" x ½"
Pellon over
hole

Bank on Santa

Fig. 2-4-G

Fig. 2-4-J

Bank on Santa

ACTIVITY 2-5: Dominick, The Monkey Bank

Materials Needed:

- 1 plastic "Leggs" hosiery container
- 1 red pipe cleaner, 12 inches long
- white felt, 5 X 5 inches
- scrape of orange felt
- black or brown rug yarn, 30 inches
- red paint
- brown spray paint
- gold paint
- blue Ivory detergent bottle cap
- 1 wooden square, 3 X 3 X 3/4 inch
- flat headed screw, 1/2 inch long
- 2 moving eyes
- green ribbon, 17 inches long by 3/4 inch wide
- play money
- ice pick
- sand paper
- glue
- scissors

Directions for Making:

STEP 1:   Wash and dry the Leggs hosiery holder. Spray all over with brown paint. Let dry. Paint an oval on one side with gold paint. (See Fig. 2-5A.)

STEP 2:   Lay a piece of paper over the pattern in the book, trace and cut out. Lay the pattern on appropriate color of felt, pin, and cut out.

STEP 3:   Cut a square of wood 3 X 3 X 1/2 inches; sand the edges until smooth.

STEP 4:   Lay the ice pick on the burner of an electric stove and heat very hot. Make a money slot by laying the hot pick in place on top of the plastic egg. (See Fig. 2-5B.)

STEP 5:   Poke a hole in the bottom of the egg with the hot ice pick and a hole on either side, and one in front about 1/2 inch above the rim on the top half of the egg. (See Fig. 2-5C.) Put the screw through the hole in the bottom of the egg and screw tight to the board. (See Fig. 2-5D.)

STEP 6:   Cut the pipe cleaner into three 4-inch pieces. Using two of the pieces shape the wire into ear shapes, twist the ends together and glue into the holes on the side of the head for ears. (See Fig. 2-5E.)

STEP 7:   Make a circle of the remaining 4-inch piece of pipe cleaner. Twist the ends together and glue into the hole in the front for a nose.

STEP 8:   To make the eyes, lay the large white felt oval on the table (Pattern B). Glue the smaller oval in place (Pattern C), and glue a moving eye on top. Let dry and then glue in place on the monkey's face. Do the other eye the same way.

STEP 9:   Glue the white horseshoe type piece of felt onto the face for a nose under the pipe cleaner ring, leaving the rounded part free.

STEP 10: Glue the white mouth in place. Draw a red line with paint in the center. (See Fig. 2-5F.)

STEP 11: Make the hair from yarn. Measure 30 inches of yarn, fold in half, then fold in half again until the yarn is 2 inches long. Tie in the middle and cut at both ends. (See Fig. 2-5G.) Glue in place on top of head.

STEP 12:   Glue a detergent bottle cap in place for a hat.

STEP 13:   Glue the ribbon around the edge of the board. Glue play money on the ribbon and over the top of the board.

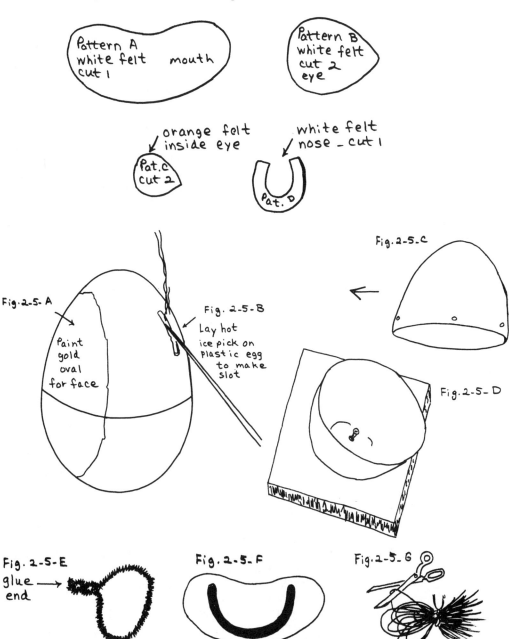

Pattern A
white felt
cut 1   mouth

Pattern B
white felt
cut 2
eye

orange felt
inside eye

white felt
nose _ cut 1

Pat.c
cut 2

Pat. D

Fig.2-5-C

Fig.2-5-A

Paint
gold
oval
for face

Fig. 2-5-B
Lay hot
ice pick on
plastic egg
to make
slot

Fig.2-5-D

Fig.2-5-E
glue
end

Fig.2-5-F

Fig.2-5-G

ACTIVITY 2-6: Grink, the Green Gremlin Bank

Materials Needed:

- "Leggs" hosiery container
- 2 moving eyes, 3/4 inch size
- scrap of red felt
- green felt
- 1 green metallic pipe cleaner, 12 inches long
- one 3 X 3 X 3/4 inch piece of wood
- green spray paint
- 17 inches red ribbon, 1/2 inch wide
- play money
- 1 metal screw, 1/2 inch long
- glue
- scissors
- ice pick

Directions for Making:

STEP 1: Wash and dry the hosiery container. Open the egg shape and spray the top and bottom on the outside with green spray paint. Let dry.

STEP 2: Lay the ice pick on the burner of an electric stove and heat until very hot. Lay on the top side of the egg to make a money slot. Also punch a hole at the large end of the egg shape and two holes at the smaller end of the egg for antennas to go in. (See Fig. 2-6A.)

STEP 3: Cut a 3 X 3 inch square from 3/4 inch lumber. (Use the pattern from Activity 5, Dominick, the Monkey Bank.) Measure to the center and put a dot. Put a screw down through the bottom of the egg and screw the egg tight to the board. CAUTION: Don't tighten the egg too much as it might split. (See Fig. 2-6B.)

STEP 4: Lay a piece of paper over the patterns in the book. Draw and cut out. Lay the pattern on felt—green ears and red nose and mouth. Cut the nose and ears with regular scissors and the mouth with pinking scissors.

STEP 5: Glue the nose and mouth onto the egg opposite the money hole. Glue on the moving eyes and green ears. Glue just enough of the top of the nose to hold. Leave the bottom free.

STEP 6: Cut the green pipe cleaner into three 4-inch pieces. Use two pieces and twist a curl in one end of each. (See Fig. 2-6C.) Poke the opposite end into the holes on the bank. Put glue on this end and hold until the antennas will stand upright.

STEP 7: Glue the red ribbon around the block of wood. When it has dried, glue play money around the ribbon and over the top of the board next to the bank.

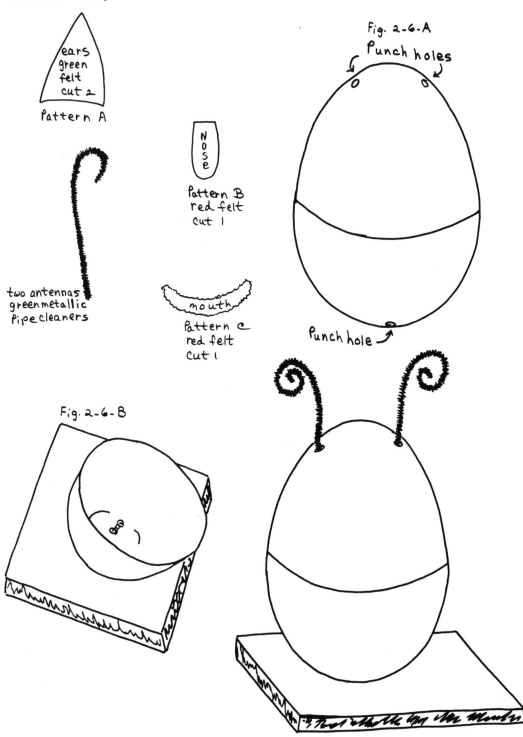

ears
green
felt
cut 2

Pattern A

two antennas
green metallic
Pipe cleaners

NOSE

Pattern B
red felt
cut 1

mouth

Pattern C
red felt
cut 1

Fig. 2-6-A
Punch holes

Punch hole

Fig. 2-6-B

Fig. 2-6-C

ACTIVITY 2-7: Gordy, The Clown Bank

Materials Needed:

- 1 Maxim coffee jar and lid
- 1 plastic drinking cup, 3 inches tall
- 1 artificial bug
- scrap of red felt
- black felt, 2 X 4 inches
- green felt, 3 X 5 inches
- gold braid or fringe 10 inches long
- white spray paint
- 1 cotton ball pom-pom nose, 1 inch in diameter, green
- glue
- scissors

Directions for Making:

STEP 1:   Remove the lid from the coffee jar, wash inside and out; dry.

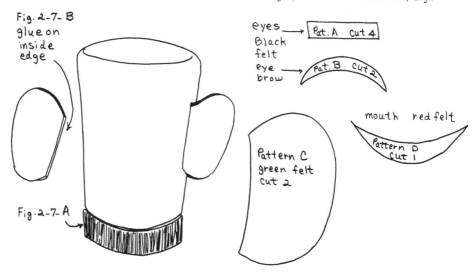

Fig. 2-7- B
glue on
inside
edge

eyes ⟶ Pat. A cut 4
Black
felt
eye ⟶ Pat. B cut 2
brow

mouth   red felt
Pattern D
cut 1

Pattern C
green felt
cut 2

Fig. 2-7- A

STEP 2:   Spray the jar on the outside with white spray paint. Let dry.

STEP 3:   Lay a piece of paper over the patterns in the book, trace and cut out. Use straight pins to fasten patterns to different color felt and cut out.

STEP 4:   Glue the piece of gold fringe or braid around the lid. Let dry. (See Fig. 2-7A.) Screw lid back on again.

STEP 5:   Cut a fake fur strip 2 X 4 inches for hair. Glue this around the bottom end of the jar.

STEP 6:   Glue a plastic cup on top of hair for a hat, open side down. Let dry. On the front side of the cup hat add the bug.

STEP 7:   To glue the green ears to each side of the face, put a line of glue on inside edge of ears and press onto the jar. Hold in place until the glue will hold. (See Fig. 2-7B.)

STEP 8:   Fluff the hair around the clown face; leave the hair long at the side.

STEP 9:   To put money into the jar, unscrew the lid, put in the money and screw the lid on again.

ACTIVITY 2-8: Arabella Bank

Materials Needed:

- 1 tall Pringle potato chip can
- white felt 3 X 4 inches
- yellow fake fur, 1/2 X 10-1/2 inches
- 2 moving eyes, 3/4 inch size
- red spray paint
- scissors
- glue

Directions for Making:

STEP 1:   Remove the lid; be sure the outside of the can is wiped free of dust. Spray the can with a good grade of red spray paint. It may need a second coat of paint to cover letters. Let dry.

STEP 2:   Lay a piece of paper over the patterns in the book for nose and mouth, trace and cut out. Pin patterns to white felt and cut out.

STEP 3:   Lay the plastic lashes on the table, glue the moving eyes onto the lashes and then glue to one side of the can along with the felt nose and mouth.

STEP 4:   Put the lid onto the can; use a sharp knife, and cut an oblong X for a money slot close to one side of the lid. (See Fig. 2-8A.)

STEP 5:   Cut a narrow strip of yellow fake fur 1/2 inch wide and glue around the top of the can for hair.

STEP 6:   Use a pretty contrasting color ribbon bow and fasten to the top of the lid in front of the money slot.

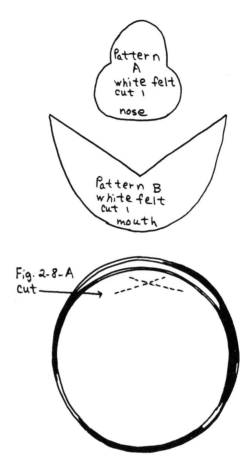

Pattern
A
white felt
cut 1

nose

Pattern B
white felt
cut 1
mouth

Fig. 2-8-A
cut

Chapter 3

Colorful Bookmarkers to Encourage Pride in Reading

Even children who don't read yet, or who are just beginning to read, find making and owning bookmarkers appealing. They are so easy to make they are fun for everyone, and they help children understand why books and reading are important.

ACTIVITY 3-1: Worm

Materials Needed:

- 1 white plastic meat tray
- 2 moving eyes, 3/16 inch size
- 1 inch fake fur
- felt, any color, 3 X 8 inches
- 3 buttons, small size
- glue
- black felt marker pen
- red felt marker pen
- scissors

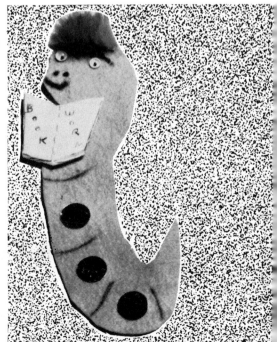

43

Directions for Making:

STEP 1:   Using patterns A and B draw around patterns with pencil. Cut out. Cut worm from felt and the book from a plastic meat tray.

STEP 2:   Draw on the nose, eyelashes and mouth, using felt marker pens, using red for the mouth and black for the rest.

STEP 3:   Glue on 2 moving eyes.

STEP 4:   Glue on 1/4 inch strips of fake fur. This can be added to the top of the head, or from top of head down between the eyes.

STEP 5:   Using the black felt marker pens, draw curving lines across the body of the worm for body lines. (See Fig. 3-1A.)

STEP 6:   Glue the 3 buttons in between the body lines, or cut 3 circles from felt or colored paper and glue on.

STEP 7:   On the tiny book, with the black felt marker pen, write: BOOK WORM. Outline the edges of the book with black. Glue book in place on body. (See Fig. 3-1B.)

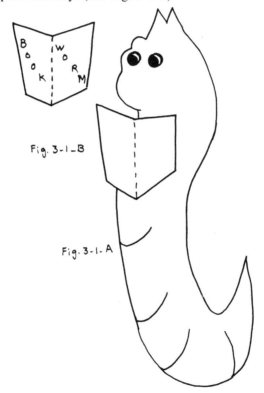

Fig. 3-1-B

Fig. 3-1-A

ACTIVITY 3-2: Ribbon Bookmarker

Materials Needed:

- 1 piece of white satin ribbon, 6 X 1-1/2 inches
- cardboard strip, 6 X 1-1/2 inches, lightweight
- tiny decals or pictures cut from greeting cards
- glitter

- glue
- typewriter
- pinking scissors

Directions for Making:

STEP 1: Onto the ribbon, type or print a verse from the Bible or a rhyme, such as:

> *If this book mark should come to roam*
> *Rescue it and send it home*
> > *to: (Name)*
> > *(Address)*

STEP 2: With pinking scissors, cut off both ends of the ribbon.

STEP 3: Add glue to the top and bottom edges of the ribbon and add glitter. Let dry.

STEP 4: Glue a small decal or picture at the top above the verse and one at the bottom.

STEP 5: Glue the ribbon to the piece of lightweight cardboard.

ACTIVITY 3-3: Dog, Fish and Chicken

Materials Needed:

- Plastic meat tray
- ribbon pieces, 8 X 1-1/2 inches
- scissors
- glue
- black felt marker pen

Directions for Making:

STEP 1: Copy Patterns A, B and C from the book, by laying a white piece of paper over the pattern and drawing the outline. Cut out the pattern.

STEP 2: Cut the bottom from a white plastic meat tray.

STEP 3: Draw the patterns onto the plastic meat tray, cut out carefully.

STEP 4: Outline with black felt marker pen.

STEP 5: Glue animals at the top of pieces of ribbon.

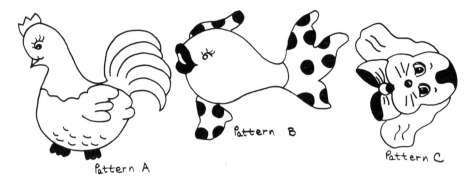

Pattern A   Pattern B   Pattern C

ACTIVITY 3-4: Sad Dog

Materials Needed:

- plastic meat tray, 8-1/2 X 10-1/2 inches
- 2 small moving eyes, 3/16 inch size
- felt marker pen
- glue
- pinking scissors

Directions for Making:

STEP 1:   Using straight scissors, cut the center from a plastic meat tray.
STEP 2:   Using pinking scissors, cut a strip 2-1/2 inches wide the length of the tray.
STEP 3:   Using pattern A, draw the dog face at the top of the bookmark.
STEP 4:   If making sad dog, glue 2 small moving eyes to face.
STEP 5:   With felt marker pen, write, ''This is where I left off,'' down the length of the bookmark.

ACTIVITY 3-5: Ribbon and Plastic Ring Marker

Materials Needed:

- 1 piece ribbon, 12 inches long X 3/4 inch
- 1 piece ribbon, 18 inches long X 3/4 inch
- 1 plastic ring
- needle and thread

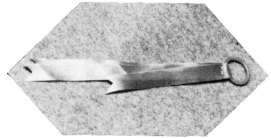

Directions for Making:

STEP 1:   Cut the ribbon, one 12 inches long and one 18 inches long.
STEP 2:   Thread the ribbon through the plastic ring. Pull ribbon together so there will be two 9-inch pieces and two 6-inch pieces. (See Fig. 3-5A.)
STEP 3:   Sew the ribbon together at the plastic ring.
STEP 4:   Notch the ends of the ribbon.

Fig. 3-5 A

ACTIVITY 3-6: Tongue Depressor Bookmarker

Materials Needed:

- 1 tongue depressor, wooden
- 1 used card
- glue
- scissors

Directions for Making:

STEP 1:   From a used card, cut a picture of a child, bird or animal.

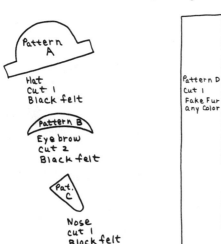

STEP 2:   Glue one end of a tongue depressor to picture. Let dry.
STEP 3:   To use as a marker, put the depressor stick inside the book, leaving
           the cutout at the top of the book.

ACTIVITY 3-7: Hermie, The Hairy Bookmarker

Materials Needed:

- 1 piece fake fur, 1-1/4 X 8 inches, any color
- 1 moving eye, 1 inch size
- black felt, 3 X 5 inches
- sharp scissors
- glue

Directions for Making:

STEP 1:   Cut a strip of fake fur 1-1/4 X 8 inches long. (Follow directions for
           cutting fake fur—Hint No. 4.)
STEP 2:   Using a piece of paper, trace the patterns and cut out: Pattern A for a
           hat, Pattern B for the eyebrow, and Pattern C is the nose. Cut from
           black felt.
STEP 3:   Comb fur until smooth, before adding features.
STEP 4:   Glue the hat in place at one end of the fake fur. Glue the eyebrow on
           next and then the eye and the nose. Make a profile with the nose
           sticking out.

ACTIVITY 3-8: Pearl, The Perky Toucan Bookmarker from Felt and Paper
Clips

Materials Needed:

- 6 or 7 paper clips 1-1/4 inches long
- 1 moving eye
- scraps of red, purple and yellow felt
- needle and thread
- glue
- 1 tiny twig

Directions for Making:

STEP 1: Draw the pattern for Pearl and cut out. Cut the body from purple felt, beak from yellow, wing from red felt.

STEP 2: Glue the wing and beak in place on the body. Add the eye.

STEP 3: Sew the body to the first paper clip at the top of the wing and at the bottom of the body.

STEP 4: Spring the paper clip slightly open and push onto the page of the book to hold your place.

STEP 5: Glue the twig behind the feet at the bottom edge.

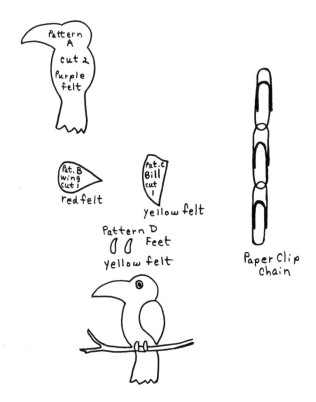

Chapter Four

Toys and Games Created from Material Found in Every Home

Many of these games and toys have educational value, teaching mathematics skills as well as sportsmanship. Children in our class enjoy making these toys and games as much as they enjoy playing with them when they are finished.

ACTIVITY 4-1: Ball Games from Detergent Bottles

Materials Needed:

- 1 "Sta Puff" plastic bottle
- rick rack and bias tape, any color
- 1 two-inch Styrofoam ball
- 30 inches of string or yarn
- felt for cutouts
- knife or scissors to cut plastic bottle
- 1 large-eyed needle
- glue

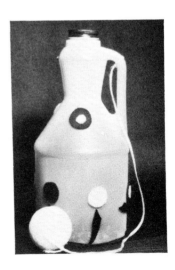

Directions for Making:

STEP 1: Wash jug inside and out with warm soapy water, rinse, and let dry. Scrape any glue off the outside of the jug.

STEP 2: Cut the bottom from the plastic jug, using the bottom line as a guide. (See Fig. 4-1A.)

STEP 3: Glue bright colored bias tape around the sharp cut edge.

STEP 4: Decorate with felt cutouts, rick rack or paint on a design with felt marker pens.

STEP 5: Cut a piece of twine string 24 inches long for a younger child or 30 inches for older children.

STEP 6: Using a large-eyed needle, thread the string through the center of the ball and tie the string to the handle of the jug. (See Fig. 4-1B.)
NOTE: This toy teaches coordination. Have contests to see who can catch the ball the most times.

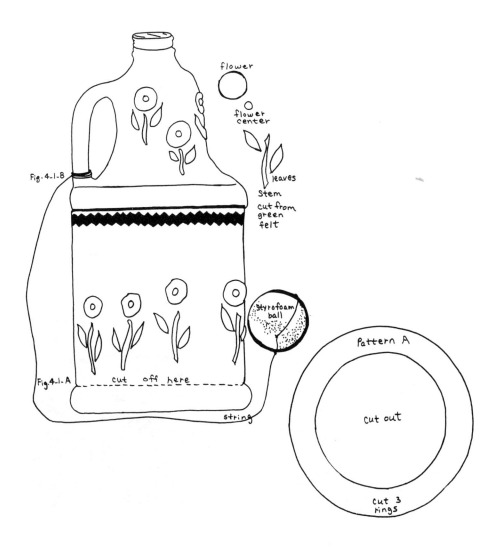

flower

flower center

leaves

Stem cut from green felt

Fig. 4-1-B

Styrofoam ball

Pattern A

cut out

Fig. 4-1-A   cut off here

string

cut 3 rings

ACTIVITY 4-2: Mrs. B's Ring Toss Game

Materials Needed:

- 3 "Mrs. Butterworth's" syrup bottles with lids
- silver glitter
- heavy cardboard
- scissors
- glue
- glue brush

Directions for Making:

STEP 1:   Remove the label from the syrup bottles, wash and dry.

STEP 2:   Cover the lids with glue and sprinkle with silver glitter. Put on bottles again.

STEP 3:   Write the numbers 3, 4 and 5 on the apron of the three bottles with glue and cover with glitter.

STEP 4:   Make three rings from heavy cardboard, using Pattern A. To make rings heavier, cover one side with glue and wind yarn around circle.

STEP 5:   To play the game, let each person have three rings or hoops and try to ring the bottle tops with them. Add up the numbers when finished. If a player rings one 3, one 4 and one 5 bottle, give him 10 extra points.

ACTIVITY 4-3: Add and Subtract Fish Game

Materials Needed:

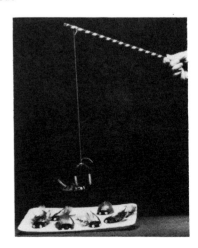

- 9 bottle caps
- magnet
- stick or dowel, 18 inches long
- 26 inch string
- felt marker pens, black and red
- 2 moving eyes for each fish
- bright feathers
- black spray paint
- glue

Fig. 4-3-A

Directions for Making:

STEP 1: Make the fish bodies by spraying 9 bottle caps black. Let dry.

STEP 2: Glue 2 tiny moving eyes on one side of the cap about 3/4 of an inch apart.

STEP 3: On the opposite side of the cap, glue on a pretty colored feather for a tail. Add a feather on each side for fins.

STEP 4: Cut round pieces of paper and glue to the inside of the caps, using Pattern A. Make numbers 1, 2, 5, 6, 8 and 9 in black and the numbers 3, 4 and 7 in red.

STEP 5: Tie a piece of string around one end of a magnet. Tie the other end to a stick or a dowel. (See Fig. 4-3A.)

STEP 6: To play the game, arrange the fish in a plate or box. Let each player have three turns to try and pick up the fish. Count the numbers of the underneath side. Add them together. The player with the highest count wins. Red numbers are to be subtracted from the score.

This game will help teach children to add and subtract. For children of pre-school age, have all of the fish numbered 1 and 2.

ACTIVITY 4-4: Toss Ball Game

Materials Needed:

- one 2-gallon ice cream carton
- 5 plastic balls or bean bags
- wallpaper or Contac paper
- black felt marker
- score sheet
- pencil
- glue
- scissors
- needle and thread

Directions for Making:

STEP 1:   Wash and dry the empty ice cream carton.

STEP 2:   Measure around the outside of the carton and cover with Contac paper or glue on wallpaper.

STEP 3:   After the paper dries, cut the letters *Toss Ball* from black construction paper and glue around the center of the carton. (See Fig. 4-4A.)

STEP 4:   Cut numbers 1, 2, 3, 4 and 5 from black felt and glue one number to each ball, or bean bag, or draw on with black felt marker pen. (See Fig. 4-4B.)

STEP 5:   To make bean bags, cut two 4-inch circles from material using Pattern A. Turn right sides together and sew edge, leaving a 2 inch opening. Then turn right side out and fill with beans. Finish sewing around the bag.

STEP 6:   To play the game, give each child all the bags or balls. Set the container on the floor. Measure a distance of ten feet; for smaller children, a shorter distance could be allowed.

Let each one throw all the balls or bags into the carton. Add up the numbers of the ones which go in and stay in. Play five games —each player would throw 25 bags or balls. The one with the highest score would win.

If several children are playing, choose up sides and have two containers.

STEP 7:   How to make a score sheet: Cut strips of paper, 3 X 4 inches. Put the players' names at the top of the sheet. Make like sample sheet, Pattern B.

Fig. 4-4-A

TOSS

BALL

Fig. 4-4-B

12345

Pattern A

4 inch Circle
for bean bag

Cut 2

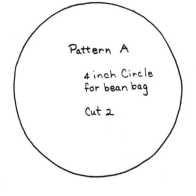

Pattern B

SCORE SHEET	
Name	
Game 1	
Game 2	
Game 3	
Game 4	
Game 5	
	total

ACTIVITY 4-5: Penny Ante Game

Materials Needed:

- Styrofoam sheet, 1 X 10 X 20 inches, or can be wood slab
- 8 small plastic animals (The animals may be purchased in a variety store)
- 1 felt marker pen
- 5 pennies for each player
- score sheet
- Elmer's glue

Directions for Making:

STEP 1: Using Pattern A and a felt marker pen, draw the 8 circles on the sheet of Styrofoam or wood.

STEP 2: Glue the plastic animals to the center of the circles.

STEP 3: Draw numbers 1 through 8 inside the circles. Set the game on a card table.

STEP 4: Give 5 pennies to each player. Let each one throw his pennies and count up the score.

STEP 5: Make a score sheet as in Pattern B.

STEP 6: Let each player have 3 turns per game. The one with the highest number of points wins the game.

Pattern B

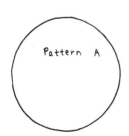

Pattern A

Name	Name
1	1
2	2
3	3
Total	Total
1	1
2	2
3	3
Total	Total
1	1
2	2
3	3
Total	Total
1	1
2	2
3	3
Total	Total
1	1
2	2
3	3
Total	Total
1	1
2	2
3	3
Total	Total
1	1
2	2
3	3
Total	Total
1	1
2	2
3	3
Total	Total

ACTIVITY 4-6: Doll Beds from Margarine Tubs

Materials Needed:

- 2 plastic oblong margarine tubs
- 2 two-prong paper fasteners
- bright, small print material
- 24 inches bright colored rick rack
- 1 square same print 5 X 5 inches
- needle and thread
- glue and brush
- scissors
- pinking scissors

Directions for Making:

STEP 1:   Wash margarine tubs and dry thoroughly.

STEP 2:   Leave one tub as is, cut the other one in half. (See Fig. 4-6A.)

STEP 3:   Using the pinking scissors, cut a strip of material 3 X 20 inches and one 5 X 5 inches.

STEP 4:   Sew bright colored rick rack or lace around the bottom of the material.

STEP 5:   With a needle and thread, gather the top side so it will be 15-1/2 inches long. (See Fig. 4-6B.)

STEP 6:   Using a quick-drying glue, glue this material to the top edge of the whole margarine tub. (See Fig. 4-6C.) Set aside to dry.

STEP 7:   Using the square of material, hem one edge and sew either rick rack or lace onto this piece. (See Fig. 4-6D.)

STEP 8:   Cover the half tub with glue; add this piece of material, leaving the edge with lace or rick rack opposite the cut edge.

STEP 9:   Press material down firmly. Fold the corners to fit and trim off any excess material. Let dry. (See Fig. 4-6E.)

STEP 10:   Punch 2 holes, one on either side in the margarine tub, about 2 inches from the end of the tub, just under the rim. (See Fig. 4-6F.)

STEP 11:   Punch holes in the half tub, about 1/2 inch up and 1/2 inch back from the end with the trimming on it. (See Fig. 4-6G.)

STEP 12:   Put a paper fastener into the holes, one on either side. Spread the prongs apart.

STEP 13:   Add a small pillow, mattress, blanket and a tiny doll.

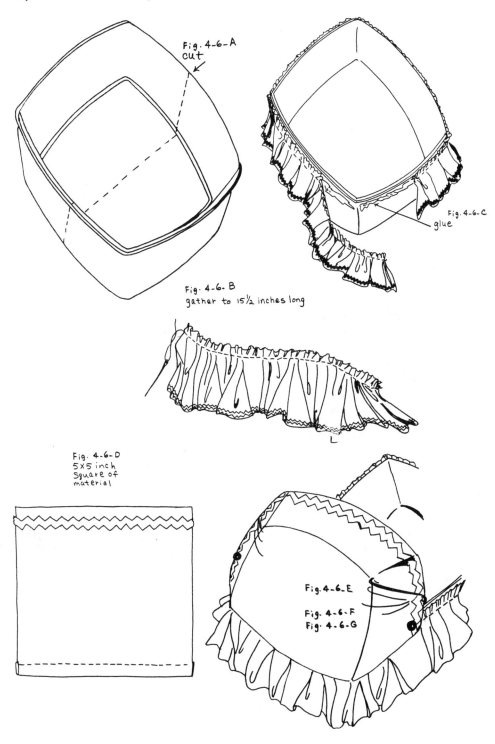

Fig. 4-6-A
cut

Fig. 4-6-C
glue

Fig. 4-6-B
gather to 15½ inches long

Fig. 4-6-D
5x5 inch
square of
material

Fig. 4-6-E

Fig. 4-6-F
Fig. 4-6-G

ACTIVITY 4-7: Child's Play Bucket

Materials Needed:

- 1 plastic gallon size bleach jug
- 2 paper fasteners
- ice pick
- black marker pen
- small pieces of felt
- pattern for deer or pig, or use other animals or flowers
- scissors
- glue

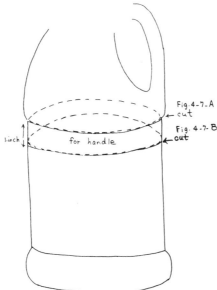

Fig. 4-7-A
← cut

Fig. 4-7-B
← cut

1-inch
for handle

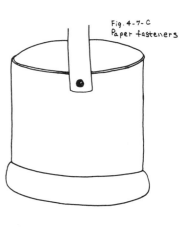

Fig. 4-7-C
Paper fasteners

blue
yellow

red

Pink
yellow

green

green

Directions for Making:

STEP 1: Remove label and scrape off the glue. Wash and dry the jug.

STEP 2: Cut the bleach jug at the rim, under the handle. (See Fig. 4-7A.)

STEP 3: Measure down one inch and cut this strip off. This will be used as a handle. (See Fig. 4-7B.)

STEP 4: Using the ice pick or sharp pair of scissors, punch a hole in the end of the strip and one in the jug. Do the same to the opposite end and side of the jug.

STEP 5: Stick a paper fastener into the hole in the jug and strip. Spread the two prongs apart. Turn the jug halfway around and repeat. (See Fig. 4-7C.)

STEP 6: Draw pictures on outside of bucket with felt marker pens or cut flowers from felt and glue on. (These buckets may be used to carry crayons, fruit, sand, etc.)

ACTIVITY 4-8: Let's Make a Pinwheel Toy

Materials Needed:

- 1 piece of paper 5 X 5 inches
- 1 straight pin
- 1 pencil with an eraser or a dowel
- 1 sequin
- box of Crayolas
- scissors

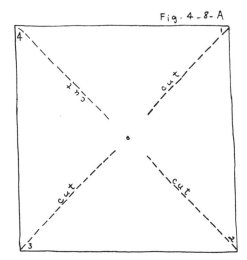

Fig. 4-8-A

Directions for Making:

STEP 1:   Cut a square of paper 5 X 5 inches, using the pattern.

STEP 2:   Starting at the corner marked 1, follow the dashes and cut up to 1/2 inch from the center. Mark a dot in the center. (See Fig. 4-8A.)

STEP 3:   Do the same with Nos. 2, 3 and 4.

STEP 4:   Pull No. 1 corner to the center and hold. Do the same with Nos. 2, 3 and 4.

STEP 5:   Hold the corners to the dot and stick a straight pin through a sequin, through the paper and into a dowel or pencil eraser.

STEP 6:   Using Crayolas, draw pictures, flowers, etc., to decorate the pin wheel.

ACTIVITY 4-9: Clown Head Bean Bag

Materials Needed:

- white felt, 5 X 10 inches
- red fake fur strip 1/2 X 6 inches
- scrap of red felt
- 2 moving eyes, 3/4 inch size
- 1 cup of beans
- needle and thread
- pinking scissors
- glue

Directions for Making:

STEP 1:   Lay a piece of typing paper over pattern in the book. Trace and cut out.

STEP 2:   Pin Pattern A on white felt and cut out with pinking scissors. Cut mouth (Pattern B) and nose (Pattern C) from red felt with straight scissors.

STEP 3:   Sew around the edge of the felt, starting at Fig. A and sew to Fig. B.

STEP 4:   Fill the face with beans and finish sewing the top of the bag shut.

STEP 5:   Glue on the moving eyes, glue the nose and mouth in place.

STEP 6:   Cut a strip of red fake fur 1/2 X 6 inches. Cut into two 3 inch pieces. Glue along the side of the face in front of the ears.

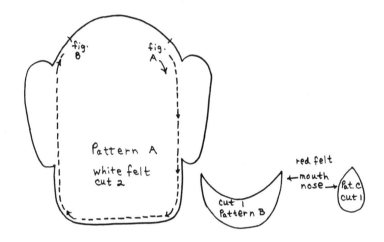

ACTIVITY 4-10: Lion Head Bean Bag

Materials Needed:

- yellow felt, 4 X 5 inches
- orange fake fur, 3 inch circle
- 1 cup of beans
- 2 moving eyes, 1/2 inch size
- needle and thread
- straight pins
- pinking scissors
- felt marker pens
- glue

Directions for Making:

STEP 1:   Lay a piece of typing paper over the patterns in the book, trace and cut out.

STEP 2:   Lay Pattern A on yellow felt, pin in place and cut out with pinking scissors.

STEP 3:   Sew from Fig. A around the triangle to Fig. B. Fill the Bag with beans and continue to sew across the top, from B to A.

STEP 4:   Cut a 3-inch oval, using Pattern B, from fake fur. Cut a 2-inch oval from the center. Be careful not to cut the long fur.

STEP 5:   Lay the oval shape onto the small end of the felt. (See Fig. 4-10A.) Stitch around the edge of the fake fur on the inside of the oval.

STEP 6:   Stitch carefully around the outside edge of the fur (see Fig. 4-10B), being careful not to get the fake fur under the thread. Smooth the fur out around the oval shape.

STEP 7:   Add moving eyes inside the small oval and draw on a face with a felt marker pen.

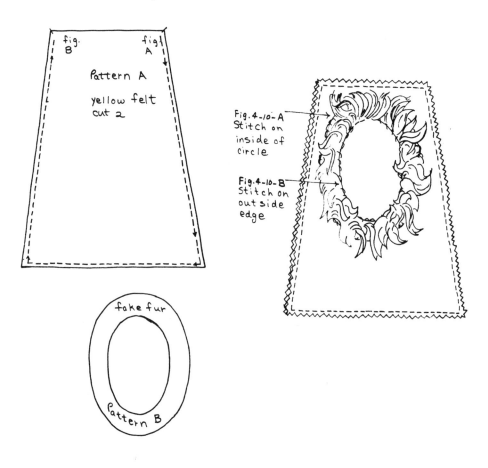

fig. B   fig. A

Pattern A

yellow felt

cut 2

Fig. 4-10-A
Stitch on
inside of
circle

Fig. 4-10-B
Stitch on
outside
edge

fake fur

Pattern B

ACTIVITY 4-11: Smiles Bean Bag

Materials Needed:

- white felt, 10 X 5 inches
- scraps of red felt
- yellow fake fur, 1 X 3 inches
- 2 moving eyes, 3/4 inch size
- 1 cup of beans
- needle and thread
- 4 straight pins
- glue
- scissors

Directions for Making:

STEP 1: Lay a piece of typing paper over the patterns in the book, trace and cut out.

STEP 2: Lay Pattern A onto white felt, pin with straight pins and cut out with pinking scissors.

STEP 3: Sew circle with needle and thread 1/4 inch from edge, from Fig. 1 around the circle to Fig. 2, to the other arrow.

STEP 4: Fill the bag with beans; finish sewing the circle closed.

STEP 5: Cut the mouth (Pattern B) and the nose (Pattern A) from red felt. Glue onto the circle face.

STEP 6: Glue on the moving eyes.

STEP 7: Cut the fake fur and glue at the top of the face for hair.

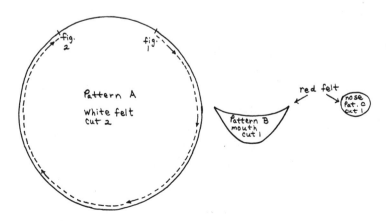

Chapter Five

Beautiful and Simple to Make Decorations

These decorations for the home are novel and attractive. With all their beautiful colors, these arrangements are easily made and they add color and brightness anywhere they are placed.

Mothers, grandmothers and elderly people appreciate getting them as gifts.

ACTIVITY 5-1: Flower Arrangement

Materials Needed:

- 3 plastic egg cartons, one each color, pink, yellow, white
- 1 plastic meat tray, 5 X 7 X 1 inch
- 1 Styrofoam block, 2 X 2 X 1 inch, or 1 round margarine tub
- tiny flowers and flower peps
- wire or pipe cleaners cut in 4 inch lengths
- 3 or 5 bright colored plastic flowers
- 3 pieces plastic greenery
- floral tape
- piece of net, 4 X 20 inches, different colors
- ice pick
- scissors and pinking scissors

Directions for Making:

STEP 1: Turn the plastic meat tray upside down and wire the Styrofoam block or the round margarine tub into the center. If using a tub, punch 3 holes evenly spaced around the rim.

STEP 2: Put the wire through the holes and through the bottom of the meat tray. Twist the ends together underneath the meat tray. (See Fig. 5-1A.)

STEP 3: Using the pinking scissors and the straight scissors, cut the different forms for flowers from the colored plastic cartons. (See Fig. 5-1B.)

STEP 4: Punch a hole in the bottom of the egg cup flower with an ice pick or sharp scissors. Add a stem to the small flower or flower pep by adding a four-inch wire stem or pipe cleaner. To add the stem, twist the end of the wire and the stem on the small flower or pep together. Poke the resulting stem through the hole in the egg cup.

STEP 5: Cover the wire with floral tape.

STEP 6: Stick the stem into the Styrofoam base or punch holes with an ice pick into the margarine tub.

STEP 7: In the center of each arrangement add a spray or two of green leaves.

STEP 8: Make as many flowers as desired. Place stems where they look best.

STEP 9: Cut the net into 2 X 4 inch pieces; using a pipe cleaner or the wire, tie in the center and add them where they are needed.

STEP 10: Cut off the stems of 3 or 5 small bright colored plastic flowers to 6 inch lengths. Add them where extra color is wanted.

Fig. 5-1-B

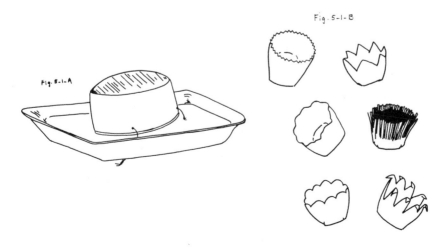

Fig. 5-1-A

ACTIVITY 5-2: Owl Note Holder

Materials Needed:

- heavy drapery material, 10 X 12 inch piece
- light cardboard
- 2 large moving eyes, 1 inch size
- small pad
- contrasting material, 4 X 5 inches (different color)
- 2 X 5 inch piece orange felt
- 2 X 4 inch piece green felt
- material 1 X 2 inches
- pencil
- glue
- paper punch
- pinking scissors

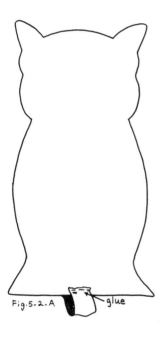

Fig. 5-2-A   glue

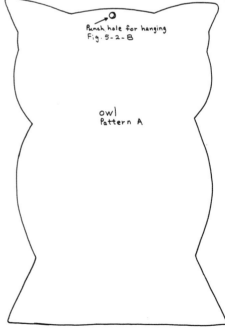

Punch hole for hanging
Fig. 5-2-B

owl
Pattern A

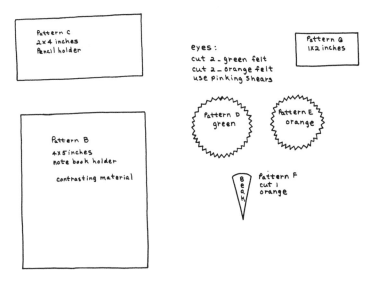

Pattern C
2 x 4 inches
Pencil holder

eyes:
cut 2 – green felt
cut 2 – orange felt
use pinking shears

Pattern G
1 x 2 inches

Pattern D
green

Pattern E
orange

Pattern B
4 x 5 inches
note book holder

contrasting material

Beak

Pattern F
cut 1
orange

Directions for Making:

STEP 1: Using Pattern A, cut the owl shape from lightweight cardboard (such as a tablet back).

STEP 2: Cover the cardboard with glue and lay it on the 10 X 12 inch piece of material. (Be sure to put glue to the edges of the cardboard.) Have the material with the design down, laying flat on the table.

STEP 3: Press material down to remove any air bubbles. Weight it with a heavy book for 15 minutes.

STEP 4: Cut the material around the cardboard shape with the pinking scissors.

STEP 5: Using the contrasting material, Pattern B, cut a pocket from the 4 X 5 inch material using the pinking scissors.

STEP 6: Cut eyes from green and orange felt with pinking scissors, using Patterns D and E, and a beak from orange felt using straight scissors (Pattern F).

STEP 7: Lay the green circle on the bottom, glue on orange circle to the center of the green one. Glue a moving eye to the centers of the orange circles.

STEP 8: When the owl shape made from cardboard and material has dried, glue the eyes to the face with the bill in the middle, close to the bottom of the eyes.

STEP 9: Cut the 1 X 2 inch piece of material (Pattern G), fold in the middle and glue at the bottom in the center of the owl. (See Fig. 5-2A.) This is the pencil holder.

STEP 10: Outline the 4 X 5 inch piece of material with glue on both edges and bottom. Lay this material in the center of the owl. This is the pocket to hold the note pad. Be sure the pocket is even with the bottom of the owl.

STEP 11: When glue is dry, insert the cardboard back of the note pad into the pocket.

STEP 12: With a paper punch (see Fig. 5-2B), make a hole at the top of the owl head in the center. Hang the owl up.

ACTIVITY 5-3: Hanging String Holder

Materials Needed:

- 1 plastic yogurt cup
- ball of string
- black ribbon, 1/4 inch x 12 inches
- 2 used birthday cards with flowers, small animals or birds
- bow of Christmas ribbon, either pink or red
- silver glitter
- glue
- black spray paint
- scissors
- sharp pointed knife or scissors

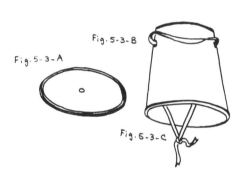

Directions for Making:

STEP 1:   Wash yogurt cup and lid inside and out. Dry and paint the outside black. Let dry.

STEP 2:   From the used cards, cut out the design to be used on the holder.

STEP 3:   Remove the lid from the holder. Using the sharp point of the knife or scissors, make a hole in the exact center of the lid (see Fig. 5-3A), and one on either side of the bottom of the cup (see Fig. 5-3B).

STEP 4:   Thread the ribbon through the two holes at the bottom sides of the cup. Pull both ends of the ribbon to the open end of the cup. Tie the ends together tightly, as this will be the hanger. (See Fig. 5-3C.) Pull ribbon until the tied ends are in the center. Keep the ribbon straight so the holder will set even.

STEP 5:   Put a narrow line of glue around the top and bottom edge of the cup. Sprinkle on glitter.

STEP 6:   Add the ball of string into the cup. Thread one end of the string through the hole in the lid and replace the lid.

STEP 7:   Glue the cutouts onto the cup.

STEP 8:   Peel the paper from the back of the ribbon bow and glue the bow between the 2 ribbon hangers.

ACTIVITY 5-4: Bird Cage

Materials Needed:

- 2 small birds
- 8 metallic pipe cleaners
- 1 Styrofoam circle, 6 inch size
- 1 twig, 4 inches long
- 1 plastic ring, 1 inch size
- 3 flower sprays with small flowers
- 3 individual flowers

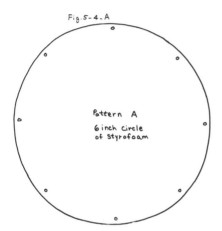

Fig. 5-4-A

Pattern A
6 inch circle
of Styrofoam

Directions for Making:

STEP 1: Lay the Styrofoam circle on the table and stick the ends of the pipe cleaners into the foam across from each other. Then follow Pattern A and insert the ends of the pipe cleaners where marked. (See Fig. 5-4A.)

STEP 2: Wire two artificial birds onto a twig; stick into the middle of the foam circle.

STEP 3: Cut the stems from the flower picks and push the ends into the foam around the twig with the birds attached.

STEP 4: Push the stems of the other flowers into the foam where added color is needed.

STEP 5: Using a plastic ring, fold the top ends of the pipe cleaners over the ring. Add a bright flower to the top in the center of the ring.
To even the sides of the bird cage, push the pipe cleaners into the foam circle. (See Fig. 5-4B.)

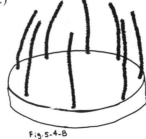

Fig. 5-4-B

ACTIVITY 5-5: A Different Vase

Materials Needed:

- 8 empty bathroom tissue roles
- soda pop can with lid removed
- gold spray paint
- 8 sprays of plastic flowers
- 2 heavy rubber bands
- plaster of Paris, 3 cups
- 1-1/2 cups water
- used birthday and anniversary cards
- waxed paper
- scissors
- glue

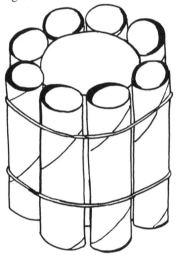

Fig. 5-5-A

Directions for Making:

STEP 1:   Remove one end of a soda can. Wash and dry.

STEP 2:   Select 8 bathroom tissue rolls. Make sure they are the same size around and the same length.

STEP 3:   Cover the outside of the can with a good, quick-drying glue. Put on a lot of glue. Set the tissue rolls around the can and hold them in place with 2 heavy rubber bands, one at the top and one at the bottom until glue sets. (See Fig. 5-5A.)

STEP 4:   Remove the rubber bands. Place the can and rolls in the middle of a newspaper. Spray paint the entire surface.

STEP 5:   Cut flower sprays, small animals, children, etc., from used cards and glue one on each tissue roll.

STEP 6:   Place onto a piece of waxed paper. Mix plaster of Paris and water to thick cream consistency.

STEP 7:   Spoon the plaster carefully into the rolls. Fill the rolls one half full. Place a spray of flowers into the plaster and let dry.

STEP 8:   Fill the can in the center 2/3 full of water. Make a bouquet of fresh flowers and put in the can.

ACTIVITY 5-6: Milk Carton Flower Holder

Materials Needed:

- 1/2 gallon cardboard milk carton
- sharp knife or razor blade
- glue and brush
- shell macaroni
- back of a tablet
- gold or silver spray paint
- blue, green or red spray paint
- staple gun
- Styrofoam, 3 X 3 X 1 inch square, or 1/2 or a 3 inch Styrofoam ball
- green stem of fern or leaves
- flowers
- miniature bird

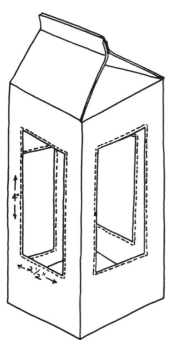

Fig. 5-6-A
cut windows 2½x4 inches
use pattern A

Directions for Making:

STEP 1: Wash and rinse 1/2 gallon milk carton. Let dry. Scrape off wax from container, using a sharp knife.

STEP 2: Using a sharp knife or razor blade, cut a window 2-1/2 X 4 inches from the middle of each side of the milk carton, using Pattern A. (See Fig. 5-6A.)

STEP 3: Measure down from the top rim of the carton 1 inch. Do not put macaroni on this space.

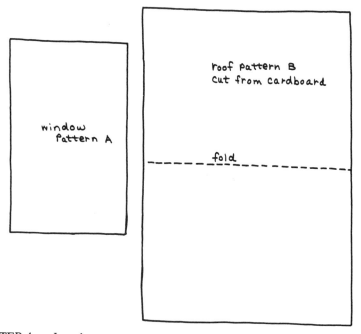

STEP 4:   Lay the carton on one side. Working on a small area at a time, cover with glue and add small shell macaroni, bump side up.

STEP 5:   Cover the milk carton on all 4 sides with glue and macaroni. Set aside to dry.

STEP 6:   Cut a piece of cardboard 4-1/2 X 6-1/2 inches. The back of a tablet or a shirt box can be used. Use Pattern B. Fold cardboard in the middle.

STEP 7:   Starting at the fold, glue shell macaroni onto the cardboard in rows. This is the roof of the holder. Let dry.

STEP 8:   Spray paint the milk carton either gold or silver.

STEP 9:   The roof may be sprayed with red, blue or green. Spray both sides of the roof, the plain side and also the one with macaroni on it.

STEP 10:   Staple the top of the milk carton together. Put glue on both sides and place the roof on. Hold for a few minutes until glue sets up.

STEP 11:   Cut a square from Styrofoam 3 X 3 X 1 inches or cut a Styrofoam ball in half. Glue into the bottom of the milk carton.

STEP 12:   Insert the ends of the greenery and flowers into the Styrofoam through the windows. Let the flowers hang out.

STEP 13:   Punch a hole in the roof at the top of the carton and stick the wire stem of the bird into the carton.

STEP 14:   Chenille bugs or butterflies can be added to the flowers.

ACTIVITY 5-7: Clothespin Flower Basket

Materials Needed:

- one pound nut, coffee or candy can
- spring clothespins
- 2 rubber bands
- Styrofoam block, 1 X 4 X 4 inches

- copper spray paint
- tie wire
- flowers, any color (should be the kind that drape down—5 or 7 sprays)
- glue

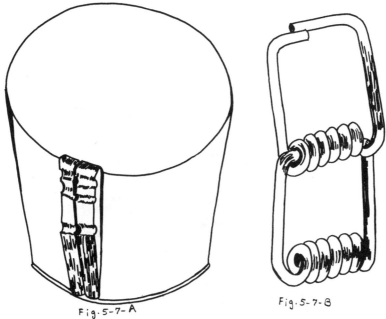

Fig. 5-7-A

Fig. 5-7-B

Directions for Making:

STEP 1: Wash and dry tin cans inside and out.

STEP 2: Separate the 2 wooden parts of the clothespins from the metal springs. Save the springs for the handle.

STEP 3:   Working in a small area, cover the can with glue and lay the separated wooden parts of the clothespins onto the can, being sure all the pins face the same way, with the grooves to the outside. Be sure the pins are even on the bottom. (See Fig. 5-7A.)

STEP 4:   Use a rubber band to hold the pins in place until the glue is dry.

STEP 5:   To make the handle, start at the spring end of the clothespin; put the end with the loose wires into the holes on the *2nd* spring. Do this to all the springs. (See Fig. 5-7B.)

STEP 6:   Take off the rubber bands. Fasten a piece of tie wire around the bottom groove. Pull tight and twist ends together. Cut off excess wire.

STEP 7:   Around the top groove measure the tie wire. Leave an extra inch; cut off.

STEP 8:   Push both ends of the spring handle onto the tie wire. Wrap wire around can. Arrange the spring handle so there will be one end on opposite sides. This wire should be in the top groove; pull tight and twist the ends of the wire together.

STEP 9:   Spray paint the entire surface of the can, springs and clothespins. Let dry.

STEP 10: Set the can onto the piece of Styrofoam and cut a circle to fit into the bottom of the can. Glue and let dry.

STEP 11: Push the ends of the flowers into the Styrofoam; let hang down.

ACTIVITY 5-8: Window Box from Plastic Egg Carton

Materials Needed:

- 1 plastic egg carton, green
- small plastic flowers with short stems
- sequins and glitter
- plaster of Paris
- bowl for mixing and spoon
- scissors
- ice pick

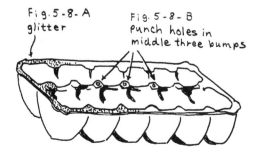

Fig. 5-8-A
glitter

Fig. 5-8-B
Punch holes in
middle three bumps

Directions for Making:

STEP 1: Remove the lid from the egg carton, also the hinge from the other side of the carton.

STEP 2: Decorate the carton with glitter around the top edge by putting a line of glue and sprinkling on glitter. Add sequins for color on the outside of the egg cups. (See Fig. 5-8A.)

STEP 3: In the middle 3 bumps, punch a hole with an ice pick, and stick three taller flowers into these holes. Cut stems no longer than 3 inches. (See Fig. 5-8B.)

STEP 4: Fill each egg cup with plaster of Paris and set small flower heads into each cup.

ACTIVITY 5-9: Window Shadow Box

Materials Needed:

- Styrofoam circle, 6 inch diameter
- clear plastic food container, 2 X 4-1/2 X 6 inches
- 1 wax candle tree, 3 inches tall
- blue spray paint
- silver glitter
- 3 plastic flowers
- 2 small deer on wire stems
- 2 plastic sprays of green leaves
- 1 sequin half moon
- 2 bird sequins
- glue

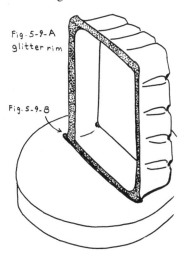

Fig. 5-9-A
glitter rim

Fig. 5-9-B

Directions for Making:

STEP 1: Remove the thin plastic lid from the top edge of the container. Wash inside and out, rinse and dry.

STEP 2: Using blue spray paint, cover the outside first, let dry, and then spray the inside of the box and let dry.

STEP 3:   Set the edge of the box onto the plastic circle. Measure, and using sharp pointed scissors, draw a line for the rim to fit into.

STEP 4:   Outline the rim of the box on three sides with glue and cover with silver glitter. Let dry. (See Fig. 5-9A.)

STEP 5:   Glue stars and moon at the top back of the box. If the half moon sequins are hard to find, cut a moon from paper, glue and glitter it, and glue it in place in the box.

STEP 6:   Cut a piece of ribbon, 1 X 19 inches; glue and pin it around the foam circle.

STEP 7:   Put glue onto the rim of the box, place rim into the line drawn on the circle (see Fig. 5-9B) and let dry.

STEP 8:   Cut the wire stem from one deer about two inches long. Insert the end of the wire into the Styrofoam circle in front of the box; cut the wire from the second deer 1-1/2 inches long. Insert the wire through the box and into the Styrofoam. Set so the feet are even with the box.

STEP 9:   Set the wax candle tree into the box at the back of one deer.

STEP 10:   Cut two sprays of plastic leaves and put on either side of the box in the background.

STEP 11:   Cut the stems from three bright colored plastic flowers, 1 inch long. Poke a hole for the stems and glue into the foam at the front of the box.

STEP 12:   (Optional) Set the sequin birds so they face each other in the foam in front of the flowers.

Chapter Six

Easily Made Gifts for Family and Friends

For a child, making a gift that is both pretty and useful is a wonderful experience. To be able to say "I made this" and to give it to someone with love, is a heartwarming part of growing up. These gifts are neither hard to make, nor very expensive. All they really cost is a little time.

ACTIVITY 6-1: Mother's Day Gift

Materials Needed:

- 1 fiesta plastic dish from the Dairy Queen
- 14 plastic flower heads, bright colors, on short stems
- plaster of Paris
- water
- 2 sprigs of plastic fern
- 4 or 5 tiny flowers, such as forget-me-nots, etc.
- sequins

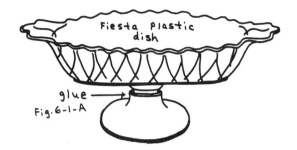

Directions for Making:

STEP 1: Glue the stand onto the boat shape. (See Fig. 6-1A.)

STEP 2: Cut small flower heads off. Cut the stems about 2 inches long. Leave any leaves or greenery on the flowers.

STEP 3: Make one stem about 3 inches long.

STEP 4: Mix the plaster of Paris and water to thick cream consistency. Fill the boat 3/4 full.

STEP 5: Working quickly, set the tall flowers in the center and on each side add the plastic ferns. Then add the rest of the flowers in a bright color arrangement around the outside edge of the boat.

STEP 6: Let set until dry. Add a ribbon bow on the leg or add sequins around the stand.

ACTIVITY 6-2: A Gift for Dad

Materials Needed:

- 90 Popsicle sticks
- 1 empty tuna can
- 1 Campbell's soup can
- 2 Vienna sausage cans—all with labels removed
- 100 inches bright colored rick rack, 2-3/4 yards
- 8 rubber bands
- used birthday cards with flowers, birds or butterflies
- sharp knife
- black felt marker pen
- scissors
- glue

Directions for Making:

STEP 1: (This project is a harder one; have help from a leader or parent.) Remove the lids from the 4 cans, take off the labels, wash and dry.

STEP 2: Lay 20 straight Popsicle sticks in a row, making sure the ends are even. Glue 6 sticks in place. (See Fig. 6-2A.) Let dry. This is the platform for the gift.

STEP 3: Turn the platform over and glue the rick rack from corner to corner. Criss cross in the center. This helps to hold the sticks in place. (See Fig. 6-2B.)

STEP 4: Glue 22 Popsicle sticks around the soup can. Stretch 2 rubber bands, one at the top and one at the bottom of the can. Let dry.

STEP 5: Glue rick rack around the top of the can down one inch and a row around the bottom of the can.

STEP 6: Glue this can to one end of the platform in the center between the rick rack. (See Fig. 6-2C.)

STEP 7: Glue a cut out paper flower or decal on the front side of the can.

STEP 8: Measure a Popsicle stick 2-1/2 inches from one end. Crease with a sharp knife. Turn the stick over and place the knife blade behind the crease and break the stick in two. Smooth off both cut ends of the stick with a knife or sandpaper.

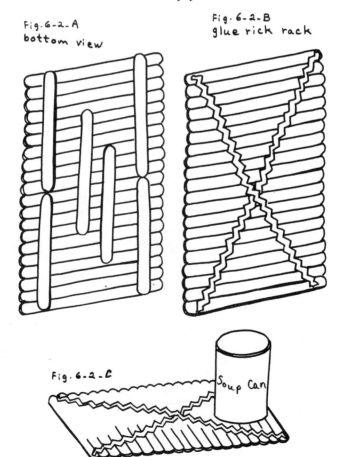

Fig. 6-2-A
bottom view

Fig. 6-2-B
glue rick rack

Fig. 6-2-C

Soup Can

STEP 9:   Using this stick for a measure, cut 42 sticks in this same way. Keep the 2-inch pieces for the tuna cans.

STEP 10:   Glue 21 sticks 2-1/2 inches long around the Vienna sausage cans; stick two rubber bands around to hold and let dry. Put glue at the top and bottom rim of the can.

STEP 11:   Using the 2-inch Popsicle sticks, glue these around the tuna can. It takes 28 pieces. Add the rubber bands until dry. Be sure the rounded end is at the top of the can.

STEP 12:   Glue rick rack around the top and bottom edges of these cans. Remove the rubber bands.

STEP 13:   Cut flowers, birds, butterflies, etc., from old greeting cards or use a felt marker pen and write "Stamps" on the tuna can; "pins" and "paper clips" on the sausage cans; and "Pens and pencils" on the soup can.

STEP 14:   Glue the two sausage cans next to the soup can and the tuna can at the front end of the platform.

ACTIVITY 6-3: A Gift for Dad or Granddad

Materials Needed:

- 1 plastic deer
- 1 3-1/2 inch foil tart pan
- 1 plastic poinsetta
- 2 plastic leaves
- small Christmas beads
- plaster of Paris and water
- felt
- silver glitter
- sharp scissors
- glue
- waxed paper, 4 inch square

Fig. 6-3-A
cut bottom
from
foil plate

Fig. 6-3-B
make hole for
flower stem

Directions for Making:

STEP 1:   Using a narrow brush, cover the petals of the poinsetta with glue. Sprinkle on glitter. Set aside to dry.

STEP 2:   Using sharp scissors, cut the bottom from a small foil plate. (These are found in some T.V. dinners. See Fig. 6-3A.)

STEP 3:   Using the sharp end of the scissors, poke a hole about 1/3 inch from the bottom of the pan. (See Fig. 6-3B.)

STEP 4:   Mix the plaster and water to thick cream consistency. Set the pan on a piece of waxed paper with the cut end up.

STEP 5:   Carefully fill up the pie pan with plaster.

STEP 6:   Poke the stem of the poinsetta flower into the hole. (Step 3.)

STEP 7:   Let the plaster set for three minutes. Set the deer figurine into the plaster just so its feet won't show.

STEP 8:   On the back side of the deer, stick 2 stems of plastic leaves.

STEP 9:   Let the plaster dry. Remove the waxed paper. Draw around the outside rim of the tart pan, and cut a piece of felt to fit.

STEP 10:   Around the outside rim of the pan, glue Christmas beads.

ACTIVITY 6-4: A Gift for Teacher

Materials Needed:

- 1 oblong papier-maché berry basket, quart and a half size
- wheel and shell macaroni
- sequins
- foil wrap
- silver spray paint
- glue
- ingredients for cookies

Directions for Making:

STEP 1:   Glue the wheel macaroni around the rim on the berry basket. (See Fig. 6-4A.)

STEP 2:   Cover the sides of the basket with small shell macaroni, glued on. Let dry. (See Fig. 6-4B.)

STEP 3:   In the hub on each wheel glue a green, red or blue sequin.

STEP 4:   Line the middle of the berry basket with foil wrap. Bake a dozen cookies of the two varieties given, using the recipes given below.

STEP 5:   After the cookies have cooled, fill the basket, cover with plastic wrap and add a ribbon bow at the top.

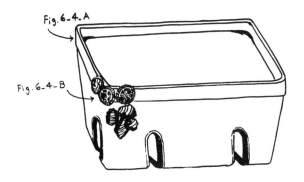

Fig. 6-4-A

Fig. 6-4-B

Snicker Doodles

1 cup shortening	2-3/4 cups flower
2-1/2 cups sugar	1 teaspoon baking powder
2 eggs	1 teaspoon baking soda
	1/2 teaspoon baking soda

Cream together the shortening, sugar and eggs. Sift together the remaining ingredients and stir into the first mixture. Roll the dough into small balls the size of walnuts. Then roll the balls in a mixture of 2 tablespoons sugar and 3 teaspoons cinnamon. Place on an ungreased cookie sheet; bake for 8 to 10 minutes in a 400° oven.

Yield: 5 dozen cookies.

Oatmeal Crunchies

1-1/2 cups flower	1-1/4 cups packed brown sugar
2 teaspoons baking soda	1 egg
1/2 teaspoon salt	1/4 cup milk
dash of cinnamon	1-3/4 cups quick-cooking oatmeal
1 cup shortening	1 cup chopped walnuts

Measure flour, salt, soda and cinnamon into flower sifter. Cream shortening with the brown sugar until fluffy in a large bowl; beat in the egg and milk. Sift in the flour mixture, blending well to make a thick batter. Fold in the rolled oats and walnuts.

Drop by teaspoonsfull, 3 inches apart, on a greased cookie sheet. Bake in a moderate oven (350°) for 12 minutes or until lightly browned. Remove from the cookie sheet and cool completely on a wire rack.

ACTIVITY 6-5: A Gift for a Shut In

Materials Needed:

- 1 clay or plastic flower pot
- 1 large flower spray with at least 5 flowers and 2 buds
- 6 fern sprigs
- foil paper, 18 X 18 inches
- 2 yards of ribbon, 3/4 inch wide
- Popsicle stick
- plaster of Paris, amount varies according to size of pot
- water

Directions for Making:

STEP 1: Select a pot the right size for the flowers.

STEP 2: Mix the plaster of Paris and water to thick cream consistency. Fill the pot full.

STEP 3: Set the flower stem into the pot. Add the fern sprigs around the flower. On one side of the pot stick the Popsicle stick into the plaster. This stick is used to tie the ribbon to. Let set until the plaster hardens.

STEP 4: Cut a piece of foil 18 X 18 inches. Lay flat on the table. Set the flower pot into the center. Pull the corners of the foil up around the pot, folding foil so it will fit tight.

STEP 5: Tie the ribbon around the foil at an angle, low at the back side; bring to the top of the pot and tie around the Popsicle stick at the front to hold. Make a pretty bow. (See Fig. 6-5A.)

Fig. 6-5-A

ACTIVITY 6-6: Recipe Holder

Materials Needed:

- 1 small glass dish or lid from a spray paint can with a wide mouth
- 1 colored plastic fork
- 2 small flowers
- small figurine
- plaster of Paris, 1 cup
- small bowl and spoon
- water, 1/2 cup

Directions for Making:

STEP 1:   Have all the materials ready, as plaster sets up very quickly.

STEP 2:   Put about 1/2 cup water into the bowl. Add plaster of Paris and mix to the consistency of heavy cream. Pour into the glass or spray can lid. Container should be full. (Plaster may be colored by adding 5 or 6 drops of food coloring to the water.)

STEP 3:   Using the plastic fork, stick the handle end into the plaster, at the back of the glass.

STEP 4:   In front of the fork, add the figurine, by sticking it down into the plaster.

STEP 5:   Add a flower on each side of the fork, between the fork and the figurine.

STEP 6:   Insert a recipe card between the first and third tines on the fork. (This holds recipe firmly and if recipe is written on both sides of the card, container may be easily turned around. Recipes are easily changed and this keeps them clean.)

ACTIVITY 6-7: Recipe Holder with Dowel

Materials Needed:

- 1 wooden dowel, 8 X 1/2 inch diameter
- glass or small container
- 2 small flowers
- small figurine
- sandpaper
- 1 tall flower
- 1 clothespin

Fig. 6-7-A
glue clothespin
to dowel

- small mixing bowl and spoon
- spray paint, color desired
- 1/2 cup water
- 1 cup plaster of Paris
- glue

Directions for Making:

STEP 1: Using sandpaper, smooth one side of the dowel the length of the clothespin.

STEP 2: Glue clothespin to the dowel, where it has been smoothed off. (See Fig. 6-7A.)

STEP 3: Spray paint over all—clothespin and the dowel.

STEP 4: In the bowl mix a half cup of water with the cup of plaster to heavy cream consistency. Pour into glass or small container.

STEP 5: Set the dowel to the back of the container.

STEP 6: Stick the stems of the 2 small flowers into the plaster, one on each side of the dowel. The tall flower should be in back of the dowel. Add the figurine to front side of container.

STEP 7: To use the holder, open the end of the clothespin and insert the recipe card.

ACTIVITY 6-8: Snow Man Gift Holder

Materials Needed:

- 1 Styrofoam ball, 2 inches
- Styrofoam ball, 1-1/2 inches
- 2 small moving eyes, 1/4 inch size
- a 12 inch red chenille stick
- 1 small red Christmas ball for nose
- small top hat
- 1 round margarine tub
- 1 bright colored feather
- 2 pieces white pipe cleaner, 1 inch long
- 3 large red sequins

- 1 pin
- glue
- piece of bright colored material or ribbon, 1/2 X 8 inches
- ice pick
- scissors

Directions for Making:

STEP 1: Wash and dry plastic margarine tub.

STEP 2: Set the 2 inch Styrofoam ball on the edge of the tub and push down. Make a dent in the ball 1/3 inch deep. (See Fig. 6-8A.)

STEP 3: Remove the ball, put glue in the dent and set ball back onto the edge of the tub. Let dry.

STEP 4: Fasten the 1-1/2 inch ball to the 2 inch ball with the 2 pipe cleaners. Stick the ends of the pipe cleaners into one ball close together and stick other ends into top of 2 inch ball. (See Fig. 6-8B.)

STEP 5: Cut the 12 inch red cleaners into two parts. Stick into the 2 inch ball close to the top for arms. (See Fig. 6-8C.)

STEP 6: Using the ice pick, poke 2 holes in the margerine tub, one on each side just under the rim.

STEP 7: Into the holes, insert the ends of the chenille sticks and twist the ends together. (See Fig. 6-8D.) This will hold the snow man in place.

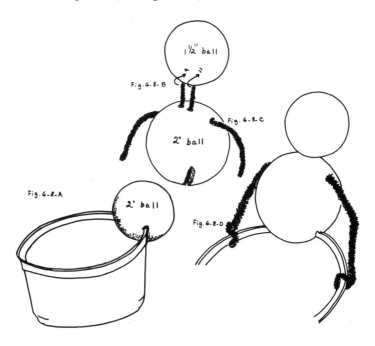

STEP 8:   Glue on a top hat.

STEP 9:   Cut a piece of material 1/2 X 8 inches. Slash the ends. Wrap around the neck of the snowman, pin on one side, leaving the ends loose.

STEP 10:   Glue on moving eyes, a rick rack mouth. Stick the end of the Christmas ball in place for a nose.

STEP 11:   Add 3 large sequins down the front for buttons.

STEP 12:   Glue a feather to the hat.

STEP 13:   Fill the margarine tub with cookies, candy or nuts. This makes a nice gift for an elderly person.

ACTIVITY 6-9: Split Pea Flower Vase

Materials Needed:

- 1 6 oz. Ajax cleanser bottle
- 1/2 cup split peas
- 5 flowers and greenery
- white spray paint
- glue

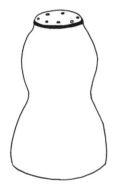

Directions for Making:

STEP 1:   Wash and dry the cleanser bottle.

STEP 2:   Put glue on a small area and cover with the split peas, with the bump side up.

STEP 3:   Cover all the bottle this way, working on a small area at a time. Let glue dry.

STEP 4:   After glue has dried, shake the can of white paint and spray the peas and bottle. Let dry. If the peas still show green, cover the second time with the paint.

STEP 5:   Make a floral arrangement by sticking the stems of the flowers down in the top of the cleanser bottle.

ACTIVITY 6-10: Santa, Small Gift Holder

Materials Needed:

- red felt or flannel, 6 X 8 inches
- pink felt, 4 X 6 inches
- silver glitter
- 2 moving eyes, 1/4 inch size
- small silver tinkle bell

- cotton
- cord for hanging
- pattern
- glue and glue brush
- plain scissors
- pinking scissors

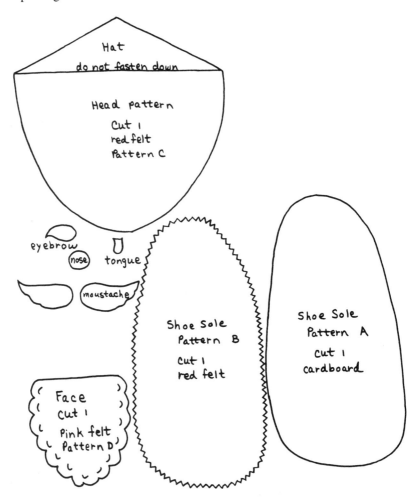

Directions for Making:

STEP 1:   Lay a piece of typing paper over the patterns, draw, and cut out with straight scissors; using Pattern A, cut the shoe sole from cardboard.

STEP 2:   With pinking scissors, cut a smaller sole from red felt, using Pattern B.

STEP 3:   Glue the red felt sole onto the cardboard sole.

STEP 4:   Using straight scissors cut out Pattern C from red felt. Glue this piece around the toe of the sole. Leave the pointed top loose.

STEP 5:   Cut out Pattern D from pink felt; glue to the center of the head pattern.

STEP 6:   Cut a red tongue from felt; glue in place; add the moving eyes and a red yarn pom-pom nose or tiny Christmas ball.

STEP 7:   Using cotton for a beard and moustache, glue in place and sprinkle silver glitter here and there on the cotton.

STEP 8:   Add a cotton band across the top of the head. In the center glue on the small silver bell.

STEP 9:   Add a cotton ball above the silver bell on the top of the hat.

ACTIVITY 6-11: Fan for Grandmother

Materials Needed:

- round card with pretty scene
- tongue depressor or Popsicle stick
- 2 staples
- staple gun
- silver glitter
- regular cardboard
- glue

Directions for Making:

STEP 1:   Draw around the card onto the cardboard. Cut out circle.

STEP 2:   Glue and glitter the highlights on the card.

STEP 3:   Glue and lay the Popsicle handle in place. Glue the card on top of the cardboard circle. Staple handle in two places. (See Fig. 6-11A.)

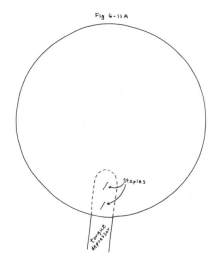

Fig 6-11A

Chapter Seven

Lovely Creations for the Holidays

Holidays are special times of the year and children love to be included in the plans and decorating. These articles are all quite simple to make, but they are very effective.

They can be made for family and friends to be used as gifts or used by the children themselves in their rooms.

ACTIVITY 7-1: Small Easter Basket

Materials Needed:

- 1 oblong margarine tub
- 2 twelve-inch chenille pipe cleaners
- ribbon, 18 inches, pastel shade
- Easter grass and candy
- little chenille chicken or rabbit
- felt cutouts—hearts, chickens, rabbits, etc.
- glitter or sequins
- paper punch
- glue
- scissors

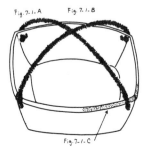

Directions for Making:

STEP 1: Wash and dry oblong margarine tub.

STEP 2: Punch holes in the tub, two at each end at the corner.

STEP 3: Using two twelve-inch chenille pipe cleaners, poke one end in a hole and twist the end up and over the rim. Twist together to tie. Do the same with the other stick. (See Fig. 7-1A.)

STEP 4: Crisscross the pipe cleaners in the center and fasten the other ends of the pipe cleaners into the opposite ends of the tubs. (See Fig. 7-1B.)

STEP 5: Tie a pretty ribbon bow where the pipe cleaners cross.

STEP 6: Apply glue with a small brush around the edge of the margarine tub and dip in glitter. (See Fig. 7-1C.)

STEP 7: Decorate the outside of the tub with felt cutouts, or sequins.

STEP 8: Fill with Easter grass and put in eggs and small cotton rabbit or chicken.

(Can be used as a party favor or gift for small child.)

ACTIVITY 7-2: Easter Treat Holder

Materials Needed:

- 1 empty quart size cottage cheese container
- 16 inches eyelet ruffling
- 1 small Easter decoration—duck, rabbit, etc., on a wire
- 1 used Easter card with cute pictures
- Easter grass
- eggs of candy, Styrofoam, or regular eggs that are dyed
- orchid spray paint
- scissors
- glue

Directions for Making:

STEP 1: Cover the outside of the cottage cheese container with spray paint. Let dry.

STEP 2: Put glue around the top rim of the container and add the eyelet ruffling.

STEP 3: Cut a design from the used card and glue to the carton.

STEP 4: Put grass into the container, fill 1/2 full. Fill up with Easter eggs.

STEP 5: Cut the wire stem from the Easter decoration, 5-1/2 inches long. Stick into the container between the eggs.

ACTIVITY 7-3: Poof Easter Baskets

Materials Needed:

- 1 gallon size bleach jug, blue
- 2 paper fasteners
- 2 clear plastic clothes bags at least 48 inches long
- string
- 2 small flowers
- grass
- Easter eggs
- 3 chenille pipe cleaners—white
- scissors
- paper punch or ice pick

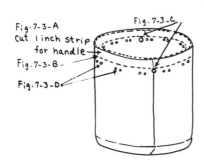

Directions for Making:

STEP 1:   Remove the label, scrape off the glue and wash and dry the jug.

STEP 2:   Cut the jug off under the handle, using the top ring as a cutting guide. (See Fig. 7-3A.)

STEP 3:   Measure down one inch from the top of the jug and cut off this strip. This is the handle of the basket. (See Fig. 7-3B.)

STEP 4:   Punch a hole in the plastic jug on the seam, one inch from the top. (See Fig. 7-3C.) Punch a hole in the plastic strip one inch from the end. Fasten to the basket with a paper fastener.

STEP 5:   Turn the basket half way around and punch holes in the other side as in step 4.

STEP 6:   Make up 12 poofs from plastic bags following directions in Hint No. 1.

STEP 7:   Cut the chenille pipe cleaners into 2 inch pieces. Make into a hairpin shape.

STEP 8:   Push a chenille hairpin where the poof is tied.

STEP 9:   Punch 12 sets of holes around the top of the plastic jug, two inches down from the top. (See Fig. 7-3D.)

STEP 10: Push the ends of the chenille hairpins into the holes, pull tight and twist ends together, inside of the basket.

STEP 11: Either staple or glue a flower at each side, at the handle.

STEP 12: Make a V notch in the handle at the top and tie on a ribbon bow.

STEP 13: Fill the basket with grass and candy Easter eggs or flowers.

ACTIVITY 7-4: May Baskets

Materials Needed:

- an assortment of detergent bottles, margarine tubs, cottage cheese containers
- flowers
- chenille pipe cleaners
- ribbon
- pieces of Styrofoam
- spray paint, pastel colors
- ice pick or sharp pointed scissors
- scissors
- staple gun

Fig. 7-4-A
cut

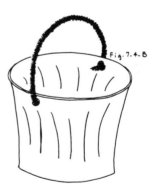

Fig. 7-4-B

Directions for Making:

STEP 1: Remove the labels from the detergent bottles; wash and dry all containers.

STEP 2: To make baskets from oblong margarine tubs, punch a hole in each of the four corners, using the ice pick. Insert the ends of two chenille pipe cleaners in the end of the tub. Crisscross the pipe cleaners and fasten other end into the opposite end of the tub. Tie a ribbon where the pipe cleaners cross and make the handle.

STEP 3: For detergent bottle baskets, cut the bottles off two inches up from the bottom. (See Fig. 7-4A.) Cut a strip of plastic 1/2 inch wide; staple to each side for handle.

STEP 4:   Cottage cheese containers are for a larger basket. Spray paint the outside. Use chenille pipe cleaners for handles by punching holes in opposite sides and twist the ends of the cleaners together. (See Fig. 7-4B.)

STEP 5:   For all containers, cut Styrofoam the size of the container. Glue bottom of Styrofoam into the basket. Insert the ends of flowers into Styrofoam to hold.

ACTIVITY 7-5: Hallowe'en Cat

Materials Needed:

- a 1/2 gallon bleach jug, any color
- black spray paint
- orange ribbon, 1 X 24 inches
- 1 three-inch Styrofoam ball
- black felt strip, 2 X 6 inches
- 2 moving eyes, 1/2 inch size
- small scrap of red and black felt
- 1 large fluffy chenille stick
- green glitter pen
- 6 toothpicks, sharp on both ends
- scissors
- black Styrofoam spray paint
- glue

Directions for Making:

STEP 1:   Remove label, scrape off glue, wash and dry bleach jug.

STEP 2:   Take the lid off the jug; spray the jug black.

STEP 3:   Spray the Styrofoam ball black. (Be sure to use a good Styrofoam spray paint as other types of paint will dissolve the Styrofoam.)

STEP 4:   Cut out oval shape from the front of the jug. (See Fig. 7-5A.)

STEP 5:   Force the ball onto the neck of the jug, using a twisting motion.

STEP 6:   Twist the ball off again, fill the hole with glue, and twist the ball back on again. Let set until dry, 1/2 to 1 hour.

STEP 7:   Cut the nose and mouth from red felt. Cut the ears from black felt. The bow tie is from orange felt, or use an orange ribbon.

STEP 8:   When the ball is dry, glue the moving eyes, nose and mouth in place. Glue and pin the ears to the top of the head, and stick toothpick whiskers in place. (See Fig. 7-5B.)

STEP 9:   Glue the fluffy chenille stick to the back of the jug for a tail.

STEP 10:   Glue the bow tie to the front of the jug under the face. Or, if using the ribbon, put ribbon under the handle in back, bring to the front, and tie.

STEP 11: Across the front of the jug, write "Trick or Treat," with the green glitter pen.

To use as a centerpiece, have an orange tablecloth, the cat in the center, and two orange candles in black candle holder on each side.

ACTIVITY 7-6: Candle Holders from Juice Cans

Materials Needed:

- 2 small juice cans
- small shell macaroni
- 2 cups plaster of Paris
- 1 cup water
- mixing bowl and spoon
- spray paint
- 2 detergent bottle caps
- 2 candles, 8 to 10 inches long
- glue

Directions for Making:

STEP 1:   Wash and dry the juice cans and detergent bottle caps.

STEP 2:   Over the outside of the juice cans, put glue and cover with small shell macaroni. Let dry.

STEP 3:   Mix plaster of Paris to thick cream consistency and fill cans full. In the center of each can, press a bottle cap.

STEP 4:   Let the plaster set up.

STEP 5:   Using black enamel paint, spray the can, macaroni, plaster and lid.

STEP 6:   Pour melted paraffin or candle wax into the bottle caps and set the candles upright. Hold for a moment or two until wax hardens.

ACTIVITY 7-7: Canes from Plastic Poofs

Materials Needed:

- 1 cane cut from heavy cardboard
- 1 paper punch, medium hole
- 2 yards white plastic
- 2 yards red plastic
- white chenille pipe cleaners
- 1 piece green ribbon, 1 yard by 5/8 inch
- string
- scissors
- ice pick

Directions for Making:

STEP 1:   Using a pair of heavy scissors or a very sharp knife and the pattern, cut a cane shape from heavy cardboard.

STEP 2:   With the ice pick or punch make holes in the cardboard at places marked on the pattern.

STEP 3:   Make 7 red poofs and 6 white poofs from plastic. (Directions for making poofs in Hints, No. 1.)

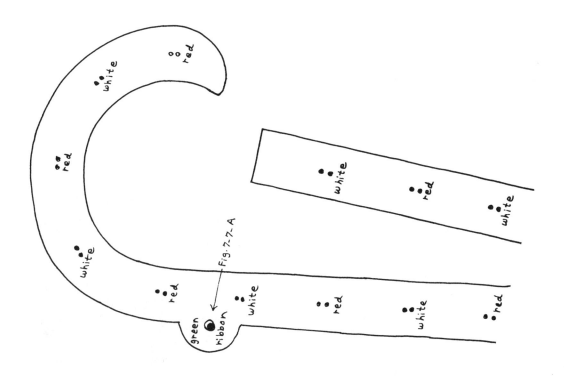

red
white
red
white
white
white
red
white
Fig. 7-7-A
red
white
green ribbon
red
white
red

STEP 4: Cut the chenille pipe cleaners into 2 inch pieces. Fold into hairpin shape.

STEP 5: Start at the bottom hole with a red poof. Push the hairpin around center of poof and stick the 2 ends of the pipe cleaner into the holes and twist ends together on underneath side.

STEP 6: Using this same procedure, cover the cane, first a red one, then a white one.

STEP 7: Tie a pretty bow from ribbon and fasten into the hole at the top side of the cane, using a 4 inch piece of chenille pipe cleaner. (See Fig. 7-7A.)

ACTIVITY 7-8: Small Christmas Decoration

Materials Needed:

- 1 small foil pie pan
- 1 small deer figurine
- 2 plastic holly leaves
- 2 small sea shells, butter clam type
- gold spray
- plaster of Paris
- water
- silver glitter

Directions for Making:

STEP 1:   Mix plaster and water to thick cream consistency. Fill the foil pie pan 2/3 full.

STEP 2:   At one edge, set 2 small shells on edge. Put into plaster about 1/3 inch. Overlap slightly.

STEP 3:   Cut the stems from the 2 plastic holly leaves. Set the leaves into the plaster on each side of the shells.

STEP 4:   Spray with gold spray paint while plaster is still wet.

STEP 5:   Before plaster sets up, set the small deer figurine in front of the shells.

STEP 6:   Add glue and sprinkle silver glitter over all.

ACTIVITY 7-9: Candle Holder for Child to Make

Materials Needed:

- 1 small 5 inch cereal bowl
- 2 cups plaster of Paris
- 1 candle, 6 inches long
- 4 small fir cones
- glitter, silver or gold
- 4 one-inch Christmas balls
- 4 egg cups cut from plastic egg carton
- scissors
- glue

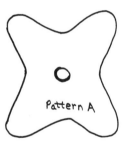

The small hole is made as the Christmas balls are pushed into the egg cups.

Directions for Making:

STEP 1:   Cut 4 cups from plastic egg cartons, using Pattern A. Put glue around the edge of each cup and dip in glitter. Set aside to dry.

STEP 2:   Select 4 little fir cones the same size. Using a brush, add glue here and there on the tips of the leaves of the cones. Dip into glitter.

STEP 3:   When all glue and glitter are dry, mix plaster to thick cream consistency. Fill the cereal bowl full.

STEP 4:   Set the candle into the center of the bowl.

STEP 5:   Set the glittered egg cups into the plaster, around the candle. Space them evenly with the open side out.

STEP 6:   In between the egg cups, stick the small cones into the plaster with the large ends in toward the candle. (Work fast because plaster sets up very quickly.)

STEP 7: Let the plaster set up. While you are waiting, take the hanger wires from 4 Christmas balls.

STEP 8: Apply glue around the holes and dip the end of the ball into glitter. Let dry.

STEP 9: Glue the Christmas ball into the egg cup, with glitter end facing to the outside.

ACTIVITY 7-10: Mrs. Santa Sucker Centerpiece

Materials Needed:

- 4 red candy suckers
- 1 large candy sucker
- 1 plastic drinking cup
- 1 Styrofoam ball, 2 inch size
- dacron cotton
- red spray paint
- 2 moving eyes
- tiny white flower on 1/2 inch stem
- ice pick
- glue

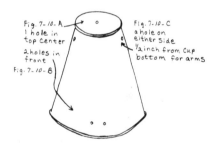

Fig. 7-10-A
1 hole in top center

2 holes in front
Fig. 7-10-B

Fig. 7-10-C
a hole on either side
1/2 inch from cup bottom for arms

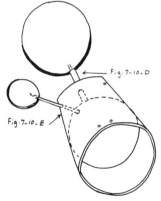

Fig. 7-10-D

Fig. 7-10-E

Directions for Making:

STEP 1: Spray the plastic cup red. Let dry.

STEP 2: Using the ice pick, punch a hole in the top center of the cup (see Fig. 7-10A); 2 holes in the front (see Fig. 7-10B); and one hole on either side of the cup, 1/2 inch from the cup bottom (see Fig. 7-10C).

STEP 3: Set the Styrofoam ball inside of the cup. Push the sucker stick through the hole in the top of the cup down into the ball. (See Fig. 7-10D.)

STEP 4:   Push the sticks through the other four holes, two in the top, and two in the bottom for hands and feet. Stick into the ball. (See Fig. 7-10E.)

STEP 5:   Glue cotton around the bottom of the cup, around the neck, and around the face.

STEP 6:   Add the moving eyes, nose and mouth.

STEP 7:   Glue a small green bow or small sprig of plastic holly to the cotton hair at the top.

STEP 8:   Glue the tiny white flower on the face for a nose. Leave stem end pointing out.

ACTIVITY 7-11: Horse Head Candy Cane Holder

Materials Needed:

- felt (any color, 4 X 8 inches)
- rick rack, large bump, 4-1/2 inches, or fake fur 1/8 X 4 inches
- 1 moving eye (1/4 inch) or large sequin
- colorful cord or yarn 18 inches long
- 1 candy cane, 5¢ or 10¢ size
- felt marker pen, black and red
- scissors
- glue
- straight pins

Directions for Making:

STEP 1:   Lay a piece of typing paper over pattern in book, trace and cut out. Pin the pattern to a double thickness of felt; using plain scissors, cut out the head. Sew around the head starting at A and sew to B, leaving the bottom open. (See Fig. 7-11A.)

STEP 2:   Glue the rick rack or fake fur onto the neck of the horse for a mane, starting just below the ear and going to the bottom of the neck. (See Fig. 7-11B.)

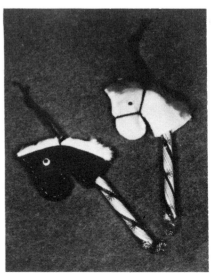

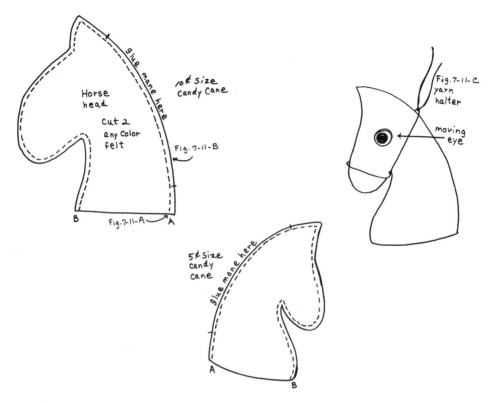

STEP 3: Glue on the moving eye or sequin. Insert the crook of the cane into the curved part of the felt head.

STEP 4: Using the cord or yarn, make a halter. (See Fig. 7-11C.) Fold cord in half. Make a loop over the nose of the horse and tie one knot under the chin; put one string up on each side of the head. Tie a double knot at the top of the mane. Tie both ends together at the very top for a hanger.

STEP 5: Using the felt marker pens, add features to the head, such as eyelashes, nostrils and mouth.

ACTIVITY 7-12: Tissue Box Christmas Creche

Materials Needed:

- 1 empty tissue box with oblong hole cut out
- 14 small shell macaroni
- wheel macaroni
- elbow macaroni
- green sequins
- 3 inch Styrofoam ball
- 1 six-inch circle of Styrofoam, 1 inch thick
- star, 1-1/4 inch
- Styrofoam block, 3-1/4 X 4 inches
- small red poinsettia
- red ribbon, 1 X 20 inches

- 4 small white rosebuds
- 2 figurines, 3 inches tall
- 1 figurine, 5 inches tall
- gold Christmas beads, 20 inches
- gold Styrofoam spray paint
- green flower sequins
- straight pins
- glue

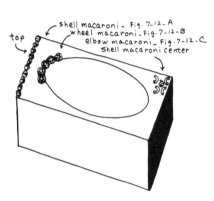

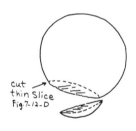

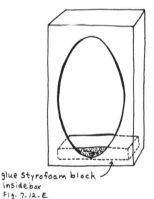

glue Styrofoam block
inside box
Fig. 7-12-E

Directions for Making:

STEP 1: Glue 10 small shell macaroni across the top of the box, shell side up. (See Fig. 7-12A.)

STEP 2: Glue the wheel macaroni around the oblong hole on the front of the box. (See Fig. 7-12B.)

STEP 3: Put four elbow macaroni in each corner of the box with a small shell macaroni in the center. (See Fig. 7-12C.)

STEP 4: Cut a thin slice from one side of the Styrofoam ball. (See Fig.

7-12D.) Glue in place, setting the flat side of the ball onto the top of the box.

STEP 5: Glue the box onto the Styrofoam circle at the back of the circle.

STEP 6: Using gold Styrofoam paint, spray the box, circle, ball and macaroni. Let dry.

STEP 7: Glue the Styrofoam block inside the box in the bottom end. (See Fig. 7-12E.)

STEP 8: Glue the gold beads around the bottom and sides next to the Styrofoam circle and around the ball on top of the box.

STEP 9: Glue a green sequin to the hub of each wheel macaroni.

STEP 10: Pin the star at the top front on the Styrofoam ball.

STEP 11: Glue the red ribbon around the foam circle; pin to hold until dry.

STEP 12: Glue the green flower sequin in place at the top of the oblong hole.

STEP 13: Cut the stem from the poinsettia, leaving stem at least one inch long. Stick this stem into the foam circle at the bottom of the oval opening.

STEP 14: Glue the two small figurines in place, one on either side of the box at the front.

STEP 15: Glue the large figurine onto the Styrofoam block inside the box.

STEP 16: Stick the stems of the four small white roses into the foam by the side of the two small figurines, next to the box.

ACTIVITY 7-13: 3 Ring Pretzel Tree Decorations with Silver Glitter

Materials Needed:

- 1 pretzel for each decoration
- silver, green, red and blue glitter
- 6 inches of white thread
- glue and brush
- an ornament hanger

3 Ring Pretzels

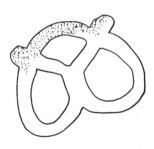

Directions for Making:

STEP 1: Lay the pretzels on a piece of newspaper. Cover one side of pretzels with glue. Sprinkle on glitter to cover. Let dry.

STEP 2: When glue has dried, turn the pretzels over and glue and glitter the other side. Let dry.

STEP 3: After glue and glitter have dried, set the pretzel on its side. Cover remaining bare spaces with glue and cover the pretzel completely with glitter. Let dry.

STEP 4: Tie a piece of thread through the top ring of the pretzel. Tie other end onto an ornament hanger. Hang on the tree. Several of these in different colors add a lot of color and shine to any tree.

Chapter Eight

Keepsake Jewelry and Holders

Children like jewelry for play and for "dress up." The items in this chapter take little time to make, but are pretty and practical.

The treasure chest could be used by boys to hold a collection such as rocks, stamps, etc. The jewelry box could become a gift for mother, sister or a girl friend.

ACTIVITY 8-1: Marble Jewelry

Materials Needed:

- 1 marble
- 1 sixteen-inch chain with fastener
- 1 large size jump ring
- 1 bell cap
- liquid glass glue
- 1 X 4 X 4 inch Styrofoam square

bell cap

jump ring

brass curtain ring

Directions for Making:

STEP 1: Open the prongs of the bell cap enough so the marble will set between them.

STEP 2: Using a good, quick-drying glue for glass or metal, put glue on the marble and set into the bell cap between the prongs.

STEP 3: Push the top of the bell cap into the Styrofoam so it will set up and hold the marble until the glue dries.

STEP 4: Open the jump ring and fasten the bell cap to the necklace chain.

ACTIVITY 8-2: Necklaces

Materials Needed:

- 1 sixteen-inch chain, either gold or silver
- 1 brass ring for curtains, 1-1/4 inch
- 1 teaspoon full of plastic crystalettes
- 1 large size jump ring
- aluminum foil
- cookie sheet

Directions for Making:

STEP 1: Cover the bottom of a cookie sheet with aluminum foil.

STEP 2: Lay the brass curtain ring onto the foil.

STEP 3: Fill the ring with plastic crystalettes.

STEP 4: Turn oven to 300° and cook crystals for 10 minutes.

STEP 5: When the crystals have cooked and fused together, remove from oven and cool.

STEP 6: Using a large size jump ring, fasten the curtain ring to the chain.

ACTIVITY 8-3: "It" Pins

Materials Needed:

- 1 piece fake fur, 1-1/2 X 1 inch
- 1 medium size safety pin
- strip of plastic, 1/2 X 2 inches, cut from plastic bleach jug
- needle and thread
- 1 large hole paper punch
- scissors
- glue

Directions for Making:

STEP 1:   Cut a piece of fake fur 1-1/2 inches by 1 inch, using a razor blade.
           (See Fig. 8-3A.) Cut on the back side of the fur—see Hint No. 4.

STEP 2:   Turn the fur side to the outside, make a roll and sew the two ends
           together, leaving the cone shape 1-1/2 inches long.

STEP 3:   Sew a safety pin, with the head up and the back side of the pin in,
           into the seam. (See Fig. 8-3B.)

STEP 4:   Cut a piece 1/2 X 2 inches from a plastic jug. Using the paper punch,
           cut the plastic into a pair of glasses, with straight pieces on the sides.
           Sharpen both ends.

STEP 5:   Glue the glasses to the front of the fur, bending the plastic and
           sticking ends into the fur.

STEP 6:   Add a hat, flowers, ribbon, etc., for decorations.

STEP 7:   Small moving eyes may be added instead of the glasses.

Fig. 8-3-A   Fig. 8-3-B

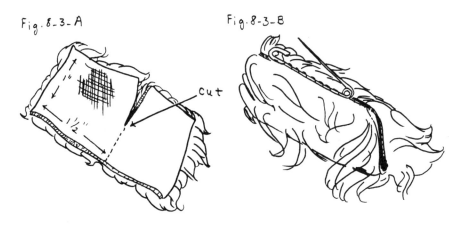

Fig. 8-3-C

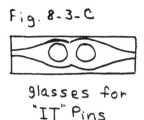

glasses for
"IT" Pins

ACTIVITY 8-4: Little Happies

Materials Needed:

- 3-inch circles of fake fur, any color
- 2 large moving eyes or large sequins, 3/4 inch size
- ribbon, sequins, spangles, feathers, etc.
- red felt scraps
- glue
- old comb

Basic
Pattern
for all Happies

cut 2
hands
pink felt

cut 2
wings
white felt

cut 1
tongue
red felt

cut 1
nose
red felt

cut 1
nose
red felt

cut 1
feather

glitter

Directions for Making:

STEP 1: Using a pair of sharp pointed scissors, cut a 3-inch circle from fake fur.

STEP 2: Comb the fur till smooth. Part the hair about 1 inch from top side, part in the middle; add ribbon bows, eyes, felt nose and mouth for a girl.

STEP 3: Add enlarged felt hands, ribbon bows, feathers, etc. What can be made is limited only by the imagination of the person.

ACTIVITY 8-5: Leaf Name Pins

Materials Needed:

- 1 piece heavy cardboard, 4 x 4 inches
- macaroni letters
- pin back
- green paint
- sharp knife
- silver glitter
- glue
- glue brush

Directions for Making:

STEP 1: Lay a piece of typing paper over the pattern, trace and cut out.

STEP 2: Trace the pattern onto the cardboard, and cut out with sharp scissors.

STEP 3: Spray paint the leaf green—give two coats of paint. Let each coat dry before spraying again.

STEP 4: Spread the glue around the edge of the leaf; sprinkle on silver glitter.

STEP 5: Select the macaroni letters for each name and lay them in a line across the leaf. Glue on.

STEP 6: On the back side of the leaf, glue a pin back in the center of the leaf pin. (See Fig. 8-5A.)

ACTIVITY 8-6: Play Earrings

Materials Needed:

- plastic bleach jug or detergent bottle
- 1 pair earring screws with drop hooks
- 2 large jump rings
- glitter and sequins
- sharp scissors
- glue
- small paper punch

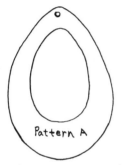

Pattern A

jump ring

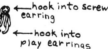

←—hook into screw earring

←—hook into play earrings

Directions for Making:

STEP 1: Remove label, wash and dry plastic bottles.

STEP 2: Make a pattern like Pattern A on paper and cut out.

STEP 3: Lay the pattern on the jug, draw two, and cut out. Punch holes at the top of loops with small paper punch. (See Fig. 8-6A.)

STEP 4: Cover one side of the loops with glue and sprinkle on glitter. Let dry.

STEP 5: (Optional) After the glue has dried, add sequins for more color.

STEP 6: Using a large jump ring, push ring through the hole in the loop and into the drop hook on the earring screw. Push jump ring together to hold earring.

ACTIVITY 8-7: Plaster of Paris Pins

Materials Needed:

- a used card with a cute picture of an animal, bird or flower
- plaster of Paris
- safety pin
- oil

- tablespoon
- clear plastic spray paint

Directions for Making:

STEP 1:   Wash and dry tablespoon. Grease the inside of the spoon with oil. (See Fig. 8-7A.)

STEP 2:   Cut a picture from a used card. Be sure it will fit inside of spoon. (See Fig. 8-7B.)

STEP 3:   Turn the picture over in the spoon so the picture side is in the bottom next to the oil. (Be sure to remember which end is up.)

STEP 4:   Mix enough plaster of Paris and water to fill the spoon. Mix to heavy cream consistency.

STEP 5:   Set the safety pin into the plaster. Be sure the pin end will fit into the pin head.

STEP 6:   When the plaster has set, remove from the spoon and let dry.

STEP 7:   Spray with clear plastic spray paint.

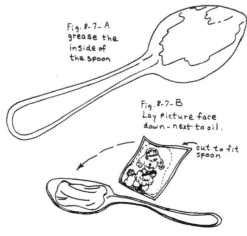

Fig. 8-7-A
grease the
inside of
the spoon

Fig. 8-7-B
Lay picture face
down - next to oil.

cut to fit
spoon

ACTIVITY 8-8: Crown for Dolls

Materials Needed:

- 1 plastic bleach jug, any color
- 2 staples and staple gun
- glitter, silver
- pencil
- sequins
- gold spray paint
- sharp scissors
- glue

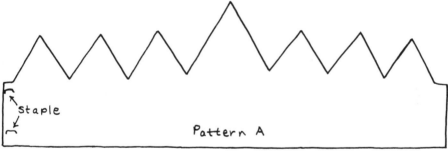

staple

Pattern A

Fig. 8-8-A

Directions for Making:

STEP 1: Remove label, wash and dry plastic bottle.

STEP 2: Lay a piece of typing paper onto pattern, trace and cut out.

STEP 3: Using sharp scissors, cut the jug down the seam and lay the pattern on the jug. Draw around Pattern A with a pencil.

STEP 4: Cut out the crown, set on a newspaper and spray gold inside and out. Ley dry.

STEP 5: Overlap the ends of the crown and staple together. (See Fig. 8-8A.)

STEP 6: Put a line of glue around the points. Dip into silver glitter.

STEP 7: Using different colored sequins, make a design on the crown. Glue in place.

ACTIVITY 8-9: Child's Crown and Pillow

Materials Needed:

- 1 gallon size plastic bleach jug
- sequins
- glitter
- felt marker pen
- glue
- sharp scissors
- plastic tape
- yarn
- 16 inches material
- cotton or nylon hose
- cardboard, 4 inch square

Place — cut out — on center seam of jug.

Pattern A

cut 1 then
turn pattern
in reverse to
cut other side.

Pattern B
Cut 2

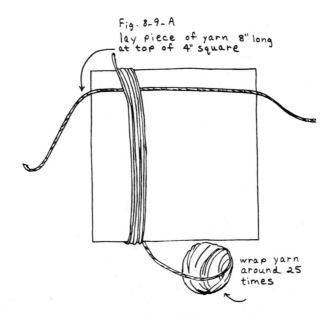

Fig. 8-9-A
lay piece of yarn 8" long
at top of 4" square

wrap yarn
around 25
times

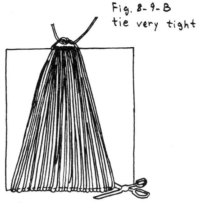

Fig. 8-9-B
tie very tight

cut yarn at bottom
Fig. 8-9-C

Fig. 8-9-D

Directions for Making:

STEP 1:   Lay a piece of typing paper on Pattern A and cut out.
STEP 2:   Lay the cut out pattern on top of the bleach jug. Tape in place. Using felt marker pen, outline the pattern; cut out, using sharp scissors. Staple the two ends together.
STEP 3:   Around the outside edge of the crown, spread a thin line of glue and cover with glitter. Put glitter around the holes in the front of the crown.
STEP 4:   Decorate with sequins, any way wanted.
STEP 5:   Make a pillow to set crown on, using Pattern B. Cut two pieces of material, 8 X 8 inches. Turn right sides together. Sew around edge, using a 3/8 inch seam. Leave a 3 inch opening. Turn material right side out and stuff pillow with cotton or nylon hose. Do not fill too full. Finish sewing the edges of the pillow.
STEP 6:   Make 4 tassels and sew one to each corner.
STEP 7:   To make a tassel, cut a piece of cardboard four inches square.
STEP 8:   Cut a piece of yarn 8 inches long. Lay at the top of the 4 inch piece of cardboard. Wrap yarn around the cardboard 25 times. (See Fig. 8-9A.)
STEP 9:   Pull the ends of the 8 inch piece of yarn together and tie at the top. Tie very tight. (See Fig. 8-9B.)
STEP 10: Using sharp scissors, cut the yarn at the bottom of the 4 inch square. (See Fig. 8-9C.)
STEP 11: Cut another piece of yarn 6 inches long and tie around the yarn one inch from the top. (See Fig. 8-9D.)

ACTIVITY 8-10: Treasure Chests

Materials Needed:

- 1 empty cigar box with lid attached
- 4-inch piece of picture molding (can be obtained from any builder's supply store or lumber yard)
- 2 pretty pictures from old calendars
- macaroni wheels and shells

- gold metallic spray paint
- sequins, either green or blue
- white enamel spray paint
- scissors
- glue

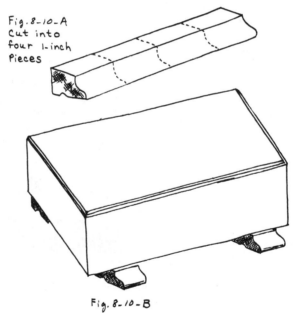

Fig. 8-10-A
Cut into
four 1-inch
Pieces

Fig. 8-10-B

Directions for Making:

STEP 1: Using either a hand saw, jig saw or coping saw, cut the picture molding into 4 one inch pieces. (See Fig. 8-10A.) These are the legs of the chest.

STEP 2: Glue the picture molding onto the box, one on each end, on the long side about one inch from the end of the box. (See Fig. 8-10B.) Let set until dry.

STEP 3: Open cigar box, spray inside with white paint. Spray the inside of the lid also. Let dry. If necessary spray the inside again. Be sure all writing is covered with paint.

STEP 4: Close the lid, and use macaroni wheels to make an outline around the top of the box, keeping in a straight line.

STEP 5: Glue macaroni shells around the sides and ends of the box. This can be covered or make a design with the macaroni. Let dry.

STEP 6: When glue has dried, close the lid and spray the outside of the box and macaroni two times with gold spray paint. Let dry.

STEP 7: Cut a picture from an old calendar to fit inside of the wheel macaroni frame on top of the lid. Glue on.

STEP 8: On the hubs of the wheel macaroni, glue bright colored sequins.

STEP 9: Cut another picture to fit the inside of the lid. Glue on.

This box can be used as a jewelry box, hankie box or treasure chest.

ACTIVITY 8-11: Jewelry Boxes

Materials Needed:

- 2 plastic boxes the same size, 2 X 4-1/2 X 5-1/2 inches, such as containers for jello or potato salad
- silver glitter
- 3 small bright colored flowers with leaves
- 6 tiny contrasting color flowers
- 2 plastic rings, any color, 1/2 inch size
- 2 small pieces cotton
- ice pick
- glue and brush

Directions for Making:

STEP 1: Remove label and plastic covering from the top of each box. Wash and dry inside and out.

STEP 2: Using a small brush, put glue in each indentation on the outside of the boxes and cover wtih glitter. (See Fig. 8-11A.)

STEP 3: Put the two rims of the boxes together, heat the ice pick on a stove burner, and make a hole on the rim of the back side of the box. (See Fig. 8-11B.) Be sure to keep the edges even. Punch 3 holes in the top of one box for flower stems. (See Fig. 8-11C.)

STEP 4: Using a sharp knife, cut the plastic ring apart. (See Fig. 8-11D.)

Spread the ends apart and slip the cut edges into the holes for hinges. Move the cut place on the ring half way around so the ring won't slip out. (See Fig. 8-11E.)

STEP 5:   Glue a small piece of cotton on the back side of the plastic leaves. Set close to the holes on the one box, stick the stems of the flowers into the holes.

STEP 6:   Glue the stems of the contrasting flowers in place on the box top.

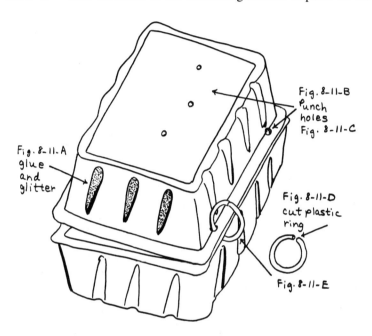

Fig. 8-11-B
Punch holes
Fig. 8-11-C

Fig. 8-11-A
glue
and
glitter

Fig. 8-11-D
cut plastic
ring

Fig. 8-11-E

Chapter Nine

Appealing Party Favors and Centerpieces

Children get more fun out of parties when they help to make the party favors and centerpieces themselves. These articles are all bright and pretty when they're finished, and they cost very little to prepare.

ACTIVITY 9-1: Individual Flower Holder Party Favor

Materials Needed:

- 1 empty bathroom tissue roll
- 1 cutout from a greeting card
- 14 Popsicle sticks
- 1 cup plaster of Paris
- 1/3 cup water
- 1 small square of waxed paper, 4 x 4 inches
- 1 tall flower, 5 inch stem, and several short flowers
- plastic greenery
- scissors
- glue
- spray paint, silver or gold

Directions for Making:

STEP 1: Glue the Popsicle sticks around the paper roll. Be sure sticks are even at top and bottom. Add a rubber band at the top and one at the bottom over the sticks. Let set until dry. (See Fig. 9-1A.)

STEP 2: Cut out a picture from a used greeting card.

STEP 3: Cut off the stems of the flowers to desired length. Make into an arrangement.

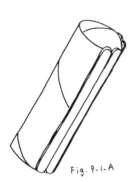

Fig. 9-1-A

STEP 4:   After glue has dried on the roll, remove the rubber bands. Spray the sticks with a metallic spray paint. Let dry.

STEP 5:   After paint is dry, glue the greeting card cutout on the front of the holder.

STEP 6:   Set the holder onto the waxed paper square. Mix plaster of Paris to thick cream consistency. Fill the paper roll, being careful not to spill any on the outside of the container.

STEP 7:   Make the flower arrangement by sticking the stem ends of the flowers into the wet plaster. Work fast because the plaster hardens very quickly. After it sets up, the stems cannot be poked into it.

These may be used as a small gift for Mother or Grandmother, or as a party favor.

ACTIVITY 9-2: Plaster Flower Holder

For a party favor or small prize

Materials Needed:

- 1 plastic flower spray
- 1 sprig of lily of the valley, plastic
- 2 short stems of leaves or plastic fern
- waxed paper, 8 inch square
- plaster of Paris, 1/2 cup, and 3 tablespoons of water
- piece of felt for bottom of plaster

Directions for Making:

STEP 1:   Mix the plaster and water very thick.
STEP 2:   Lay the waxed paper on the table. Pour the plaster in a glob onto the paper.
STEP 3:   Add the flower in the center. Put the lily of the valley in front, and add leaves or fern on each side.
STEP 4:   When plaster is dry, cut a piece of felt to fit on the bottom of the plaster.

ACTIVITY 9-3: Rabbit Head Party Favor

Materials Needed:

- 1 fibre egg carton
- 2 small plastic eyes, 1/4 inch size
- felt marker pen, black
- Easter grass
- tiny bird candy eggs
- scissors and glue

Directions for Making:

STEP 1:   Using a fibre egg carton, cut off the lid and cut down the center of the carton. Make two strips of 6 egg cups each. (See Fig. 9-3A.)
STEP 2:   Cut off the end cup. Cut the number 2 cup from number 3 cup. Cut in between the cups leaving a tall piece of carton fibre on each side. This forms the ears. Trim around the edges. Leave cup straight across in front. (See Fig. 9-3B.)
STEP 3:   Turn the cup so the tall part of the ears are on the back side and the cup is toward you.
STEP 4:   Pressed into the fibre are two arches, perfect shapes for eyes. Using a felt marker pen, draw an eye lash at top of each arch. Glue on the moving eyes.
STEP 5:   Put a dot for a mouth at the bottom of the face.
STEP 6:   Fill with green Easter grass and a teaspoon of candy bird eggs.

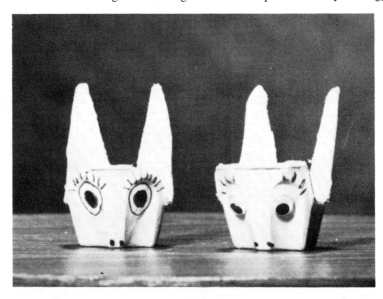

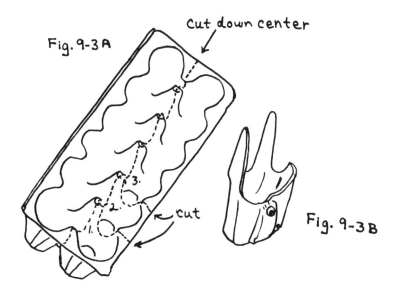

Cut down center

Fig. 9-3 A

cut

Fig. 9-3 B

ACTIVITY 9-4: Rabbit and Flower Party Favor

Materials Needed:

- 1 metallic margarine bowl
- 3 bright colored flower heads
- 4 sprigs of lily of the valley flowers, plastic
- 1 green metallic pipe cleaner, 12 inches long
- 1 Styrofoam egg, 3 inch
- 2 moving eyes, 1/2 inch size
- 4 bumps of pink chenille, each 3 inches long
- 1 flower sequin
- plaster of Paris and water
- bright colored sequins
- scrap of pink felt or foam
- black felt, 1-1/2 inch X 3 inch piece
- straight pin
- pinking scissors
- glue

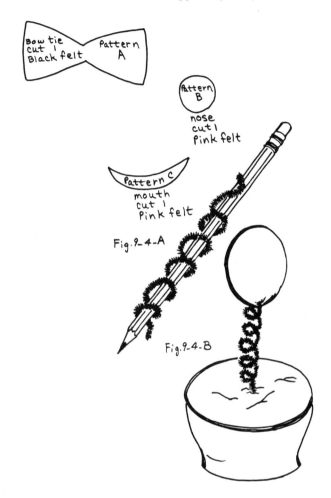

Directions for Making:

STEP 1:   Mix the plaster of Paris and water to thick cream consistency. Fill the foil bowl.

STEP 2:   Wrap the green pipe cleaner around a pencil and make a roll. (See Fig. 9-4A.) Stick one end into the Styrofoam ball and the other end into the bowl full of plaster. Hold until it sets upright. (See Fig. 9-4B.)

STEP 3:   Make an arrangement of flowers and leaves around the pipe cleaner.

STEP 4:   To make the rabbit, glue the 2 moving eyes in place on the Styrofoam egg. Cut a nose, using Pattern B, and a mouth, using Pattern C, from pink felt. Cut a bow tie from black felt, using Pattern A. Fasten the small end of the egg under the mouth with a straight pin stuck first through a flower sequin, and then into the egg.

STEP 5:   Cut the chenille bumps into two pieces, with two bumps on each. Bend the pieces in the middle and insert into the rabbit head for ears.

STEP 6:   Glue a tiny hat or flower between the ears.

STEP 7:   Around the rim of the bowl, glue a row of sequins.

ACTIVITY 9-5: Turkey Party Favor

Materials Needed:

- 1 small pine cone
- 10 brown feathers, such as Chinese pheasant feathers
- 2 small moving eyes, 3/16 inch size
- red chenille pipe cleaner
- Styrofoam, 3 X 3 X 1/2 inches
- glue
- serrated edge knife
- scissors

Fig. 9-5-A

Directions for Making:

STEP 1: Lay the pine cone on the table with the largest end toward you.

STEP 2: Using the piece of red chenille pipe cleaner, fold like the illustration to make a turkey head. (See Fig. 9-5A.)

STEP 3: Glue on the eyes, one on each side of the head.

STEP 4: Stick the chenille pipe cleaner head into the cone petals on the large end of the cone. Glue in place.

STEP 5: Cut the square of Styrofoam, using a serrated edge knife or Styrofoam cutter.

STEP 6: Glue the pine cone into the center of the Styrofoam. Let dry.

STEP 7: Stick the ends of two feathers into the cone on each side for wings. Glue in place.

STEP 8: Place other feathers into small end of the cone for tail feathers.

ACTIVITY 9-6: Christmas Tree Party Favor

Materials Needed:

- Styrofoam block, 1/2 X 4-1/2 X 5-1/2 inches
- 1 Styrofoam circle, 3 inches diameter
- 4 small red Christmas tree ornaments
- 1 silver star
- 14 inches red ribbon, 1/2 inch wide
- glue
- 5 straight pins, 1 inch long

cut
1
styrofoam

Pattern
A

Fig. 9-6-A

Fig. 9-6-A

cut 1
Styrofoam
base

Pattern
B

Directions for Making:

STEP 1:   Draw around the pattern in the book on a piece of paper; cut out. Using a 1/2 inch thick piece of Styrofoam, and a serrated edge knife, cut out the tree and the circle.

STEP 2:   Be sure the bottom edge of the tree trunk is even. Put glue on this and set in the middle of the circle. Stick 2 straight pins up through the circle into the tree trunk. (See Fig. 9-6A.)

STEP 3:   Glue the 4 red Christmas balls onto the tree.

STEP 4:   Pin and glue the star at the top of the tree.

STEP 5:   Tie a ribbon bow and pin it to the center bottom on the tree trunk.

STEP 6:   Add a green leaf at the top of the ribbon bow. Stick the stem end into the Styrofoam.

ACTIVITY 9-7: Santa Party Favor on a Soup Can

Materials Needed:

- 1 Campbell's soup can with lid removed
- pink felt, 3 X 4 inches
- red felt, 10 X 4 inches
- 2 moving eyes, 1/2 inch size
- dacron cotton
- candy and nuts
- scissors
- glue

Directions for Making:

STEP 1:   Remove one end from a Campbell's soup can—be sure the edges are smooth. If there are rough edges, hammer them down.

STEP 2:   Wash and dry the can inside and out.

STEP 3:   Cut a strip of pink felt 3 X 4 inches. Glue onto one side of the can. (See Fig. 9-7A.)

STEP 4:   Cut a strip of red felt and glue around the rest of the can. Overlap the pink a little. (See Fig. 9-7B.)

STEP 5:   Glue the eyes in place on the pink felt. Cut nose, Pattern A, and mouth, Pattern B, from red felt. Glue on.

STEP 6:   Make cotton eyebrows and moustache. Add to the face.

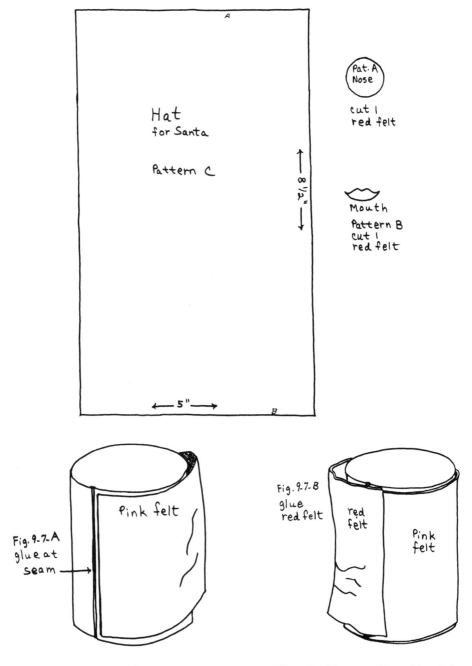

STEP 7:   Cut 2 narrow strips of cotton, 1/2 inch. Glue on either side of the face. Cut whiskers from cotton and glue at the bottom of the can.

STEP 8:   Using Pattern C, make a hat of red felt; Sew A and B together. Glue a 1/2 inch strip of cotton around the bottom edge. (See Fig. 9-7C.) Add cotton ball on top (See Fig. 9-7D.)

STEP 9:   Fill the can with candy and nuts. Set the hat on top of can.

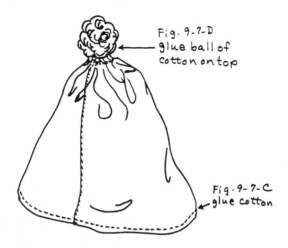

Fig. 9-7-D
glue ball of cotton on top

Fig. 9-7-C
glue cotton

ACTIVITY 9-8: Santa on a Spool Party Favor

Materials Needed:

- 1 large empty gold colored spool
- cotton
- 2 moving eyes, 1/4 inch size
- tiny red felt nose and mouth
- red felt, 3 X 5 inches
- glue
- scissors

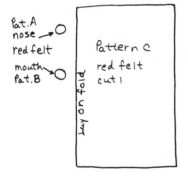

Pat.A nose — red felt

mouth — Pat.B

Pattern C

red felt

cut 1

lay on fold

Directions for Making:

STEP 1: Onto one side of the spool, glue the eyes, nose and mouth.

STEP 2: Cover the sides and back of the spool with glue. Add cotton hair.

STEP 3: Make a hat, using Pattern C. Either sew or glue edges together. Glue in place on top of spool.

STEP 4: Glue a cotton ball at the top of the hat.

STEP 5: Add a narrow strip of cotton around bottom of hat.

STEP 6: Glue cotton eyebrows and moustache to face.

There can be used as a party favor or as a tree ornament. If used as a tree ornament, punch a hole in the felt at the top of the hat. Insert Christmas tree ornament hanger.

ACTIVITY 9-9: Santa on a Bottle

Materials Needed:

- 1 tall baby food jar
- cotton
- 2 small moving eyes, 1/4 inch size
- red felt, 5 X 8 inches
- white felt, 1 X 8 inches
- green felt, 2 X 1 inch
- silver sequins
- red rick rack, 1 inch long, medium size
- scissors
- glue
- candy to fill
- pinking scissors

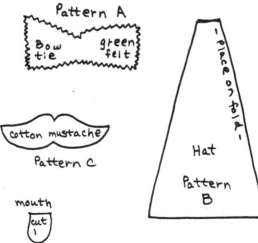

Pattern A
Bow tie   green felt

cotton mustache
Pattern C

Place on fold.
Hat
Pattern B

mouth
cut 1
Pattern D
red felt

Directions for Making:

STEP 1:   Remove label and glue from baby food jar, wash and dry inside and out.

STEP 2:   Glue on small moving eyes, 3/4 of the way up the side of the jar.

STEP 3:   Cut a small circle from red felt for the nose and glue on. Cut a mouth from red felt, using Pattern D. Glue in place.

STEP 4:   Cut the strip of white felt with pinking scissors on both sides. Glue this around the bottom of the jar.

STEP 5:   Using Pattern A, cut out a neck tie from the piece of green felt. Use pinking scissors. Glue in place under the mouth.

STEP 6:   Make a hat using Pattern B; either sew or glue into a cone shape. Fold the top down an inch. Glue to the hat and add a cotton ball to the center.

STEP 7:   In the center of the neck tie, glue a large silver sequin.

STEP 8:   Cut cotton into narrow strips. Glue to the sides of the jar on either side of the face. Make cotton eyebrows and mustache. Glue in place.

STEP 9:   Fill with candy.

ACTIVITY 9-10: Nature Centerpiece

Materials Needed:

- 1 flat rock, shaped similar to Pattern A
- 3 oval shaped rocks for bird bodies
- 3 small oblong rocks for bird heads
- 6 tiny moving eyes, 1/4 inch
- 1 piece felt, enough to cover bottom of rock, Pattern A, any color
- 3 sprays plastic fern
- 3 flat heads from plastic flowers
- blue spray paint

Directions for Making:

STEP 1:   Wash and dry all rocks thoroughly.

STEP 2:   Spray the large flat rock blue.

STEP 3:   Set the 3 oval rocks on the table and glue the small oblong shaped rocks on top at one end for a head.

Pattern A
approximate
rock shape

other rock
shapes for
birds

STEP 4:   Glue tiny moving eyes onto the head of each rock bird.
STEP 5:   Glue three sprays of plastic fern onto the back side of the large rock.
STEP 6:   Glue the three birds in place on the blue rock. Add feathers where
           they are wanted.
STEP 7:   Draw around the big rock and cut a piece of felt to fit. Glue it on the
           bottom side.
STEP 8:   Cut the stems from small, plastic, bright colored flowers. Glue here
           and there over the blue rock surface for added color.

ACTIVITY 9-11: Slipper Centerpiece

Materials Needed:

- 1 used high heel slipper
- wheel and shell macaroni
- metallic spray paint, gold, silver or copper
- oblong piece of Styrofoam, 1 X 3 X 5 inches
- assortment of flowers with different length stems
- glitter
- bright colored sequins
- plaster of Paris and water
- glue

Directions for Making:

STEP 1:   Wipe dust or dirt from an old high heel shoe. Be sure the heel is not
           run over.
STEP 2:   Around the opening of the shoe glue the wheel macaroni. (See Fig.
           9-11A.)
STEP 3:   Cover the rest of the surface of the shoe with small shell macaroni,
           oval side up. If the heel is large enough, cover it also. Let dry.
STEP 4:   When the glue is dry, spray the macaroni in the color wanted—silver
           for Christmas, gold for summer, or copper for fall.

Fig. 9-11-A
Start with
wheel macaroni

STEP 5: Cut a piece of Styrofoam so it will slip into the opening of the slipper, or fill the slipper with plaster of Paris (thick cream consistency). If using plaster, have arrangement ready to set into place since the plaster hardens very quickly.

STEP 6: Add the flowers to the shoe by sticking the flower stems into the foam or plaster. Start with plastic leaves or fern at the heel. Add other flowers according to color, height and size. (Poinsettias that are glittered and Christmas greenery for the Christmas shoe; spring flowers in pastel shades for spring and summer; and orange, red and yellow for a fall centerpiece.)

STEP 7: In the hubs of the macaroni wheels glue bright colored sequins for added color and sparkle.

ACTIVITY 9-12: Poinsettia and Cone Centerpiece

Materials Needed:

- 1 square plastic meat tray, 1 X 5 X 5 inches
- 2 large size poinsettias
- 3 green holly picks
- 1 white holly branch
- silver glitter
- plaster of Paris, 2 cups
- water, 3/4 cup
- wire cutters
- small cones
- glue

Directions for Making:

STEP 1: Spread glue on the poinsettia petals, sprinkle on glitter and set aside to dry.

STEP 2: Mix the plaster of Paris and water to heavy cream consistency. Pour into the meat tray.

STEP 3: Cut the stems of the poinsettias to the height wanted—no longer than six inches. Stick the ends into the plaster of Paris.

STEP 4: Cut the stem from the white holly branch to 4-1/2 inches. Stick in front of the poinsettias.

STEP 5: Put the green holly picks across the front top edge of the meat tray.

STEP 6: (Optional) Add small cones around flowers for fillers and to add color to the arrangement.

ACTIVITY 9-13: Berry Basket Flower Cart

Materials Needed:

- 1 pint size cardboard berry box
- 2 plastic lids from 1 pound coffee cans
- 1 large tongue depressor or Popsicle stick
- 2 brass paper fasteners, 1/2 inch long
- glitter
- flowers
- 1 piece of plastic, 3 X 3 X 1 inch or 1/2 of a 3 inch Styrofoam ball
- 2 felt flower cutouts
- glue
- scissors
- ice pick

felt flower
cut 2

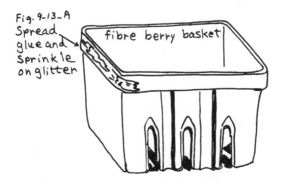

Fig. 9-13-A
Spread glue and sprinkle on glitter

fibre berry basket

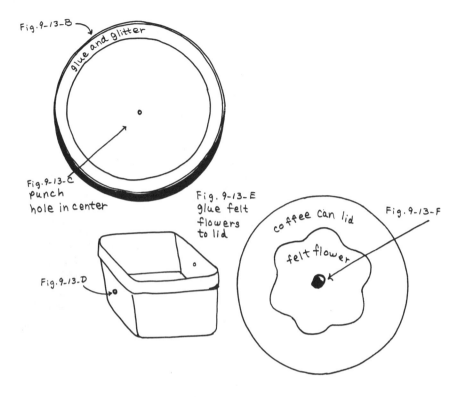

Fig. 9-13-B glue and glitter

Fig. 9-13-C punch hole in center

Fig. 9-13-D

Fig. 9-13-E glue felt flowers to lid

coffee can lid

felt flower

Fig. 9-13-F

Directions for Making:

STEP 1: Using the pattern, cut out 2 flowers from felt.

STEP 2: Around the top rim of the berry box, spread glue and sprinkle on glitter. Set aside to dry. (See Fig. 9-13A.)

STEP 3: On the inside of the coffee can lids with the groove, put glue and glitter. These are the wheels of the cart. (See Fig. 9-13B.)

STEP 4: Around the edges of the flowers, spread a thin line of glue. Sprinkle on glitter. Shake off excess glitter.

STEP 5: With the ice pick, punch a hole in the center of the lids. (See Fig. 9-13C.)

STEP 6: Punch holes in the berry basket, one on each side half way up the side. (See Fig. 9-13D.)

STEP 7: Glue the flowers to center of the lids. Let dry. (See Fig. 9-13E.)

STEP 8: Poke a hole through the center of the felt flowers.

STEP 9: Put a paper fastener through the holes in the flowers, lid and berry basket. (See Fig. 9-13F.) Spread fasteners apart on the inside of the basket.

STEP 10: Glue a tongue depressor to the bottom of the berry basket for a holder.

STEP 11: Glue a piece of Styrofoam into the bottom, inside the berry basket.

STEP 12: Make a flower arrangement by sticking the ends of plastic flowers into the Styrofoam.

ACTIVITY 9-14: Valentine Party Favor Candy Holder

Materials Needed:

- 1 small size baby food jar and lid
- 1 Valentine
- 2 dozen candy hearts
- silver glitter
- 1 rubber band
- glue

Directions for Making:

STEP 1: Glue and glitter the highlights on a Valentine.

STEP 2: Cover the lid with glue and glitter. Set aside to dry.

STEP 3: Fill the baby food jar full of candy hearts. Screw on the lid.

STEP 4: Put glue on the back of the Valentine and place on front of the jar. Hold in place with a rubber band until dry.

STEP 5: Remove rubber band. Write the name of the person to receive the bottle of candy. Set on table.

Chapter Ten

Fancy Pencil Holders

Pencil holders are a "must" in every craft class, especially if they are either pretty or practical.

All the holders in this chapter appeal to youngsters because they are different and are easily made.

ACTIVITY 10-1: Flower, Pencil, Calendar and Picture Holder

Materials Needed:

- 38 Popsicle sticks—can be obtained any place craft materials are bought
- 2 empty rollers from bathroom tissue
- school picture
- small calendar
- gold spray paint
- flowers, plastic
- 3 tablespoons plaster of Paris
- 2 rubber bands
- water
- small dish to mix plaster in
- waxed paper
- glue

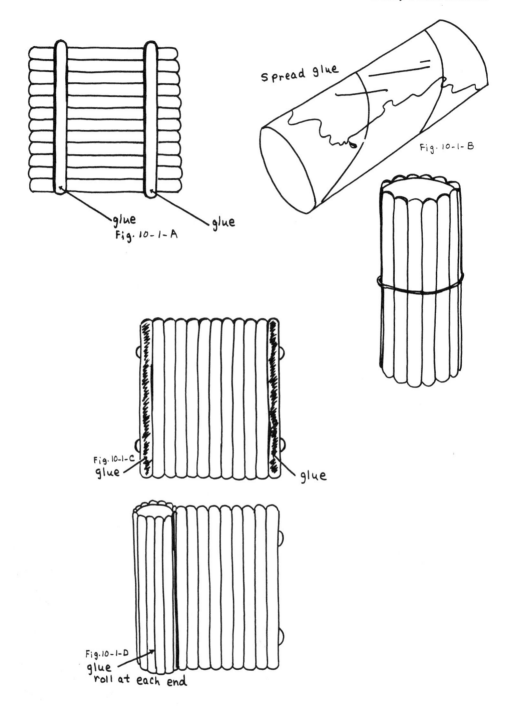

Fig. 10-1-A

glue   glue

spread glue

Fig. 10-1-B

Fig. 10-1-C
glue   glue

Fig. 10-1-D
glue
roll at each end

fill
half full and insert
stems of plastic flowers
Fig. 10-1-E

fill
1/4 inch deep

Directions for Making:

STEP 1: Lay 12 Popsicle sticks on the table in a row; be sure the ends are even. (Use a straight stick; first lay it at one end and then at the other end of the row. Make sure the ends all touch the straight stick.)

STEP 2: Using a good, quick-drying glue, cover one side of two sticks. Lay one at the top of the row of sticks about 1/2 inch from the edge. Place one at the bottom about 1/2 inch up. These sticks hold the row of sticks together, to make the back of the project. (See Fig. 10-1A.)

STEP 3: Spread glue evenly over the outside of one cardboard roll. Set flat on the table. Place 12 sticks around the roll, and hold in place with a rubber band until dry. (See Fig. 10-1B.)

STEP 4: Repeat for the second roll.

STEP 5: Set the row of sticks upright and the two sticks that hold them together are on the back side. Put glue on the two end sticks of the row on the front side. (See Fig. 10-1C.) Set a roll at each end and hold for a few seconds until the glue sets up. (See Fig. 10-1D.)

STEP 6: When glue is dry, spray over all with gold spray paint.

STEP 7: Mix the plaster of Paris to thick cream consistency and spoon very carefully into the rolls, which have been placed onto a square piece of waxed paper.

STEP 8: Fill one roll 1/2 full of the plaster and insert the stems of two or three flowers into plaster while it is still wet. (See Fig. 10-1E.)

STEP 9: Into the second roll, spoon the plaster until it has a depth of 1/4 inch. Let dry. Remove the waxed paper.

STEP 10: To the front of the holder, between the two rolls, glue a small picture at the top and a small calendar at the bottom.

STEP 11: When plaster is dry, add pencils and pens to the second roll.

ACTIVITY 10-2: Heart Pencil Holder

Materials Needed:

- piece of Styrofoam, 3 inches square by 1 inch
- 1 oblong plastic margarine tub with clear lid

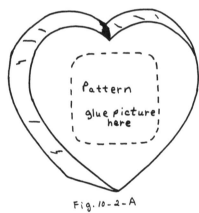

Fig. 10-2-A

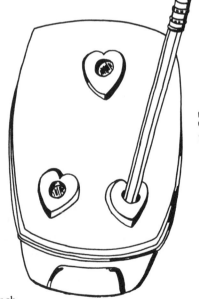

read
carefully
Fig. 10-2-B

- 1 dowel, 8 inches X 1/8 inch
- red sequins
- straight pins
- school picture, 1-1/2 X 2-1/2 inches

- red ribbon, 1/2 inch wide
- plaster of Paris, 1 cup
- red spray paint
- 2 pencils or pens
- 7 felt heart cutouts
- glue
- scissors

Directions for Making:

STEP 1:   Using a serrated edge knife or Styrofoam cutter and the heart pattern, cut the heart shape from one inch Styrofoam.

STEP 2:   Glue picture into the center of the heart shape. Put a straight pin into each corner to hold picture until it is dry. (See Fig. 10-2A.)

STEP 3:   First put a bead, then a sequin on a straight pin. Push the pin into the Styrofoam. Outline the picture first and then continue until the surface of the heart is covered.

STEP 4:   Using a narrow ribbon, 1/2 inch, starting at the top center, pin the ribbon. Go around the heart shape and back to the center again and pin.

STEP 5:   Spray the dowel red; set aside to dry.

STEP 6:   Make three holes in the lid. One in the middle to the back and one on each side in front. One is for the dowel and the two are for pencils. (See Fig. 10-2B.)

STEP 7:   Mix up enough plaster to fill the margarine tub. (1 cup of plaster to 1/2 cup of water.) Pour into the tub.

STEP 8:   Put the lid onto the tub filled with plaster. Push the dowel and pencils through the holes and into the plaster while it is still soft.
(*Caution:* Don't let the plaster harden before you push the dowel and pencils into it. Pull pencils out before it is completely set, about 10 minutes.)

STEP 9:   Force the heart onto the dowel.

STEP 10:   Add a ribbon bow an inch below the heart on the dowel.

STEP 11:   Decorate the tub and lid with felt heart cutouts, glued on.

STEP 12:   To cover the pin heads at the top of the heart, in the ribbon, stick a flower or two into the Styrofoam.

ACTIVITY 10-3: Snowman Pen and Pencil Holder

Materials Needed:

- 1 Styrofoam ball, 3 inch size
- 1 Styrofoam ball, 2 inch size
- 2 chenille pipe cleaners
- 1 Styrofoam circle, 5 inch diameter
- red ribbon
- feathers
- small hat
- 2 moving eyes, 1/2 inch size
- 3 large sequins
- 1 bump red rick rack

- piece of bright colored material for scarf, 1 X 10 inches
- sharp knife
- glue
- scissors
- pen and pencil

Directions for Making:

STEP 1:   To make the snowman, cut a thin slice from the bottom of the 3 inch Styrofoam ball (see Fig. 10-3A), using a sharp serrated edge knife. Set the 2 inch ball on top, opposite the cut edge on the 3 inch ball.

STEP 2:   Cut 2 pieces from a pipe cleaner, 2 inches long. Push one end into the 2 inch ball, and the other into the three inch ball. Push firmly together.

STEP 3:   Cut a mouth from rick rack, using one bump of large size.

STEP 4:   For a nose use a small red Christmas ball. Remove the hanger. Add glue and push into the top ball. Glue on eyes and mouth. For earmuffs, use a large bright colored sequin or cut a felt circle, glue, and pin on.

STEP 5:   Glue the 3 sequins onto the chest of the snowman. (See Fig. 10-3B.)

STEP 6:   Glue and pin the ribbon around the Styrofoam circle.

STEP 7:   Set the snowman in the center to the back side of the circle. Glue in place.

STEP 8:   Stick a 4 inch piece of chenille pipe cleaner on each side of the 3 inch ball for arms. (See Fig. 10-3C.)

STEP 9:   Make a broom by cutting a red chenille pipe cleaner 4 inches long. Glue 5 or 7 feathers at one end.

STEP 10: Fasten the broom onto one of the chenille arms by twisting one end of the arm around the handle on the broom.

STEP 11: Make a scarf from bright colored material. Wrap around neck of snowman and pin.

STEP 12: Add pen and pencils by sticking the ends into the Styrofoam circle. (See Fig. 10-3D.)
          The hat is made from a tin which comes inside a roll of paper. Wash and dry, spray paint black all over and let dry. Glue in place on snowman's head.

STEP 13: Add a perky feather at one side of hat.

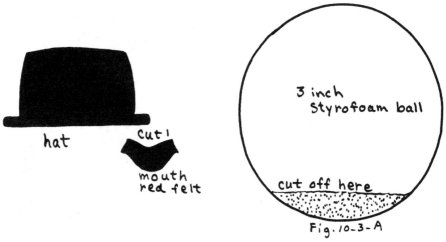

hat

cut 1

mouth
red felt

3 inch
Styrofoam ball

cut off here

Fig. 10-3-A

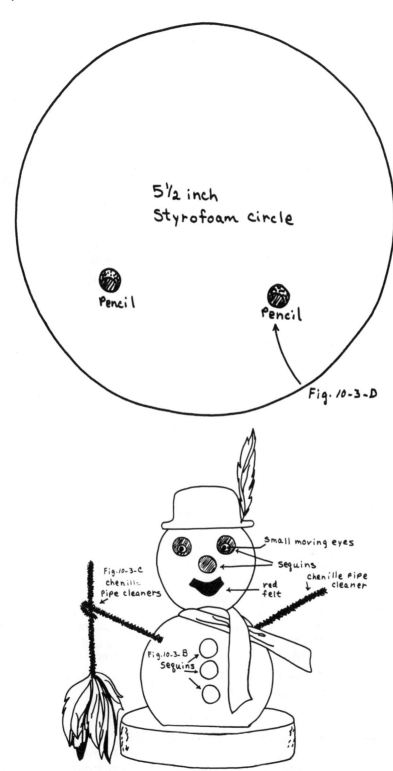

5½ inch
Styrofoam circle

Pencil

Pencil

Fig. 10-3-D

Small moving eyes

Sequins

Fig.10-3-C
chenille
pipe cleaners

red
felt

chenille pipe
cleaner

Fig.10-3-B
sequins

ACTIVITY 10-4: Pencil, Ruler and Calendar Holder on a Coffee Can

Materials Needed:

- 1/2 half pound coffee can and plastic lid
- calendar for the current year
- assortment of pens and pencils, 8
- one 12-inch ruler
- black spray paint
- sharp, narrow blade knife
- sand (optional)
- glue

Fig. 10-4-A

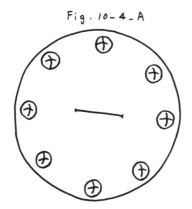

Directions for Making:

STEP 1:   Remove the plastic lid; wash and dry can.

STEP 2:   Using black spray paint, cover the outside of the can. Let dry.

STEP 3:   Set the lid back onto the can. Around the top edge of the lid, draw eight circles the size of a pencil. Space evenly. (See Fig. 10-4A.)

STEP 4:   In the center of the lid, draw a line one inch long.

STEP 5:   Using the knife, cut carefully along the one-inch line. Force the ruler into this cut. Push end to the bottom of the can, into the sand.

STEP 6:   Set the knife point in one of the circles and cut across the circle. Set knife blade on opposite side of the circle and make an "X" cut. Do this to each of the eight circles. Push the sharp point of the pens and pencils into the holes. Push them halfway down into the can. The plastic will hold the pencils upright.

STEP 7:   Put glue on the back side of the calendar and glue in place. Hold with a rubber band at the top and one at the bottom until dry. Remove the rubber bands.

STEP 8:   (Optional) A cup of sand may be added to the bottom of the can for added weight.

ACTIVITY 10-5: Pencil and Ruler Holder

Materials Needed:

- felt, 18 X 2-1/2 inches
- thread
- needle
- 4 pencils

- 1 ruler, 6 inches long
- sequins
- contrasting color felt for flowers, 5 inch square

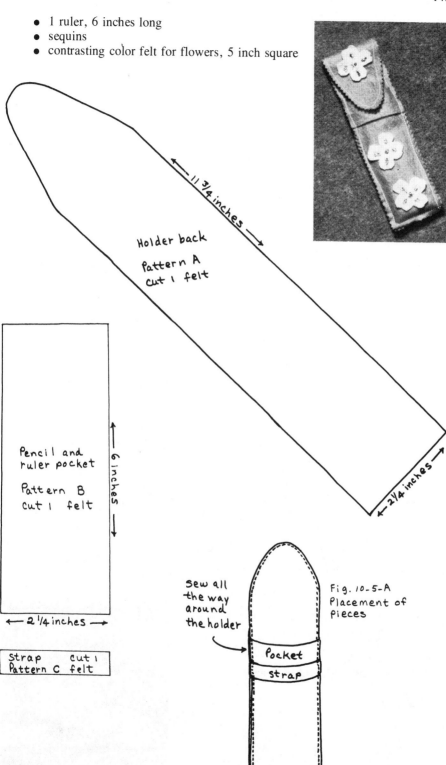

Holder back

Pattern A

cut 1 felt

11 3/4 inches

2 1/4 inches

Pencil and ruler pocket

Pattern B

cut 1 felt

6 inches

2 1/4 inches

Strap   cut 1
Pattern C felt

Sew all the way around the holder

Pocket

strap

Fig. 10-5-A
Placement of pieces

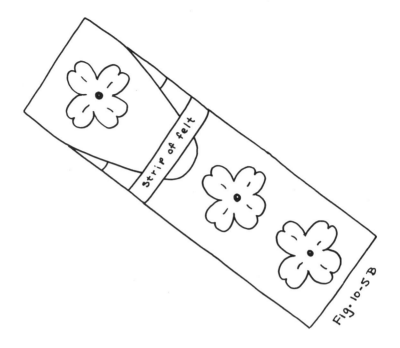

Fig. 10-5 B

Strip of felt

Directions for Making:

STEP 1: Lay a piece of typing paper over the pattern in the book. Trace and cut out. Cut all pieces from felt.

STEP 2: Lay Pattern A on the bottom, next Pattern B, and place Pattern C on top. (See Fig. 10-5A.)

STEP 3: Tack the pocket and strip in place and sew all the way around the holder.

STEP 4: Fold the top down and insert the tongue under the strip. (See Fig. 10-5B.)

STEP 5: To decorate the holder, sequins may be glued around the edge; or, cut felt flowers, using the patterns, from contrasting color felt and glue wherever they are wanted. Add glitter for color in the flower centers.

ACTIVITY 10-6: Dog Pencil Holder on a Soup Can

Materials Needed:

- 1 Campbell's soup can with lid removed
- brown yarn
- red felt
- brown felt
- 2 moving eyes, 1/2 inch size
- glue
- scissors

Directions for Making:

STEP 1: Remove the label; wash and dry soup can.

STEP 2: Starting at the bottom of the can, glue yarn around the can, to the top. Put glue on a small area and work fast. Don't bunch the yarn.

STEP 3: Lay a piece of typing paper over patterns in the book. Trace and cut out.

STEP 4: Cut the ears, Pattern A, from brown felt. Glue in place at top of the can. Leave the bottom of the ears free.

STEP 5: Cut a nose, Pattern B, and tongue, Pattern C, from red felt. Glue in place on front of the can.

STEP 6: Add the moving eyes.

STEP 7: Put in pencils and pens.

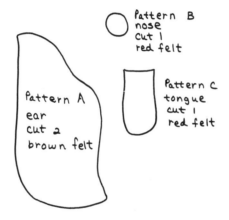

Pattern B
nose
cut 1
red felt

Pattern A
ear
cut 2
brown felt

Pattern C
tongue
cut 1
red felt

ACTIVITY 10-7: Note and Pencil Box

Materials Needed:

- tiny flowers
- 1 oblong tomato box, plastic
- tack board, any color
- scissors
- glue
- 2 Styrofoam eggs, 2-1/2 inches
- 1 plastic fork

Directions for Making:

STEP 1: Draw the Patterns A, B and C from the book by laying a piece of typing paper over the patterns and drawing around them. Cut out.

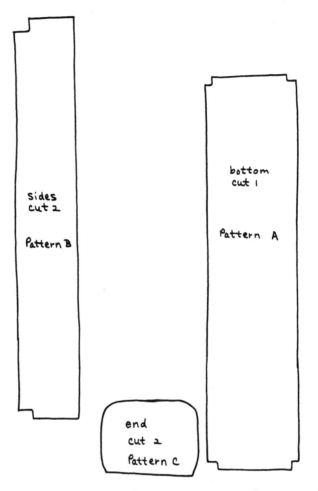

STEP 2:   Lay the patterns onto tack board and trace. Cut out carefully.
STEP 3:   Glue Pattern A onto the bottom of the tomato basket. Be sure it fits.
            Set the two sides, Pattern B, in next and glue. Last, add two ends,
            Pattern C.
STEP 4:   Cut the two Styrofoam eggs in half. Glue the larger ends, oval end
            up, one on each end. Glue the other pieces into the middle.
STEP 5:   Add pencils on one end, pens in the other by sticking the sharp ends
            into the foam egg.
STEP 6:   Stick the top end of the fork into the second egg, tines up. This is for
            notes.
STEP 7:   Add the tiny flowers into the other 1/2 egg.

ACTIVITY 10-8: Letter and Pencil Holder on a Salt Box

Materials Needed:

- Styrofoam circle, 1 X 5 inches
- salt box, empty
- gold metallic rick rack
- 5 pencils
- small calendar

- 3 rubber bands
- 3 bright colored plastic flowers
- green spray paint
- glue

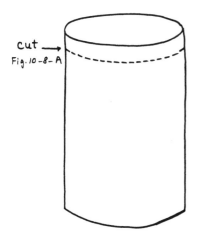

cut ⟶

Fig. 10-8-A

Fig. 10-8-B

Push
sharpened
pencils
into
foam

glue salt
box here

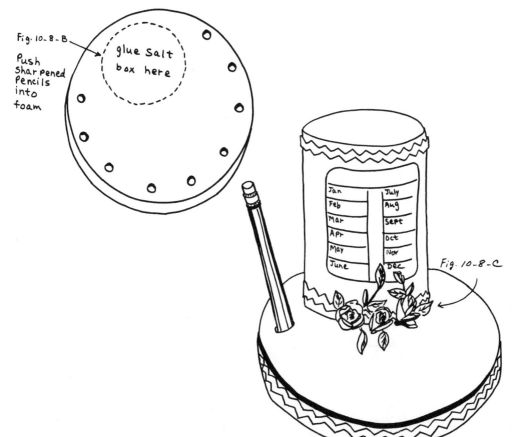

Jan	July
Feb	Aug
Mar	Sept
Apr	Oct
May	Nov
June	Dec

Fig. 10-8-C

Directions for Making:

STEP 1:   Using a sharp knife, remove the top end of the salt box. (See Fig. 10-8A.)

STEP 2:   Spray the box green. Let dry.

STEP 3:   Around the top and bottom of the salt box, glue a strip of metallic rick rack or cord. Also add one around the Styrofoam circle.

STEP 4:   Glue the box to the back side of the Styrofoam circle. (See Fig. 10-8B.)

STEP 5:   Add a small calendar to the front of the box or cut a picture from an old greeting card of a small animal or pretty child. Glue it on. Hold with 3 rubber bands until the glue dries.

STEP 6:   Around the outside edges of the foam circle push sharpened pencils into the foam.

STEP 7:   At the bottom front of the box stick the stems of the 3 flowers into the foam. (See Fig. 10-8C.)

STEP 8:   Put letters or notes in the box.

Chapter Eleven

Captivating Pictures

Here are decorative pictures and wall plaques that will brighten the walls of schoolrooms or bedrooms at home. They make attractive personal gifts, too.

ACTIVITY 11-1: Angela, The Precious Caterpillar Picture

Materials Needed:

- 1 plastic meat tray, 9 x 11-1/2 inches
- gold and green sequins (12)
- 2 small moving eyes, 1/4 inch size
- 2 small black seed beads
- 2 black chenille pipe cleaners, 12 inches long
- tiny scrap red felt
- medium black rick rack, 40 inches
- silver sequins
- 3 tiny flowers
- green and orange art foam, 2 x 12 inches each color
- black ribbon, 1/4 inch wide x 6 inches long
- straight scissors
- pinking scissors
- glue
- pattern

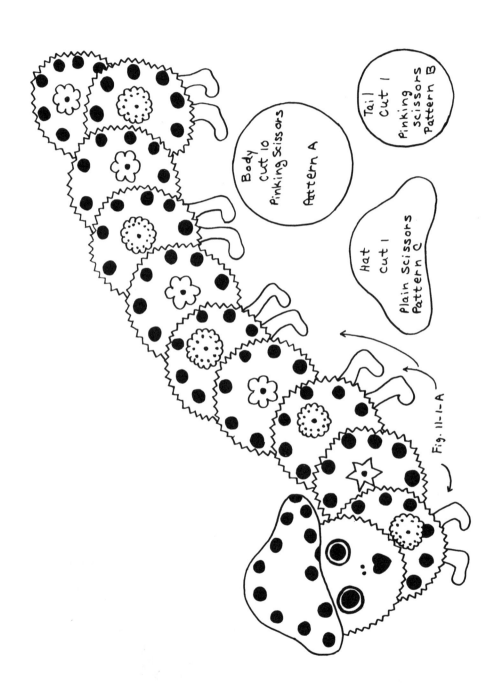

Body
Cut 10
Pinking Scissors

Pattern A

Tail
Cut 1
Pinking
Scissors
Pattern B

Hat
Cut 1
Plain Scissors
Pattern C

Fig. 11-1-A

Directions for Making:

STEP 1: Wash and dry a plastic meat tray, being sure there is no cut place or stain on it.

STEP 2: With pinking scissors, cut 6 circles from orange and 5 circles from green art foam using Pattern A. Cut one circle for tail from green art foam using Pattern B.

STEP 3: Lay the circles on the pattern to form the caterpillar, starting with the small circle at the tail end. Overlap the orange circle almost half, then overlap the orange circle with a green one, etc.

STEP 4: Using plain scissors, cut a hat from green art foam, using Pattern C. Glue to the top of the face.

STEP 5: Glue the 2 moving eyes to the face under the hat.

STEP 6: Around the edge of the green circles, space and glue 6 gold sequins, and on the orange, glue 6 green sequins. Do not glue sequins around the face.

STEP 7: Glue 2 black seed beads for nose holes and red heart from felt for a mouth.

STEP 8: To the center of the green circles, glue a gold flower sequin; to the orange circles, a leaf or pretty shaped sequin.

STEP 9: To the centers of these sequins, glue a bright colored sequin or a rhinestone.

STEP 10: Cut 10 pieces of black chenille pipe cleaner 1-1/2 inches long. Bend into an inverted L shape. These are the feet and legs of the worm. Glue two feet under No. 2, 4, 6, 8 and 10 circles. (See Fig. 11-1A.)

STEP 11: Around the edge of the hat glue on silver sequins. Add three tiny cloth or plastic flowers in the center and on each side.

STEP 12: Around the outside edge of the meat tray, glue on black rick rack for a frame and add silver sequins.

STEP 13: Lay the caterpillar in the meat tray with the head in the left hand corner. Put a small dab of glue onto each circle on the back side and hold foam in place until it is dry.

STEP 14: At the middle top of the tray, punch 2 holes 1/2 inch apart. Thread the 2 ends of a narrow ribbon through and tie on the back side of the tray for a hanger.

ACTIVITY 11-2: Bird Pictures

Materials Needed:

- one 8 x 10 inch white plastic meat tray
- 3 pieces of felt, red, pink, yellow, 2 x 4 inches each
- 1 piece green felt, 3 x 1 inch
- black rick rack, 36 inches long
- 1 piece blue felt, 6 x 6 inches
- glue and brush
- scissors

Beak.Cut 1 orange

feet.Cut 2 orange

Cut 1 green

cut 1 green

cut 1 red

cut 1 blue (yellow)

Cut 1 Pink (yellow)

Directions for Making:

STEP 1:   Using the pattern of the birds and flowers, cut them from felt. Cut the bird from blue, the flowers one each from red, pink, and blue, centers from yellow, and the stems from green.

STEP 2:   Glue the bird on the left hand side of the meat tray. First the body, then the beak, eyes and feet.

STEP 3:   Glue the flowers, stems, and centers in a row at the edge of the tray.

STEP 4:   Using a glue brush, put glue around the edge of the meat tray. Add the rick rack.

STEP 5:   Punch 2 holes in the top of the plate, using an ice pick or sharp pair of scissors.

STEP 6:   Thread the ribbon through the holes. Tie in a bow at front of the picture. Can also be used as a hanger for the picture.

ACTIVITY 11-3: Egg Carton and Meat Tray Picture

Materials Needed:

- 3 lids from pink foam egg cartons
- 1 lid from yellow foam egg carton
- 1 lid from blue foam egg carton
- 1 plastic meat tray, 9 x 11 inches
- green glitter
- sharp scissors
- Elmer's glue
- green felt marker pen
- pencil

Directions for Making:

STEP 1: Remove the lids from the plastic egg cartons.

STEP 2: Draw the patterns and cut out.

STEP 3: Using a pencil, draw the flower pot and petals, centers and blue bells on different colored cartons and cut out.

STEP 4: Arrange on the meat tray. Glue in place.

STEP 5: Cut the hinges from egg cartons, make into flower shapes, glue in place.

STEP 6: Using sharp scissors, fringe the edges of the leaves by cutting into the leaf 1/4 inch.

STEP 7: Draw the veins in the leaves and glue in place.

STEP 8: Glue and glitter the square flower centers (Pattern C). Add to flowers.

STEP 9: With the green felt marker pen, draw stems wherever needed.

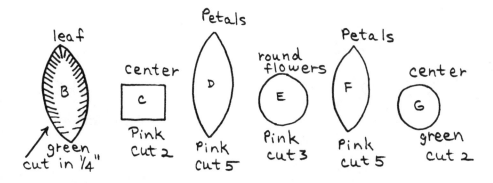

Flower

H

Pink
cut 8

Flower

I

Pink
cut 4

A
Flower Pot
cut 1
green

Flower

K

yellow
Cut 4

Blue Bells

J

Blue
cut 3

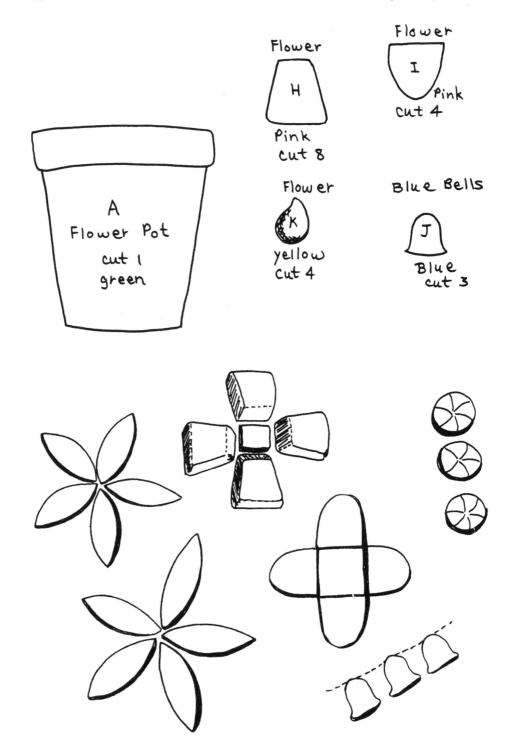

ACTIVITY 11-4: Christmas Scene in a Tray

Materials Needed:

- 1 Christmas card with a pretty picture
- 1 plastic meat tray a little larger than the picture
- gold glitter
- 1 adhesive hanger with metal eyelet (most stationery stores sell them)
- scissors
- glue

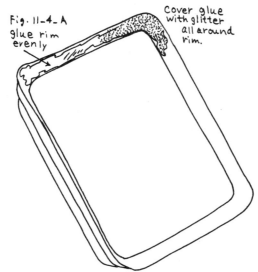

Fig. 11-4-A
glue rim
evenly

Cover glue
with glitter
all around
rim.

Directions for Making:

STEP 1: Around the rim of the plastic meat tray, spread glue evenly; cover the glue with glitter. (See Fig. 11-4A.)

STEP 2: Using an old Christmas card with a pretty scene, cut out the picture and glue to the center of the tray.

STEP 3: At the top of the picture, on the back of the tray, glue an adhesive hanger.

ACTIVITY 11-5: Flower Wall Plaque

Materials Needed:

- 1 plastic coffee can lid, 1 lb.
- crushed egg shells
- flower, open face rose
- spray paint, blue
- ribbon, 10 x 1/2 inch
- paper punch or ice pick
- glue

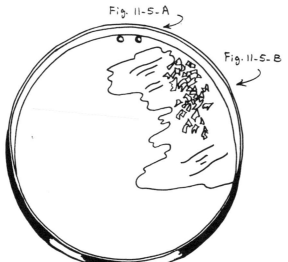

Fig. 11-5-A

Fig. 11-5-B

Directions for Making:

STEP 1: To make crushed egg shells, dry the broken empty egg shells thoroughly. To dry quickly, put in oven, 200° temperature, for 10 minutes. Put in a plastic bread bag and roll with bottle or rolling pin.

STEP 2: Lay the plastic lid on the table with the open side up.

STEP 3: Using an ice pick or paper punch, punch 2 holes in the lid 1/2 inch apart in the rim around the edge. (See Fig. 11-5A.)

STEP 4: Cover the lid with quick-drying glue. Sprinkle on crushed egg shells until the lid is covered. (See Fig. 11-5B.) Let dry.

STEP 5: Lay an open face rose in the center of the lid and either glue in place or punch holes with the ice pick and fasten with the wire around the leaves.

STEP 6: Thread the ribbon through the 2 holes that have been punched in the lid. Tie a pretty bow to hang the picture wtih.

ACTIVITY 11-6: Crushed Egg Shell Wall Plaque

Materials Needed:

- 1 plastic meat tray, 5 x 8 inches
- crushed egg shells
- 1 nylon butterfly
- rick rack
- gold spray for Styrofoam
- 8 to 10 small plastic flowers with leaves
- plastic egg carton, white or green
- glue
- scissors

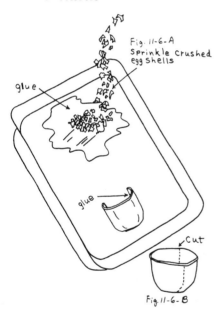

Fig. 11-6-A
Sprinkle Crushed
egg shells

glue

glue

Cut

Fig. 11-6-B

Directions for Making:

STEP 1: Cover the bottom of the meat tray with glue and sprinkle on the crushed egg shells. Let dry. (See Fig. 11-6A.)

STEP 2: To make a basket, cut a cup from an egg carton. Cut the egg cup in half and glue the cup basket to the bottom of the tray. (See Fig. 11-6B.)

STEP 3: Spray paint gold.

STEP 4: Around the rim of the meat tray, glue on a row of rick rack.

STEP 5: Fill the egg cup basket with tiny flowers.

STEP 6: Just above the flowers in the center of the tray, glue a butterfly or bug, etc.

ACTIVITY 11-7: Praying Hands Picture

Materials Needed:

- 1 white foam plastic meat tray, 4 x 7 inches
- 1 praying hands decal (most stationery stores have these or it can be cut from old Christmas cards), or draw pattern from book and color with Crayolas
- black rick rack
- black felt tip marker pen
- ribbon, 10 inches long, 1/2 inch wide
- small plastic flower
- pinking scissors
- glue
- paper punch or ice pick

Directions for Making:

STEP 1: Be sure the meat tray is clean and not stained. With the pinking scissors, cut the bottom from the plastic tray.

STEP 2: Around the outside edge, glue on the black rick rack.

STEP 3: Glue the praying hands decal to the center of the plastic frame.

STEP 4: Using a felt marker pen, write a Bible verse in the left hand corner under the hands, such as, "Be ye kind to one another," etc.

STEP 5: In the upper right hand corner, glue the plastic flower with the stem removed.

STEP 6: Punch 2 holes at the center top; add a ribbon bow for hanging.

ACTIVITY 11-8: Platter Picture

Materials Needed:

- 1 fibre board meat platter
- crushed egg shells
- flowers
- spray paint, gold or silver
- macaroni wheels

- green sequins
- chenille pipe cleaners, green
- ribbon
- ice pick
- glue

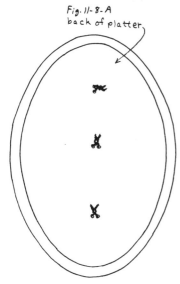

Fig. 11-8-A
back of platter.

Directions for Making:

STEP 1: Cover the bottom of the fibre board meat tray with glue and sprinkle crushed egg shells on.

STEP 2: Around the outside rim, glue on macaroni wheels or small shell macaroni and let dry.

STEP 3: After the glue has dried, spray the entire surface with either gold or silver spray paint. Let dry.

STEP 4: To the center of each hub of the macaroni wheels, glue a green sequin.

STEP 5: Into the center of the platter, fasten pretty flowers and foliage using a green pipe cleaner to hold. Poke two holes 1/2 inch apart and insert the ends of the chenille pipe cleaners through and twist together on the back side of picture. (See Fig. 11-8A.)

STEP 6: The chenille pipe cleaners should be cut in 2 inch lengths and each flower should be fastened in two or more places.

ACTIVITY 11-9: Meat Tray Pictures

Materials Needed:

- 1 white foam meat tray, 4-1/2 x 8-1/2 inches
- Christmas or birthday card with scene
- 10 inches narrow ribbon, red
- pinking scissors
- glue

Directions for Making:

STEP 1:   Wash and dry the meat tray.
STEP 2:   Turn tray over so the bottom will be up.
STEP 3:   Using pinking scissors, cut the picture from used cards.
STEP 4:   Center the picture on the tray and glue in place.
STEP 5:   At the top of the tray punch 2 holes 1/2 inch apart and insert the
           ribbon; tie in a bow knot.

ACTIVITY 11-10: Praying Silhouettes

Materials Needed:

- 2 plastic meat trays
- black baby rick rack
- 2 pieces black construction paper
- black sequins
- small pearl beads
- scissors
- glue
- narrow ribbon, 8 inches

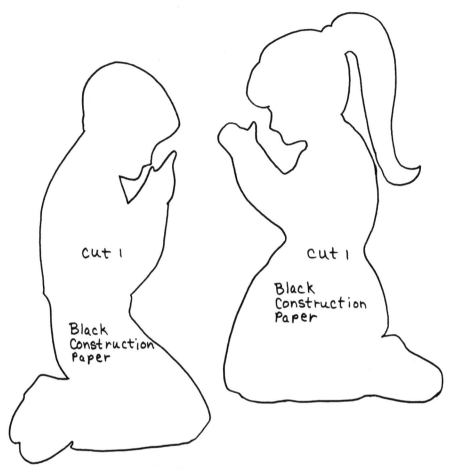

cut 1

Black
Construction
Paper

cut 1

Black
Construction
Paper

Directions for Making:

STEP 1: Using the patterns, trace the boy and girl onto black construction paper; cut out.

STEP 2: Glue the figures into the middle of the meat trays, the boy on one, the girl on the other, facing each other.

STEP 3: Glue baby rick rack around the rim of the tray.

STEP 4: Glue black sequins between the bumps of the rick rack.

STEP 5: Into the center of each sequin glue a small pearl bead.

STEP 6: For a hanger, glue a piece of ribbon to the top on the back side of the picture. Cut 2 four-inch pieces of ribbon.

ACTIVITY 11-11: Reminder Plaque

Materials Needed:

- 6 tongue depressor sticks
- 8 inches of string
- macaroni alphabet letters
- black spray paint
- sharp pointed knife

- glue
- tooth pick

Fig. 11-11-A
Pattern A

Directions for Making:

STEP 1: Lay a piece of typing paper over Pattern A in the book. Draw the outline of the plaque.

STEP 2: Lay the tongue depressor sticks on the pattern. (See Fig. 11-11A.) Glue and let dry.

STEP 3: When the glue is dry, lay the frame on a piece of newspaper. Spray with black paint. Let dry.

STEP 4: Make a hole in the two upright sticks. Use a sharp pointed knife. Set the point where the hole is marked and twist knife around and around until the hole is the size desired.

STEP 5: Push a piece of string through the holes from the front side. Make a knot in the end of the string on the back side, large enough so it won't pull back through. This is to hang the plaque with.

STEP 6: Pick out the letters from alphabet macaroni. On the first stick write:
BE KIND
2nd: BE GOOD
3rd: PLEASE
4th: THANK YOU

STEP 7: Hang up where it can be seen.

ACTIVITY 11-12: Doily Wall Hanging

Materials Needed:

- 2 ten-inch plastic doilies
- 1 five-inch plastic doily
- 40 inches black ribbon, 1/4 inch
- 1 foil pie pan, 8 inch
- flowers and leaves
- glue
- 1 straight pin

Directions for Making:

STEP 1: Lay the 5-inch doily flat. Make a flower and leaf arrangement in the center and glue in place. Set aside to dry, with a heavy book on top until the glue dries.

STEP 2: Measure 50 inches of ribbon. Fold in half and stick a straight pin on the fold.

STEP 3: Start weaving the ribbon around the edge of the two large size doilies. Pull the ribbon through the holes until the pin is at the top. Ribbon can be woven in both directions. Be sure to keep ribbon straight and smooth. Don't let it turn over.

STEP 4: Weave around about 1/2 way, and insert the foil plate inside. Finish weaving on around the edge until the ribbons meet. Tie the ends in a neat bow. Trim off the excess ribbon.

STEP 5: Using a pair of sharp scissors, snip a five inch center from the top doily.

STEP 6: Carefully glue the 5 inch doily with the flowers into the center of the bottom foil pan.

Can be hung in pairs or as a single.

ACTIVITY 11-13: A Christmas Plaque

Materials Needed:

- 1 Lux detergent bottle
- gold or silver spray paint
- red felt, 4 x 6 inches
- small Nativity scene
- 1 plastic meat tray, 6 x 8 inches
- green glitter
- silver sequins
- silver metallic rick rack
- 2 metal fasteners
- red ribbon, 12 x 1/4 inch
- glue
- sharp scissors or knife

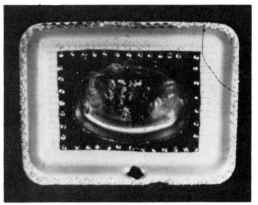

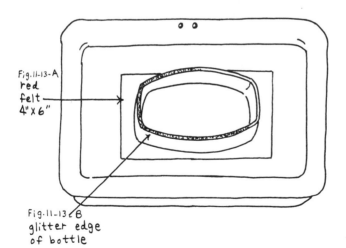

Fig. 11-13-A
red
felt
4" x 6"

Fig. 11-13 B
glitter edge
of bottle

Directions for Making:

STEP 1: Soak the detergent bottle in warm soapy water to remove the label. Wash and dry the bottle.

STEP 2: Measure up 1-1/2 inches from the bottom of the bottle. Cut off. (Use the top of the bottle to make the flower holder, in Chapter 15.)

STEP 3: Spray the bottom of the bottle gold or silver. Set the bottle bottom side up and spray all over. Let dry. Turn the cut piece over and spray the inside. Let dry.

STEP 4: Cut a piece of red felt 4 x 6 inches and glue to the center of the plastic meat tray. (See Fig. 11-13A.)

STEP 5: Around the cut edge of the bottle, make a thin line of glue and dip into green glitter. (See Fig. 11-13B.)

STEP 6: Glue the decorated detergent bottle to the felt—the long way of the bottle with the long way of the meat tray.

STEP 7: Glue silver sequins around the red felt.

STEP 8: Set the meat tray up on one side and glue curly angel hair at the bottom; let a little hair extend over the edge of the rim.

STEP 9: Glue the small manger scene into the bottle; add a silver star at the top rim over the scene.

STEP 10: Around the outside edge of the meat tray, glue silver metallic rick rack.

STEP 11: Fasten 2 metallic eyelets 1/2 inch apart in the rim of the meat tray. Add ribbon for hanging.

Chapter Twelve

Inventing Picture Frames

These picture frames are all exciting for children to make. They especially like the "Different" frame because it lets them pound, hammer and scratch—noisy to make, but quite nice when completed.

ACTIVITY 12-1: Plastic Can-top School Picture Holder

Materials Needed:

- 1 plastic lid from a 2 pound coffee can
- gold or silver spray paint
- 23 marbles
- 2 metal eyelets
- school pictures
- 12 inches ribbon, 1/4 inch wide
- glue
- eyelet pliers

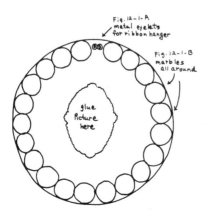

Fig. 12-1-A
metal eyelets
for ribbon hanger

Fig. 12-1-B
marbles
all around

glue
Picture
here

Directions for Making:

STEP 1: Wash and dry plastic lid.

STEP 2: Spray paint the front and back side with either gold or silver.

STEP 3: With eyelet pliers, insert 2 metal eyelets at the edge in the rim, 1/2 inch apart. (See Fig. 12-1A.)

STEP 4: Push a ribbon from the front side through to the back and tie for a hanger.

STEP 5: Put glue in the rim of the lid, and set marbles all around the outside edge. (See Fig. 12-1B.)

STEP 6: Glue a school picture in the center.

STEP 7: Set aside to dry. It should dry for three or four hours before hanging.

ACTIVITY 12-2: Plastic Picture Holder

Materials Needed:

- 1 plastic holder from a six pack of either pop or beer
- gold glitter
- 6 school pictures
- white, lightweight cardboard
- small staples and gun
- 2 inches ribbon, 1/2 inch wide, any color
- scissors
- glue

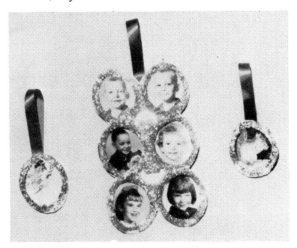

Directions for Making:

STEP 1: Lay the plastic holder in hot water for 3 minutes; dry and lay between 2 paper towels; place under a heavy book for 30 minutes.

STEP 2: Using Pattern A, cut a frame for the back of the plastic from lightweight cardboard.

STEP 3: Cut out pictures, using Pattern B. These do not need to be school pictures. They can be any kind—animals, birds, etc.

STEP 4: Cover the plastic frame with glue and spread on gold glitter. (See Fig. 12-2A.)

STEP 5: Arrange the pictures onto the cardboard and glue in place.

STEP 6: After the glue has dried, staple the plastic rings and cardboard together around the edge in several places. (See Fig. 12-2B.)

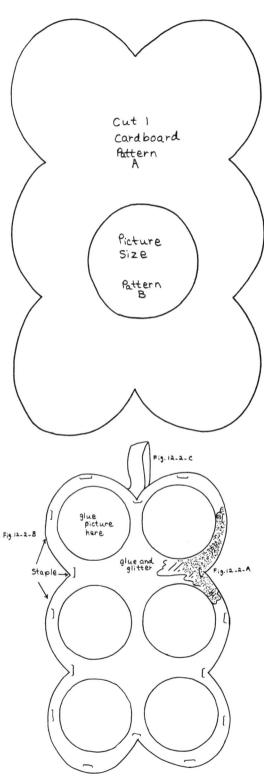

Cut 1
Cardboard
Pattern
A

Picture
Size

Pattern
B

Fig. 12-2-C

glue
picture
here

Fig. 12-2-B

glue and
glitter

Staple

Fig. 12-2-A

STEP 7: Add a ribbon hanger at the top in the middle of the two top pictures. Staple it on. (See Fig. 12-2C.)

STEP 8: These rings can make individual frames also by cutting the frames apart. Cut cardboards and pictures to fit. Glitter the plastic frame and staple together in four places. Add a ribbon hanger.

ACTIVITY 12-3: Macaroni Picture Frame

Materials Needed:

- wheel macaroni
- plastic meat tray, 5 x 6 inches
- Styrofoam spray paint, brown, gold or copper
- picture from Christmas card or magazine
- yarn, 10 inches
- darning needle
- glue

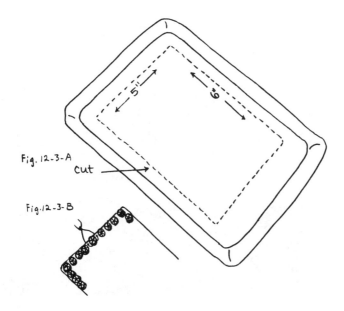

Fig. 12-3-A

cut

Fig. 12-3-B

Directions for Making:

STEP 1:   Cut an oblong piece, 5 x 6 inches, from a plastic meat tray. (See Fig. 12-3A.)

STEP 2:   Using small shell macaroni, glue a line across the top and bottom of the plastic piece and up both sides. Set aside to dry at least an hour.

STEP 3:   Spray the frame with Styrofoam spray paint. (Regular paint will dissolve the tray.)

STEP 4:   Using a picture from a Christmas card or magazine, cut to fit inside of the macaroni frame.

STEP 5:   Glue the picture into the center of the frame.

STEP 6:   Thread a darning needle through the plastic from the back side, leave a 1/2 inch space and push back through and tie a knot in the yarn, to be used for a hanger.

Another way to fix the pictures would be to color a picture in a coloring book; cut out and measure picture on a piece of cardboard; glue macaroni around the edge and spray paint the frame; then add the picture to the middle of the frame. Make a hanger as before. Wheel macaroni with sequins glued to the hubs are different. (See Fig. 12-3B.)

ACTIVITY 12-4: Bracelet Picture Frames

Materials Needed:

- 1 plastic bracelet
- 1 Christmas card with a pretty scene
- gold or silver glitter
- 12 inches of ribbon, 1/4 inch wide
- glue brush
- glue
- ice pick

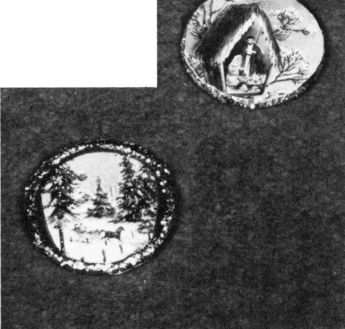

Directions for Making:

STEP 1: Lay the bracelet onto a Christmas card with a pretty scene. Draw around the bracelet; cut out the picture.

STEP 2: Using a brush, cover one side and the outside rim of the bracelet with glue.

STEP 3: Sprinkle glitter onto the glue. Let dry.

STEP 4: Glue the picture to the back side of the bracelet.

STEP 5: Make a hole at the top of the picture with an ice pick, stick a narrow ribbon through and tie a bow for a hanger.

To make a Christmas tree ornament, cut two pictures the same size as the bracelet. Glue a picture on both sides. Use a ribbon hanger.

ACTIVITY 12-5: A Different Picture Frame

Materials Needed:

- 1 board, 8 x 12 inches (size optional)
- picture, 4 to 6 inches smaller than board
- dark brown shoe polish
- an assortment of nails, screws, of different sizes
- file
- 2 snap tops from pop or beer
- hammer
- glue
- 8 inches stove pipe wire
- soft piece of cloth

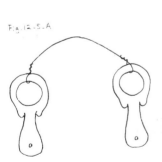

Directions for Making:

STEP 1: Cut out the picture to be used to the size wanted. Lay on the board and draw around it. Be sure to center the picture.

STEP 2: Remove the picture, and using the nails, screws, file, etc., stress the board around the frame.

To stress the board, pound nails into the board just a short way. Lay the screws on the board and hit with the hammer on the screw end. Use the file to make holes in the edges of the board. Use the nails to draw lines in the wood, using the sharp end.

STEP 3:   When all the holes and indentations have been made in the frame, use a soft piece of cloth, dip in the shoe polish, and cover the board where the frame will be. Fill all the indentations with shoe polish.

STEP 4:   Cover the back side of the picture with glue and put in place on the board. Press down to remove air bubbles from under the picture.

STEP 5:   On the back of the board, nail 2 snap tops from pop cans about 6 inches apart. Put wire through one and twist the end of the wire together. Do the same to the other snap top. This is to hang up the picture. (See Fig. 12-5A.)

ACTIVITY 12-6: Bread Fastener Picture Frame

Materials Needed:

- picture, any size, from an old calendar
- plastic bread fasteners, green and white, or any color combination
- black ribbon, 1/4 inch wide
- cardboard, same size as picture
- straight pins
- ruler
- glue

weave ribbon in and out, start at center bottom

Fig. 12-6-B   Fig. 12-6-A

Directions for Making:

STEP 1:   Select picture; measure cardboard to fit.

STEP 2:   Measure a 1/4 inch border onto the cardboard. Lay the plastic bread fasteners in a row around the cardboard—first a white and then a green one. Glue in place. Do both sides first, then top and bottom.

STEP 3:   At each corner lay an extra fastener on. (See Fig. 12-6A.)

STEP 4:   Glue the picture onto the top of the cardboard. Set aside to dry. Lay a heavy book on top until the glue has set up.

STEP 5: After the glue has dried, measure around the picture frame, measure the ribbon, add 12 inches, and cut. Fold the ribbon in the center and add a straight pin.

STEP 6: Count the fasteners in the bottom row, start at the middle, and weave the ribbon both ways, over and under. Pull ribbon through until pin is at the center. (See Fig. 12-6B.) Weave ribbon around the bottom, up one side, up to the middle top. Do the same with the other side of the picture.

STEP 7: Tie a pretty bow to hang picture by at the top, using the excess ribbon.

ACTIVITY 12-7: Round Card with Thumbtack Picture Frame

Materials Needed:

- round card, or cut a picture from something interesting
- 1 round piece of corrugated cardboard same size as pattern
- 2-inch piece of ribbon 1/2 inch wide
- 50 or more thumbtacks depending on the size of the circle
- glue
- glitter

Directions for Making:

STEP 1: Draw pattern on typing paper and cut out. Trace onto corrugated cardboard and cut out.

STEP 2: Glue the picture in place on the cardboard circle and stick thumbtacks around the picture for a frame, being sure to keep the edges of the tacks even with the edge of the picture.

STEP 3:   Highlight any part of the picture with glitter.

STEP 4:   Add a hanger to the back side of the cardboard at the top of the picture by gluing a 2-inch piece of ribbon onto the cardboard.

STEP 5:   Thumbtacks should stay if glue on picture is still wet. Otherwise, put glue around the edge of the card and push thumbtacks in so the heads rest on the cardboard. Let dry.

cut 1
corrugated cardboard

Card Size
Circle

ACTIVITY 12-8: Inexpensive Picture Frames

Materials Needed:

- any can with a lift-off top, such as Pringle potato chips or Vienna sausage can, or nut can
- school picture
- an assortment of lace, rick rack, glitter, sequins or gold braid
- glue

Directions for Making:

STEP 1:   Remove the lid from the can by pulling lid off with the ring. Wash and dry. (See Fig. 12-8A.)

STEP 2:   Twist the ring opener to the top of the lid. This is the hanger. (See Fig. 12-8B.)

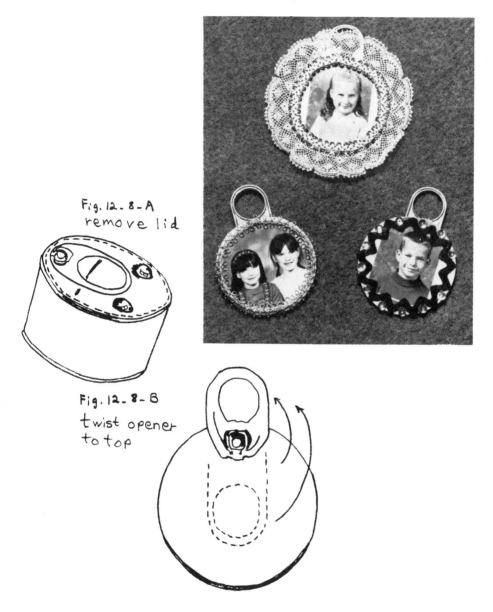

Fig. 12-8-A
remove lid

Fig. 12-8-B
twist opener
to top

STEP 3: Lay the lid on the picture, draw around and cut out. Glue the picture to the can lid, being sure the picture faces the right way and the hanger is at the top.

STEP 4: Around the edge of the can lid and picture glue either rick rack and sequins, lace or braid, or put the glue around rim and sprinkle on glitter.

STEP 5: Hang pictures in pairs or singly.

Chapter Thirteen

Clever Pin Cushions and Refrigerator Decorations

Each one of the animal novelties in this chapter is different from the rest. Children love making them, and adults find them amusing gifts, popular in any season.

ACTIVITY 13-1: Plastic Coaster Pin Cushion

Materials Needed:

- 1 pink plastic coaster, 6 inch
- 1/2 of a 3 inch Styrofoam ball
- 1/4 inch black ribbon, 24 inches long
- 7 flower sequins
- gold rick rack, 12 inches
- 6 sequins, other shapes
- cotton
- glue
- 6 straight pins
- spray paint, blue

Directions for Making:

STEP 1:   Measure black ribbon, fold in the center, put straight pin on fold. Thread the ribbon through every other loop on outside of coaster. Pull ribbon through until pin is on the coaster edge. Weave ribbon both ways until the ends meet. Tie a bow knot.

STEP 2:   Using Sytrofoam spray paint, paint the 3 inch ball. Let dry. (optional)

STEP 3:   Use a serrated edge knife and cut the ball in half.

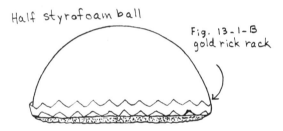

Half styrofoam ball

Fig. 13-1-B
gold rick rack

Fig. 13-1-A
glue cotton

Plastic
Coaster

STEP 4:   Glue a small wad of cotton into the coaster. Then glue the half ball to the cotton. (See Fig. 13-1A.) Glue gold rick rack around the cut edge of the ball. (See Fig. 13-1B.)

STEP 5:   On top of each bump on the coaster, where the ribbon is, glue a flower sequin.

STEP 6:   Pin 6 sequins evenly spaced around the coaster at the plastic rim on the edge.

ACTIVITY 13-2: Tuna Can Pin Cushion

Materials Needed:

- 1 tuna fish can with lid partially removed
- wheel macaroni
- 4 medium shell macaroni
- cotton
- 3 flower heads of a contrasting color
- art foam or felt, 1 piece, 8 x 8 inches
- scrap of green art foam or felt
- needle and thread
- gold spray paint
- glue
- scissors

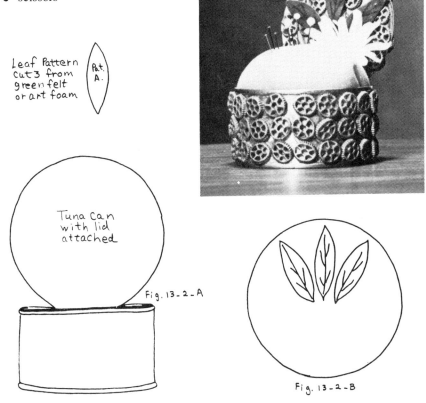

Leaf Pattern
Cut 3 from
green felt
or art foam

Pat.
A.

Tuna Can
with lid
attached

Fig. 13-2-A

Fig. 13-2-B

Directions for Making:

STEP 1: When opening the tuna can, leave the lid attached by a 1 inch strip. (See Fig. 13-2A.) Remove the label, wash and dry can and lid inside and out.

STEP 2: Around the outside edge of the can, glue on 3 rows of wheel macaroni.

STEP 3: Open the lid on the can to an upright position. In the middle of the lid, glue on 4 shell macaroni. On the back or top side of the lid, cover with wheel macaroni. Let dry.

STEP 4: Using a good grade of spray paint, paint the can, the lid, and the macaroni on front and back side.

STEP 5: Cut one piece of art foam or felt into an 8 inch square, Pattern B. Lay on the table and fill the center with cotton. Pull the material up at the 4 corners and tack at the top with needle and thread.

STEP 6: Turn the resulting ball over so the sewed place is on the bottom side and stuff and glue into the tuna can.

STEP 7: Make 3 leaves, using Pattern A from green felt or foam. Draw veins in the leaves using gold paint or a black felt marker pen.

STEP 8: Glue the leaves to the top front of the can. (See Fig. 13-2B.)

STEP 9: Stick the flowers into the can at the back side next to the lid. Add pins wherever wanted.

Pattern B
8 inch square

ACTIVITY 13-3: Can and Ball Pin Cushion

Materials Needed:

- 1 tomato sauce can, 3 inches tall
- 1 Styrofoam ball, 3 inches tall
- red velvet, 8 x 8 inches
- gold metallic braid
- 20 pearl beads
- bird and flower cutouts from a used birthday card
- 20 straight pins
- blue spray paint
- glue
- scissors

Pattern A
Cut 1
Red Velvet

Directions for Making:

STEP 1: Remove the label from the can and spray with blue paint. Let dry.

STEP 2: Using Pattern A, cut red velvet. Wrap around Styrofoam ball. Fasten with straight pins. Glue ball into the top of the can where the velvet meets.

STEP 3: Around the top and bottom edge of the can, glue gold metallic braid.

STEP 4: From a used card, cut out birds and flowers and glue in between the metallic braid.

STEP 5: Around the top of the can, add the pearl beads and pins. Space evenly. Stick a pin through each bead, then into the Styrofoam ball.

ACTIVITY 13-4: Ginny the Giraffe

(For the Refrigerator)

Materials Needed:

- 1 piece yellor or tan felt, 14 x 6 inches
- black felt, 2 x 4 inches
- 1 moving eye, 1/4 inch
- orange fake fur, 5 x 1/4 inch
- 1 black pipe cleaner
- pen, ball point
- 2 magnets, 1/2 inch long
- glue
- scissors

Fig. 13-4-A

Fig. 13-4-B

Spots from black felt

cut 1

cut 1

nose from black felt

cut 1

cut 1

Cut 1 each feet

Directions for Making:

STEP 1: Using the pattern, trace the body and spots onto paper and cut out.
STEP 2: Cut 2 giraffe bodies from tan felt and the spots and feet from black felt.
STEP 3: On one of the bodies, glue the spots in place, and also the feet. (See Fig. 13-4A.)
STEP 4: Cut a piece of black pipe cleaner for a tail, 3 inches long. Twist in a shape as in the picture and glue under the top body. (See Fig. 13-4B.) Put glue around the outside edge of the other body and place the bodies together.
STEP 5: With a pen, draw the lines onto the legs, ear and eye.
STEP 6: Glue the moving eye in place; draw on the eyelashes.
STEP 7: Add the fake fur mane and fur tip for the tail.
STEP 8: Glue 2 magnets onto the back side, one about one inch down from the top of the head and one under the largest black spot at the bottom of the tummy.

ACTIVITY 13-5: Jack, The Refrigerator Donkey

Materials Needed:

- gray felt, 5 x 13 inches
- black felt, 2 x 2 inches
- black pipe cleaner, 3 inches long
- red fake fur, 4 inches
- 2 magnets, 1/2 inch long
- 1 moving eye, 1/4 inch size
- glue
- scissors
- pen

Directions for Making:

STEP 1: Using the pattern, trace the body and hoofs onto paper and cut out.
STEP 2: Cut 2 bodies from gray felt and the tiny hoofs from black felt.
STEP 3: On one body, glue the hoofs in place and, using a pen, draw the lines on the body and ear. (See Fig. 13-5A.)

cut 2
gray felt

Donkey body

feet
cut 1
of each
Pattern

←Fig. 13-5-A

STEP 4:   Cut a 3 inch piece of black pipe cleaner and shape like the tail in the pattern and glue under the top body.

STEP 5:   Put a line of glue around the other felt body and glue the two bodies together.

STEP 6:   Add the moving eye, the fake fur mane and the tip on the tail.

STEP 7:   On the back of the donkey, one inch down from the top of the head and at the middle of the stomach 1/2 inch up from the bottom, glue the magnets.

ACTIVITY 13-6: Milly and Billy, The Refrigerator Twins

Materials Needed:

- white felt, 8 x 12 inches
- red felt, 6 x 6 inches
- blue felt, 6 x 6 inches
- green felt, 3 x 5 inches
- brown felt, 2-1/2 inches x 4-1/2 inches
- 4 moving eyes, 1/2 inch size
- magnets, 1/2 inch long
- red fake fur, 3 x 1/4 inch
- yellow fake fur, 5 x 1/4 inch
- glue
- scissors

Girl Face

Boy Face

cut 1

flower holder
background
Pattern
G.

Scallop Pattern C

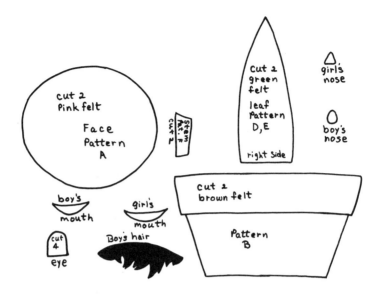

Directions for Making:

STEP 1:   Using the pattern, trace onto paper the flower pot, leaves, stems, flowers, face, nose and mouth, and cut out.

STEP 2:   Cut two flower pots from brown felt (Pattern B); 2 pink oval faces from pink (Pattern A); 2 sets of green leaves and stems (Patterns D and E); one flower from red and one from blue felt (Pattern C).

STEP 3:   Cut Pattern G from white felt and glue the leaves and stem in place.

STEP 4:   Glue the flower pot on and glue the flower in place.

STEP 5:   Into the center of each flower, glue the pink oval face.

STEP 6:   Glue the fake fur in place at the top of the heads.

STEP 7:   Glue on the eyes, felt nose and mouth.

STEP 8:   Make eyelashes and eyebrows with the ball point pen.

STEP 9:   Glue 2 magnets 1/2 inch long to the backs of each flower and pot. Glue one 1 inch up from the bottom, and the other magnet 1 inch down from the top center of the flower head.

ACTIVITY 13-7: Ronnie Rabbit Refrigerator Animal

Materials Needed:

- white felt, 5 x 12 inches
- pink felt, 3 x 3 inches
- scrap of red felt
- 2 moving eyes, 1/2 inch size
- black flair marker pen
- scissors
- glue
- 2 one-inch pieces magnetic tape

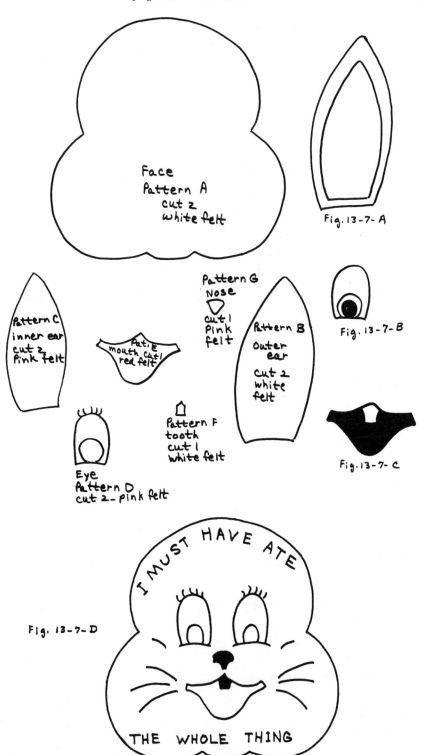

Face
Pattern A
cut 2
white felt

Fig. 13-7-A

Pattern C
inner ear
cut 2
Pink felt

Pattern G
Nose
cut 1
Pink
felt

Pat. E
mouth cut 1
red felt

Pattern B
Outer
ear
cut 2
white
felt

Fig. 13-7-B

Pattern F
tooth
cut 1
white felt

Eye
Pattern D
cut 2 - pink felt

Fig. 13-7-C

Fig. 13-7-D

I MUST HAVE ATE

THE WHOLE THING

Directions for Making:

STEP 1:   Lay a piece of typing paper over the patterns in the book, trace and cut out.

STEP 2:   Using straight pins fasten patterns to felt of the right color and cut out.

STEP 3:   Lay the two smaller pink ears onto the larger white ones and glue in place. (See Fig. 13-7A.) Lay the pink felt eyes on the table, glue on the moving eyes. (See Fig. 13-7B.) Glue the white tooth in place on the red mouth. (See Fig. 13-7C.)

STEP 4:   Lay the ears in place on top of one rabbit face, put glue around the rim of the other face and place on top of the first face. Press firmly together. Let set until dry.

STEP 5:   Glue the eyes in place on top face, then the nose and mouth. (See Fig. 13-7D.)

STEP 6:   Using a flair marker pen, or macaroni letters, write: ''I must have ate the whole thing!''

STEP 7:   Add eyelashes to top of eyes, whiskers by the mouth, lines on the face and eyebrows with the pen.

STEP 8:   Cut two one-inch pieces from a roll of magnetic tape, glue to the back side of the animal at the top and bottom.

Chapter Fourteen

Pin on Purses

Both boys and girls will use these purses. The boys will put them in their pockets, but the girls will wear them proudly on the collars of their dresses or pinned to their sweaters. The girls in our class termed them ''neat.'' Certainly they are inexpensive to make and colorful to own.

ACTIVITY 14-1: Pink Poodle Pin on Coin Purse

Materials needed:

- pink felt, 3-1/4 x 6-1/2 inches
- white felt, 3 x 8 inches
- red felt scrap
- 2 moving eyes, 3/4 inch size
- narrow pink ribbon, 4 inches
- pinking scissors
- straight scissors
- needle and thread
- large safety pin
- glue

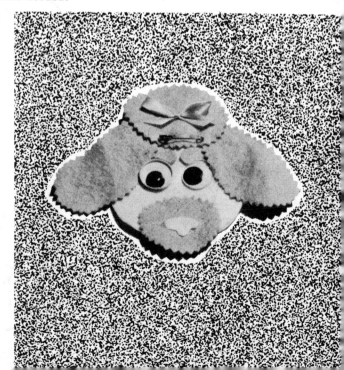

Directions for Making:

STEP 1:   Cut 2 circles from pink felt, using straight scissors and Pattern A.

STEP 2:   Using pinking scissors, cut the 2 ears, top knot and chin ruff from white felt.

STEP 3:   Use straight scissors to cut mouth from red felt and 2 eyebrows from white.

STEP 4:   Sew around the circles 1/8 inch from edge. Leave an opening 2 inches long.

STEP 5:   Glue the chin ruff to the bottom of the circle opposite the opening. Glue the ears in place and the top knot.

STEP 6:   Add the eyes and glue on eyebrows and mouth.

STEP 7:   Tie a ribbon in a knot, cut both ends on an angle. Glue in place on top knot.

STEP 8:   Fasten a large safety pin at the top next to the ribbon. Use the pin to fasten the poodle purse to child's dress, shirt or sweater.

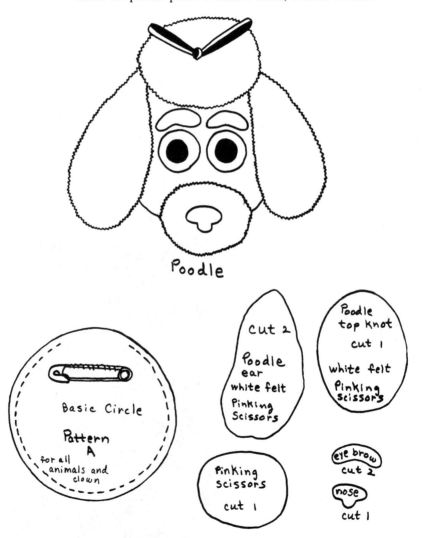

Poodle

Basic Circle

Pattern
A

for all
animals and
clown

Cut 2

Poodle
ear

white felt

Pinking
Scissors

Pinking
scissors

cut 1

Poodle
top knot

cut 1

white felt

Pinking
scissors

eye brow
cut 2

nose
cut 1

ACTIVITY 14-2: Dog Head Pin on Purse

Materials Needed:

- white felt, 3-1/4 x 6-1/2 inches
- black and red felt scraps
- brown felt, 2 x 7 inches
- white fake fur, 1/8 inch x 4 inches
- 2 moving eyes, 3/4 inch size
- glue
- scissors
- needle and white thread
- large safety pin

Directions for Making:

Follow same procedure for making poodle. Cut the circle from white felt and the ears from brown felt. Cut all pieces with straight scissors.

Sew the circle, glue on ears, eyes, nose and mouth. Add fake fur eyebrows and two tiny 1/2 inch pieces of fur to tips of ears.

Add safety pin.

ACTIVITY 14-3: Turtle Pin on Purse

Materials Needed:

- green felt, 3-1/4 x 7-1/2 inches
- black baby rick rack, 20 inches
- 2 black sequins, small size
- large safety pin
- scissors
- needle and green thread
- glue

Directions for Making:

STEP 1: Cut two 3-inch circles. Cut 4 feet, Pattern B; tail, Pattern C; and a head, Pattern D. Cut all from green felt.

STEP 2: Lay the head, feet and tail between the circles and pin to hold.

STEP 3: Sew the tail to the under circle, in the center of the opening.

STEP 4: Start sewing at the top side of the foot on the right, and sew the circles together, 1/8 inch from the edge, sewing around the top side of the other foot. Leave an opening 2 inches long, around the tail, so money can be slipped inside.

STEP 5: Lay the circles flat; make a line of glue around the edge, where the stitches are. Lay the baby rick rack onto the glue, make another line of glue 1/2 inch in toward the middle and add another row of black rick rack.

STEP 6: Outline the head with glue and add rick rack.

STEP 7: Glue 2 black sequins in place for eyes.

STEP 8: Add a safety pin below the tail, to pin to child's dress, shirt or sweater. Turtle will hang head down.

ACTIVITY 14-4: Kitty, Clown and Lion Head Pin on Purses

Materials Needed:

Clown Face:

- white felt
- black felt
- red felt
- green felt
- orange fake fur
- scissors
- needle and thread
- glue
- large safety pin

Kitty Face:

- white felt
- green felt
- black felt
- fake fur, white
- 2 tiny moving eyes, 3/16 inch size
- scissors
- needle and thread
- glue
- large safety pin
- 3 black stamens from flowers for whiskers

Lion Head:

- yellow felt
- red felt
- 2 moving eyes, 1/4 inch size
- orange fake fur
- ball point pen
- glue
- scissors
- needle and thread
- safety pin
- flower stamens

clown

Kitty

mouth
cut 1
red felt

eye
cut 2
black felt

nose
cut 1
red felt

eye
cut 2
green felt

nose
cut 1
Pink
felt

ear
cut 2
white felt

mouth
cut 1
red felt

Lion

Lion
ear
cut 2
orange felt

tongue
red felt

Directions for Making:

STEP 1: BASIC STEPS—Cut the circles from felt, white for the kitty and clown, and yellow for the lion.

STEP 2: Using the patterns for each animal, cut ears, noses, mouths and eyes.

STEP 3: Place the ears between the circles. Pin to hold, and sew around the outside 1/8 inch from edge. Leave a two-inch opening on each one.

STEP 4: Add the eyes, nose and mouth on each animal.

STEP 5: Add the fake fur to each circle around the lion face and the kitty face. Glue the fur all the way around. For the clown, put a 2 inch piece at the top, and 1-1/2 inch pieces down both sides for sideburns.

STEP 6: To make the eyes for the clown, cut a strip of black felt 1/8 x 3 inches. Cut this strip into four equal parts. Lay one strip up and down on the face and one across for each eye.

STEP 7: Fasten a safety pin at the top of each head.

STEP 8: Glue 3 stamens in the center of the kitty face for whiskers.

Chapter Fifteen

Bonus Ideas

Here's a bonus chapter full of ideas that just don't fit in the other chapters. These activities are just as interesting and as much fun as those in the other chapters. You'll find that the children will write notes to each other on the "home-made" stationery, and they'll enjoy making the holders and mats.

ACTIVITY 15-1: Flower Holders

Materials Needed:

- 1 plastic Lux detergent bottle
- 1 plastic Thrill detergent bottle
- 2 metal eyelets
- silver glitter
- decal or flowers cut from an old card
- sharp scissors
- eyelet pliers
- glue

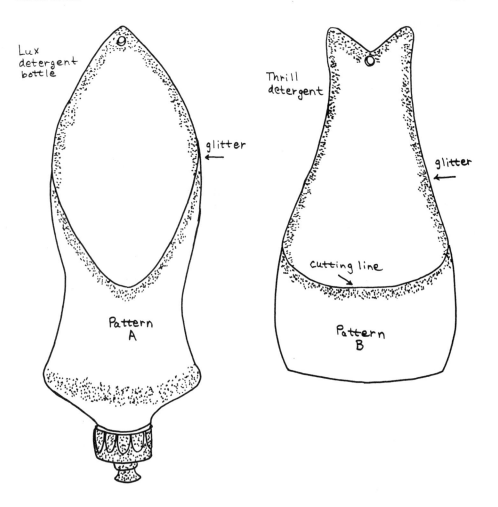

Lux detergent bottle

glitter

Pattern A

Thrill detergent

glitter

cutting line

Pattern B

Directions for Making:

STEP 1:   Soak the detergent bottles in warm soapy water to remove the labels. Wash and dry bottles.

STEP 2:   Using a sharp pair of scissors, cut the Lux or Thrill bottle off, using either Pattern A or B.

STEP 3:   Make a thin line of glue around the cut edges of the front of the bottles. Sprinkle on silver glitter.

STEP 4:   *With eyelet pliers*, punch a hole at the top of each holder and insert a metal eyelet for a hanger.

STEP 5:   Using a decal or cut a flower from an old card, glue at the top under the hanger.

STEP 6:   Water can be put into the holder for fresh flowers or plastic flowers may be used. Hang on the wall.

ACTIVITY 15-2: Hot Mat Using Bead Strings

Materials Needed:

- 1 five inch circle of cardboard
- 36 inch bead string, glass or plastic beads
- glue

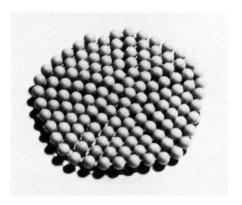

Hot Pot Mat from beads

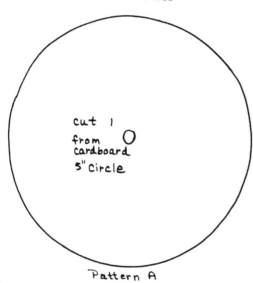

cut 1
from
cardboard
5" circle

Pattern A

Directions for Making:

STEP 1:   Using Pattern A, cut one circle from cardboard.

STEP 2:   Mark the center of the cardboard; starting at the center, glue the beads around and around until the outside edge is reached.

STEP 3: Cut one bead from the end of the string and glue into the center of the mat.

STEP 4: Let set until dry. It is ready for use.

ACTIVITY 15-3: Bobby Pin Box

Materials Needed:

- round Lux detergent bottle
- scissors or razor blade
- tiny figurine or flower
- felt marker pen
- sequins
- glitter
- glue

Fig. 15-3-B

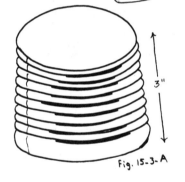

Fig. 15-3-A

Directions for Making:

STEP 1: Remove the label, scrape off the glue, wash and dry a round detergent bottle.

STEP 2: Measure up from the bottom of the bottle 3 inches. Draw a line around bottle. (See Fig. 15-3A.)

STEP 3: Using a sharp razor blade or scissors, cut off on this line. (See Fig. 15-3B.)

STEP 4: Measure down from the top rim of the bottle 1 inch, draw a line and cut top off.

STEP 5: Leave the lid on for a handle.

STEP 6: With a felt marker pen, write, "Bobby Pins," "stamps," "pins," "buttons," etc.

STEP 7: Decorate with sequins or glitter.

STEP 8: At the top of the lid, on the bottle cap, glue a tiny figurine or flower.

ACTIVITY 15-4: Macaroni Cross

Materials Needed:

- small shell macaroni
- 2 small pictures
- silver spray paint
- margarine tub, round
- small flowers
- 2 cups plaster of Paris
- cardboard
- scissors
- bowl and spoon
- 1 cup water
- glue

Directions for Making:

STEP 1:   Using Pattern A, cut a cross from corrugated cardboard.

STEP 2:   Cut 2 pictures from old Christmas cards, using Pattern B. Draw around the pictures in the center of the cross between the arms on both sides. (See Fig. 15-4A.)

STEP 3:   Working on a small area at a time, spread glue and cover with small shell macaroni with the bump side up. Outline the picture area first. Do not put macaroni in this part.

STEP 4:   Continue to cover the cross with macaroni. When first side is covered, turn the cross over and cover the second side.

STEP 5:   When macaroni and glue are dry, spray with silver paint.

STEP 6:   When the paint is dry, glue the pictures to the front and back of the cross.

STEP 7:   Fill the margarine tub full of plaster of Paris mixed to heavy cream consistency.

STEP 8:   Set the cross into the middle of the margarine tub. Press down in plaster so cross sets in the bottom of the tub.

STEP 9:   Around the bottom of the cross on both sides, add flowers and greenery. Stick the stems into the plaster.

Warning: Be sure to cover both sides of the cross with macaroni. If only one side is covered, the cross will buckle.

By adding a string or ribbon holder at the top, cross may be hung on the wall. If used for hanging, only one side needs to be covered, and the cross should not be put in a margarine tub.

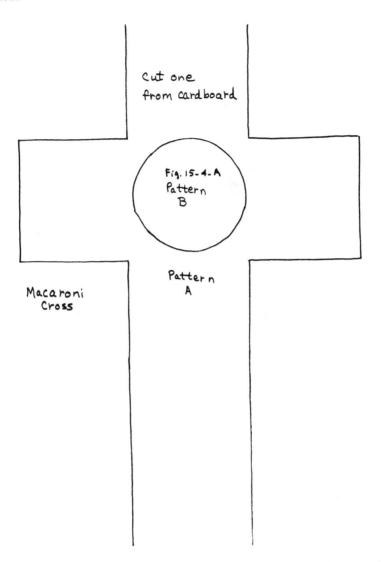

Cut one
from cardboard

Fig. 15-4-A
Pattern
B

Pattern
A

Macaroni
Cross

ACTIVITY 15-5: Key Holder on Wooden Square

Materials Needed:

- wood square, 5 x 5 x 1 inch
- school picture
- metallic picture frame (can be purchased at stationery store)
- 6 cup hooks
- ribbon
- thumbtack
- plastic spray or clear shellac (can be purchased at hardware store)
- sandpaper
- glue

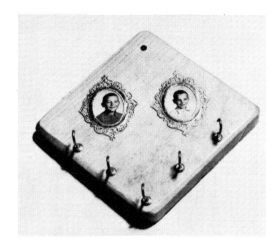

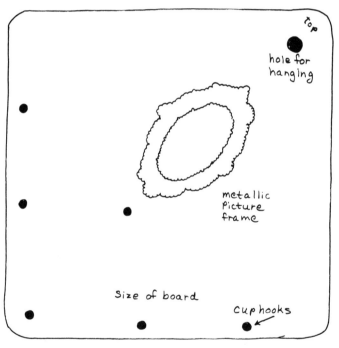

Directions for Making:

STEP 1: Cut out the square of wood. Use sandpaper to smooth off the edges.
STEP 2: Spray the board with clear shellac or plastic spray.
STEP 3: Turn the board, so there will be a point at the top and bottom.
STEP 4: Glue the picture to the board at the middle top.
STEP 5: Glue the metallic frame around the picture.
STEP 6: Screw the cup hooks into place, 3 across the middle, then 2, and at the bottom screw one.

STEP 7:   Fold the piece of ribbon in half and using a thumbtack, make a hanger on the back of the board, or bore a hole at the top and hang with a nail.

ACTIVITY 15-6: Little Hats

Materials Needed:

- detergent bottle caps
- tiny flowers
- plastic egg carton
- plastic meat tray the same color as carton
- bright colored feather
- narrow ribbon, 1/8 inch wide, any color
- white plastic meat tray
- black narrow ribbon, 1/8 inch wide
- indoor-outdoor carpet, 3 x 4 inch piece
- narrow ribbon bow, any color
- glue
- scissors

Directions for Making:

Hat No. 1:

Use a detergent bottle cap from Lemon Joy. Glue tiny flowers around the bottom edge and around the indented top.

Hat No. 2:

Cut a plastic egg cup off so the edge is even all around. (See Fig. 15-6A.) From a plastic meat tray the same color as the egg carton, cut a circle. (See Fig. 15-6B.) Glue the plastic pieces together. Glue a narrow ribbon around the egg cup. Add a feather. Glue or fasten onto animal with a straight pin.

Hat No. 3:

Cut ovals from plastic meat trays. (See Fig. 15-6C.) Cut one large and two small ones. Glue all together, one on top of the other. Glue a narrow black ribbon around the two small ovals. Glue or pin on head.

Hat No. 4:

Tie a small bow of ribbon to stem of small flowers. Stick into the head or glue on.

Hat No. 5:

Cut indoor-outdoor carpet in oval shapes. (See Fig. 15-6D.) Cut one from each pattern. Glue together. Pin or glue to head of animal or whatever.

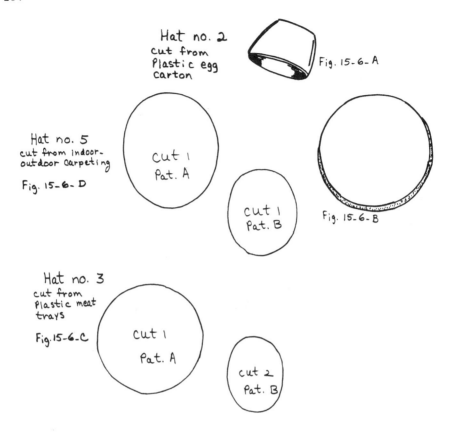

Hat no. 2
cut from
Plastic egg
carton
Fig. 15-6-A

Hat no. 5
cut from indoor-
outdoor carpeting

Fig. 15-6-D

cut 1
Pat. A

cut 1
Pat. B

Fig. 15-6-B

Hat no. 3
cut from
Plastic meat
trays

Fig. 15-6-C

cut 1
Pat. A

cut 2
Pat. B

ACTIVITY 15-7: Autograph Book

Materials Needed:

- 2 pieces cardboard, 5 x 6-1/2 inches
- 1 bright colored shoe string with metal ends
- paper punch
- 20 sheets of typing paper
- ruler
- sharp scissors
- felt marker pen
- felt flowers (optional)

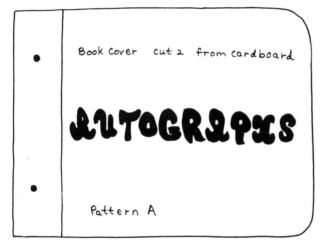

cut 30 pages this size
from typing paper

Pattern B

Book cover   cut 2   from cardboard

AUTOGRAPHS

Pattern A

Directions for Making:

STEP 1: Using a sheet of typing paper, trace and cut out Patterns A and B. Trace Pattern A onto the cardboard; use sharp scissors or knife and cut out. Place Pattern B onto the sheets of typing paper, trace and cut out.

STEP 2: Measure one inch from the back side edge of the Pattern A. Lay a ruler on this line and using the sharp end of the scissors, cut through the top layer of paper on the cardboard.(Be very careful not to cut anything but the top layer of paper.) Turn the cardboard over and lay a ruler on the back side and make a crease.

This will let the book open up. On the side away from the cut, put a small X with a pencil. This is the front of the book and will be the top.

STEP 3: Using the paper punch, poke 2 holes where indicated on Patterns A and B.

STEP 4: Lay the 20 pages of typing paper together, making sure all the edges are even.

STEP 5: Lay the bottom cardboard on the table; place the sheets of paper on

STEP 6:

STEP 7:

STEP 8:
STEP 9:

top, making sure the pages are lined up with the holes on the bottom. Be sure to place the cardboard over with the X on top so the book will open.

Using the shoe string, poke the end with the metal on it down through the hole on top, through the paper pages and out the bottom. Go to other side and push the metal end of the shoe string up through the bottom, on through the paper pages up through the top of the album and tie the shoe lace in a bow knot on the top.

Using the felt marker pen, write ''Autographs'' on the front side. Either use the pattern shown or draw the letters freehand.

Felt flowers may be glued on for decoration, or leave as is.

Ask friends to write in the book and sign their names. The verses included here may be used, or make up more of your own.

VERSES:

You are the sunshine of my life.
I love you more each day.
I'd like to lock you in my heart
And throw the key away.

When you are old and cannot see,
Put on your specs and think of me.

Remember me when this you see,
Though many miles apart.
Remember me when this you see,
And place me in your heart.

When I am dead and in my grave,
And when my bones are rotten,
This little book will tell of me,
When I am quite forgotten.

When you are sitting on a stump,
Remember me before you jump.

When you grow old and ugly
As people sometimes do,
Remember that you have a friend
Who is old and ugly too.

If on this page you chance to look
Think of me and close the book.

Roses are red, violets are blue,
Sugar is sweet and so are you.

When the golden sun is setting,
And the path no more is trod,
May your name in gold be written,
In the autograph of God.

Love many, but trust few.
Always paddle your own canoe.

When the golden sun is setting
And your mind from care is free,
When of loved ones you are thinking,
Will you sometime think of me?

When evening draws its curtains
And pins them with a star,
Remember me dear friend
Although I may be afar.

In the golden chain of friendship
Regard me as a link.

Your friend 'till the pillow slips and the butter fly's.

With all good wishes,
Forget me not.

Long may you live,
Happy may you be,
Blessed by 40 children
20 on each knee.

When the sun of life is setting
And my time on earth is o'er,
I hope you will meet me someday
Upon the other shore.

The ring is round.
It has no end.
So is the love for you,
My friend.

Y Y U R
Y Y U B
 I C U R
Y Y 4 me.

A friend in need
Is a friend indeed.

When Rocks and rills divide us
And you no more I see,
Remember it is (your name)
That often thinks of thee.

ACTIVITY 15-8: Baby Food Jar Book Ends

Materials Needed:

- 12 small size baby food jars and lids
- 12 flowers, with open faces, if possible
- liquid glass glue
- 2 pieces of wood, 1 x 5 x 7 inches
- black spray paint
- metallic rick rack, 36 inches, bright color
- quick drying clear glue

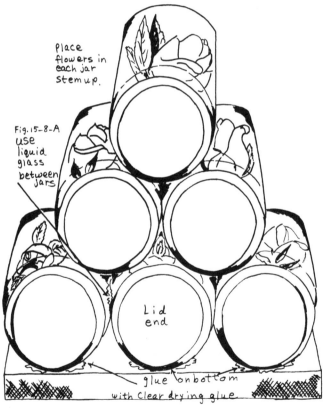

place
flowers in
each jar
stem up.

Fig. 15-8-A
use
liquid
glass
between
jars

Lid
end

glue on bottom
with clear drying glue

Directions for Making:

STEP 1:   Remove the labels and glue from 12 baby food jars. Wash and dry
            lids and jars.

STEP 2:   Spray the jar lids black, inside and out. Let dry.

STEP 3: Set the 12 jars on the table. Into each jar press a plastic flower, stem end up. (Any type of flower may be used—open roses, orchids, or flowers with flat faces.)

STEP 4: Screw the lids into the jars. Cut two pieces of wood, 1 x 5 x 7 inches. Sand the edges of the wood until it is smooth.

STEP 5: Using a glue that dries quickly and dries clear, cover a strip on 3 jars about 1 inch wide. Lay these jars onto the board, across the wide way, being sure the lids are flush with the back of the board (3 jars are 7 inches wide). To keep them straight, set a jar or can on each side of the board until the glue has dried—3 to 4 hours or longer.

STEP 6: On the sides of the jars where they touch, trickle a thin layer of liquid glass glue.

STEP 7: Do the same with the other board and 3 jars.

STEP 8: Start the next row of jars after the first 3 jars and glue have set up. Put the glass glue where the jars will touch. On the first row there are 3 jars, the next row will have 2 jars, with 1 on top. Let dry overnight. (See Fig. 15-8A.)

STEP 9: Around the edge of the wood, glue a strip of metallic rick rack.

STEP 10: Add a bug or butterfly onto each board in the center.

ACTIVITY 15-9: Decorating Note Paper

Materials Needed:

- 6 or 8 sheets of typing paper
- 12-inch ruler
- used cards with flowers, birds, children or animals
- scissors
- glue
- envelopes, 3-1/2 x 5-1/2 inches, for each note paper

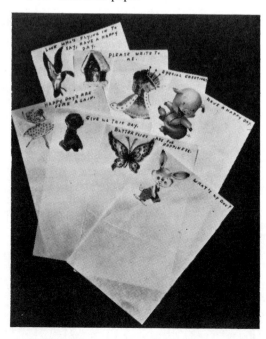

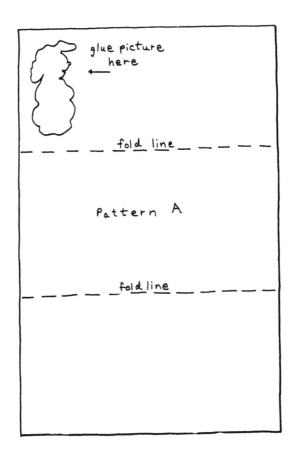

Directions for Making:

STEP 1:   Select the used cards with the decoration desired and cut out design.

STEP 2:   Lay a piece of typing paper on the table. Fold in the middle.

STEP 3:   Open the paper and lay a ruler on the fold. Pull from top edge and pull the paper in two.

STEP 4:   Select the cutout design and glue in place at the top left of a sheet of paper.

STEP 5:   Write a line at the top side of the paper such as, a card with butter-flies: "Butterflies are for happiness." A bird: "Look who's flying in to say, have a happy day." A child praying: "Give us this day." A rabbit: "What's up Doc?" Other animals: "Special greetings and have a happy day." Think of other things to write.

STEP 6:   After letter is written on the paper, fold as in Pattern A. Put in an envelope. These may be purchased at any variety store.

Portfolio of Instant
Tracing Patterns

The following patterns can be traced directly from the pages. In some cases, where the shape of the pattern is round, or the same on both ends, we have provided "half-patterns." In these cases you trace half onto a large piece of paper, then turn it around (180°) and trace the other half. Other patterns are in sections which can be combined.

A

Pattern for mouth
red felt
cut 2

B

Pattern for
nose end
red felt
cut 1

Pattern for
nose cone
cut 1
from center of
fibre egg carton

ACTIVITY 1-1

Black felt

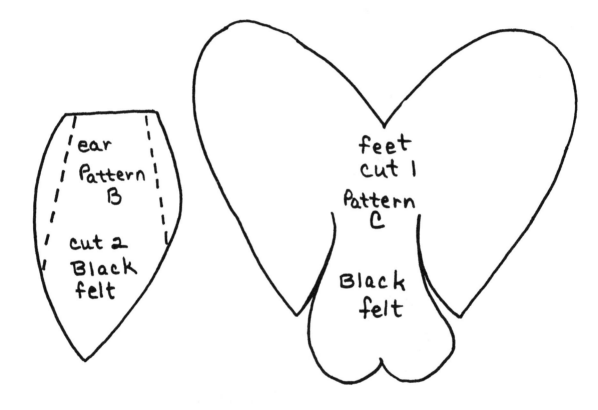

Pattern A
glue baby rickrack
on top and bottom

ear
Pattern
B

cut 2
Black
felt

feet
cut 1
Pattern
C

Black
felt

tongue

Pattern
D
red felt
cut 1

eyelash
Pattern E
cut 2
Black felt

nose

Pattern F
Black felt
cut 1

ACTIVITY 1-3

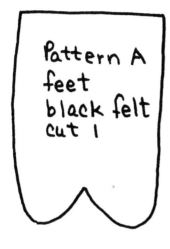

Pattern A
feet
black felt
cut 1

Pattern B
face
black
felt
cut 1

nose → ▽
red felt
cut 1
Pattern C

Pattern D
ear
cut 2
Black
felt

ACTIVITY 1-7

Feet
Pink felt
cut 1 for
each rabbit

nose
cut 1
for each
rabbit

pink
felt

ACTIVITY 1-8

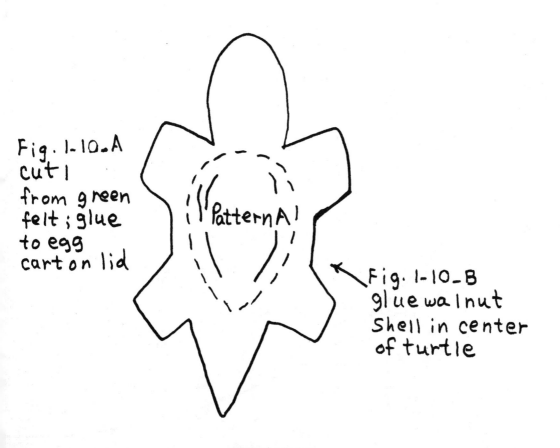

Fig. 1-10-A
cut 1
from green
felt; glue
to egg
carton lid

Pattern A

Fig. 1-10-B
glue walnut
shell in center
of turtle

ACTIVITY 1-10

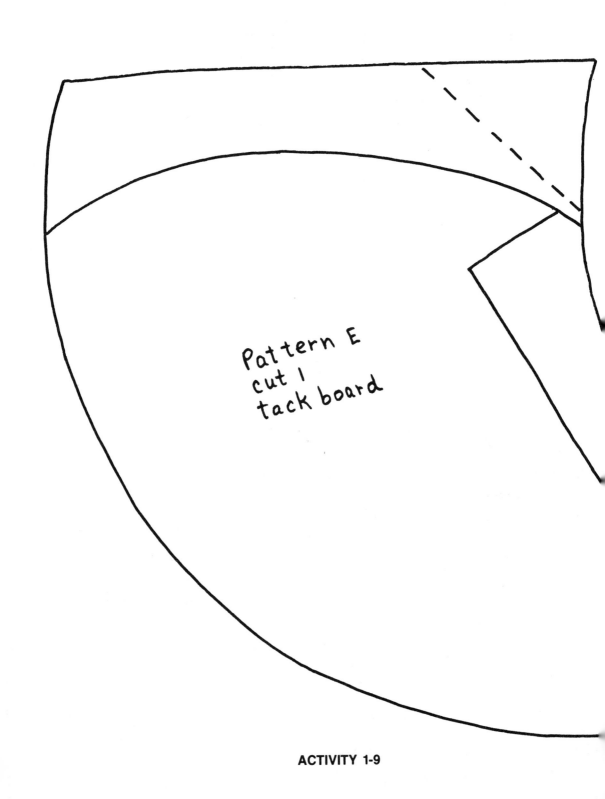

Pattern E
cut 1
tack board

ACTIVITY 1-9

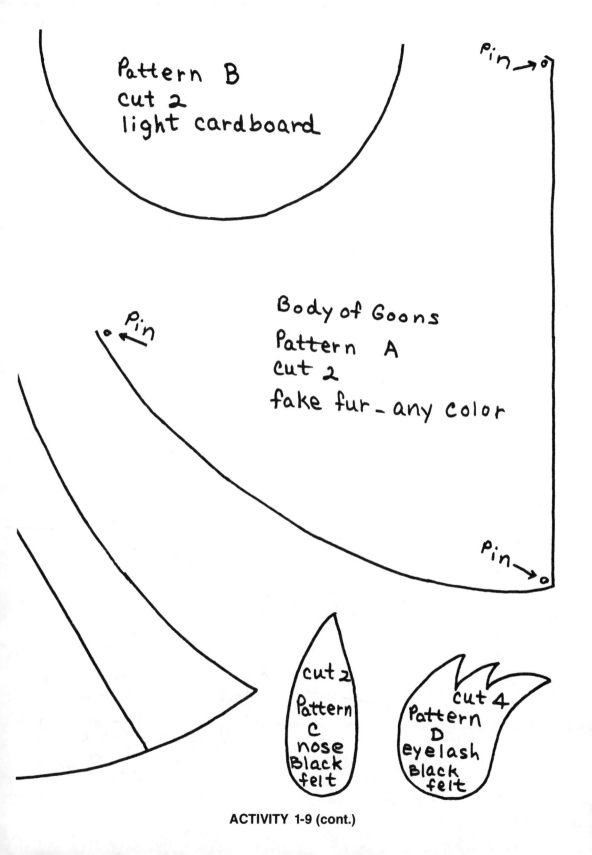

Pattern B
cut 2
light cardboard

Pin →o

Pin →

Body of Goons
Pattern A
cut 2
fake fur — any color

Pin →o

cut 2
Pattern C
nose
Black felt

cut 4
Pattern D
eyelash
Black felt

ACTIVITY 1-9 (cont.)

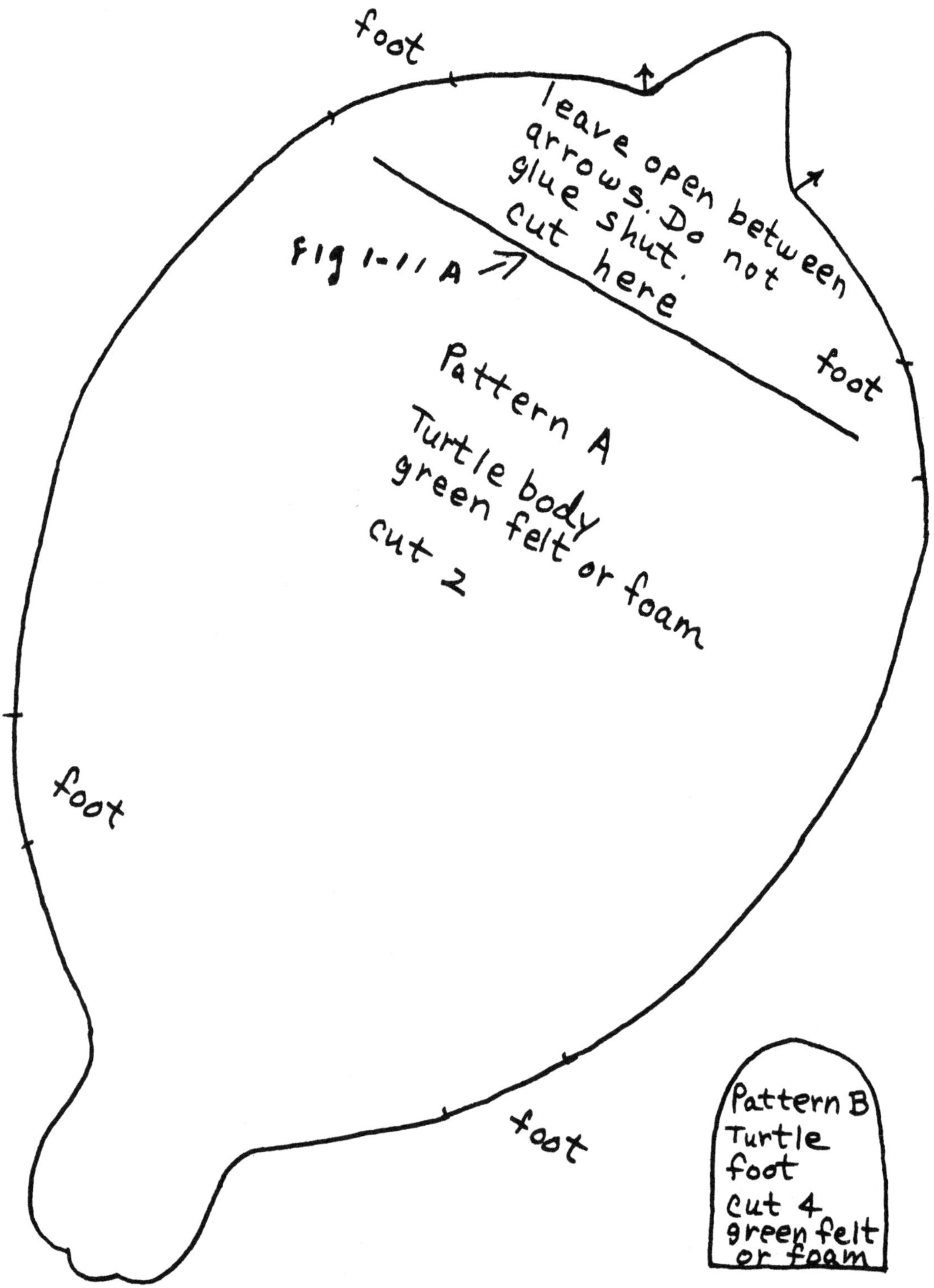

foot

leave open between arrows. Do not glue shut.

Fig 1-11 A → cut here

foot

Pattern A
Turtle body
green felt or foam
cut 2

foot

foot

Pattern B
Turtle
foot
cut 4
green felt
or foam

ACTIVITY 1-11

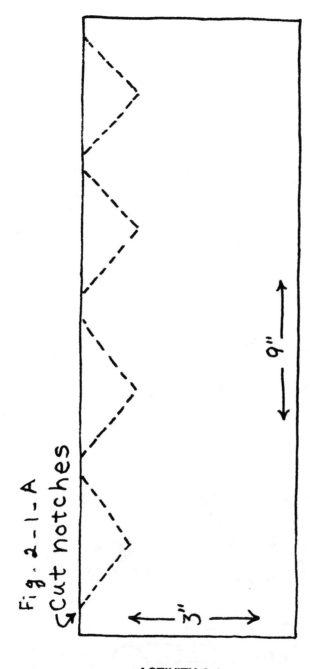

Fig. 2-1-A
Cut notches

9"

3"

ACTIVITY 2-1

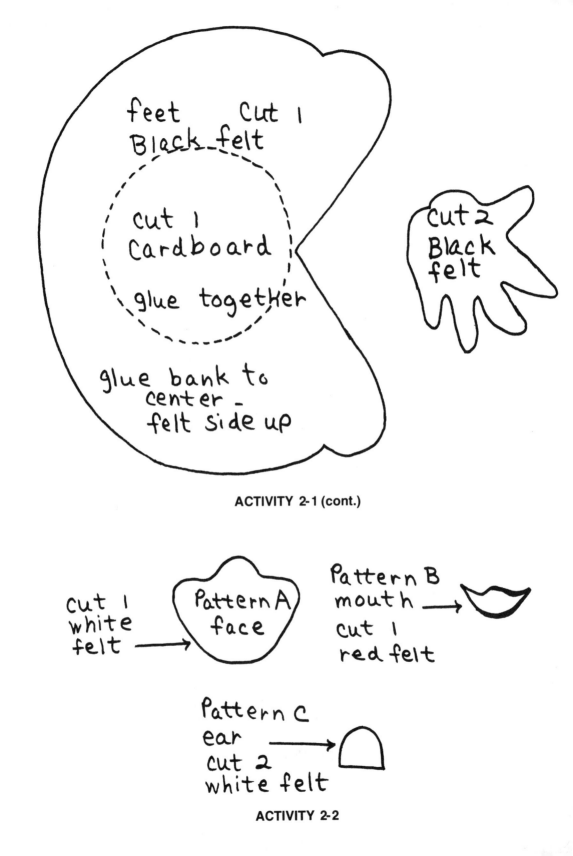

feet   Cut 1
Black felt

cut 1
Cardboard

glue together

glue bank to
center -
felt side up

Cut 2
Black
felt

ACTIVITY 2-1 (cont.)

cut 1
white
felt ——→

Pattern A
face

Pattern B
mouth ——→

cut 1
red felt

Pattern C
ear ——→
cut 2
white felt

ACTIVITY 2-2

ACTIVITY 2-3

Fig. 2-4A

Bank o a Santa

ACTIVITY 2-4

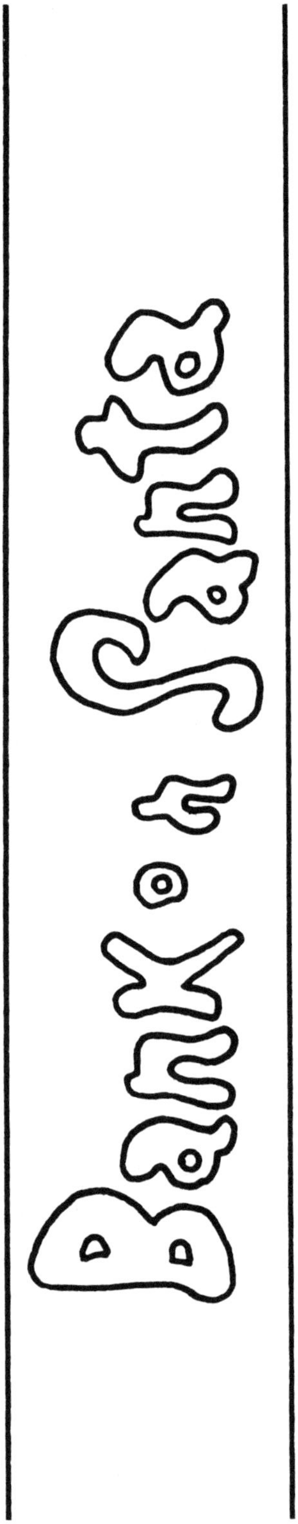

Pattern A white felt cut 1   mouth

Pattern B white felt cut 2 eye

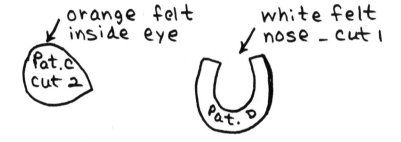

orange felt inside eye

Pat. C cut 2

white felt nose - cut 1

Pat. D

Fig. 2-5-F

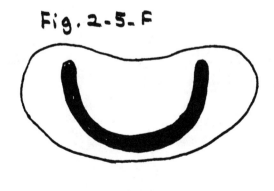

ACTIVITY 2-5

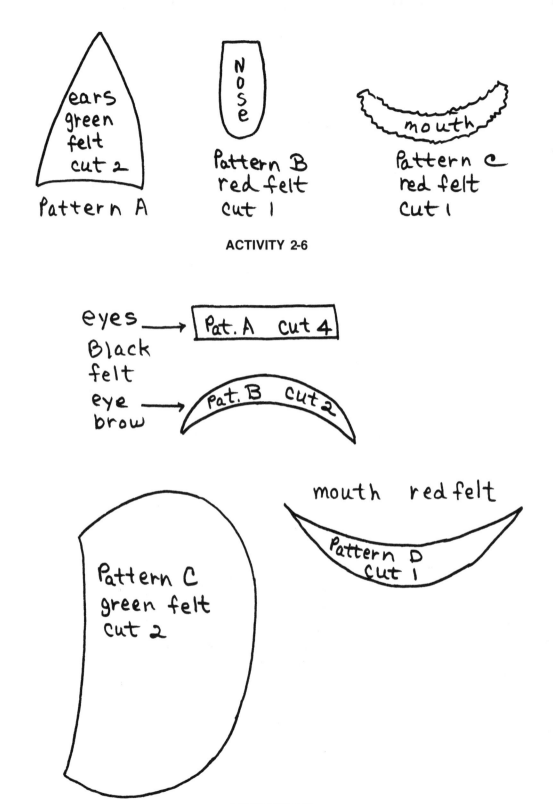

ears
green
felt
cut 2

Pattern A

NOSE

Pattern B
red felt
Cut 1

mouth

Pattern C
red felt
Cut 1

ACTIVITY 2-6

eyes ⟶ Pat. A   Cut 4
Black
felt
eye ⟶ Pat. B   cut 2
brow

mouth   red felt

Pattern D
Cut 1

Pattern C
green felt
cut 2

ACTIVITY 2-7

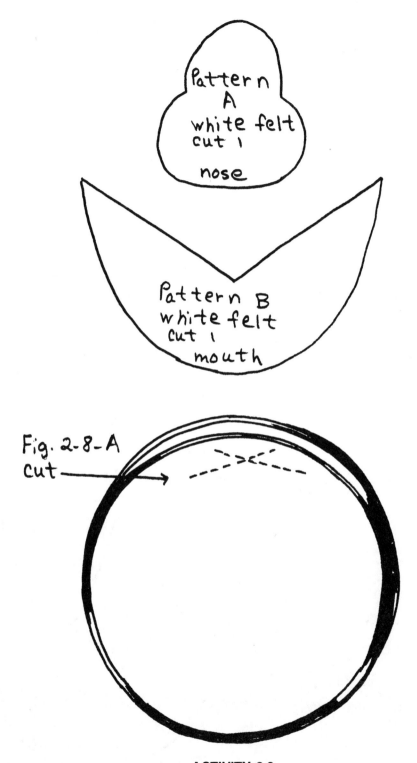

Pattern
A
white felt
cut 1

nose

Pattern B
white felt
cut 1

mouth

Fig. 2-8-A
cut

ACTIVITY 2-8

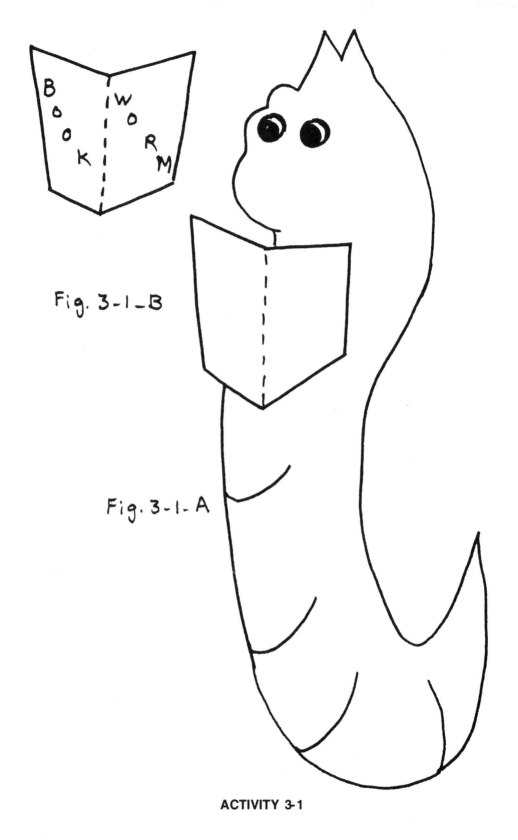

B
O
O
K
W
O
R
M

Fig. 3-1-B

Fig. 3-1-A

ACTIVITY 3-1

Pattern A

Pattern B

Pattern C

ACTIVITY 3-3

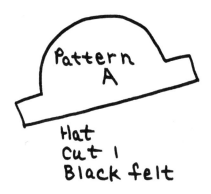

Pattern
A

Hat
Cut 1
Black felt

Pattern B

Eye brow
Cut 2
Black felt

Pat.
C

Nose
cut 1
Black felt

Pattern D
Cut 1
Fake Fur
any Color

ACTIVITY 3-7

Pattern A
cut 2
Purple felt

Pat. B
wing
cut 1
red felt

Pat. c
Bill
cut 1
yellow felt

Pattern D
Feet
yellow felt

Paper Clip
Chain

ACTIVITY 3-8

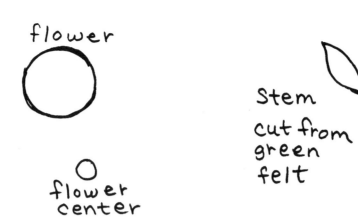

flower

flower center

Stem cut from green felt

leaves

ACTIVITY 4-1

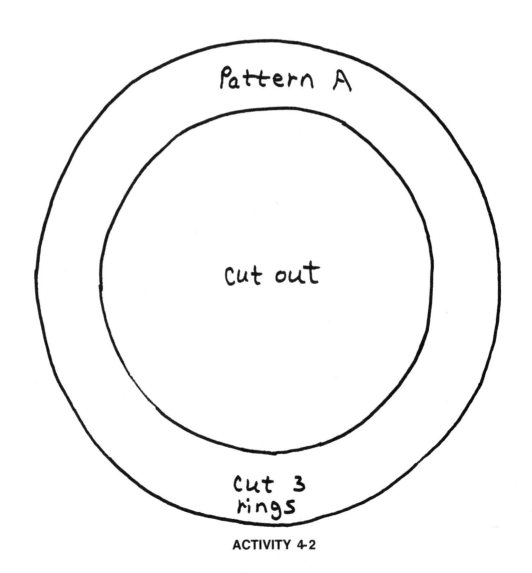

Pattern A

cut out

Cut 3 rings

ACTIVITY 4-2

Fig. 4-4-A

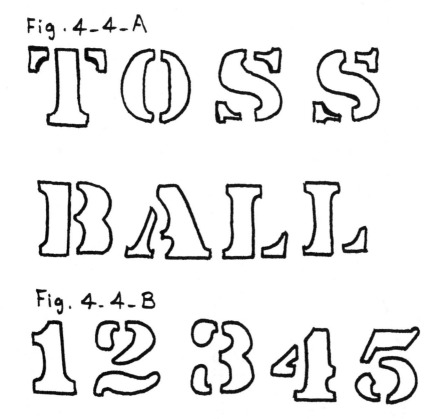

TOSS
BALL

Fig. 4-4-B

12345

ACTIVITY 4-4

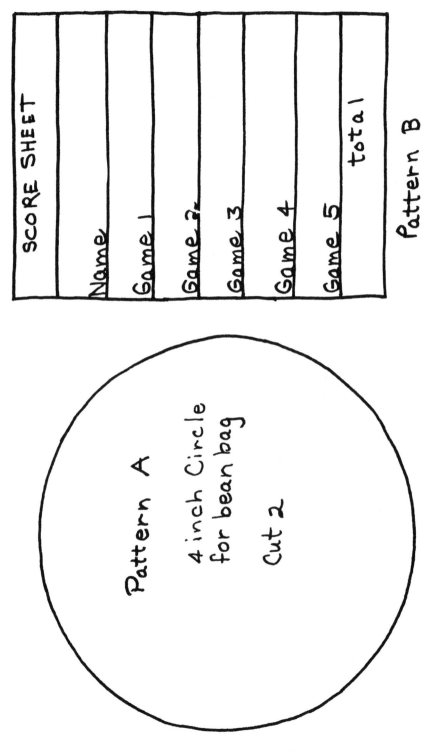

SCORE SHEET

Name	Game 1	Game 2	Game 3	Game 4	Game 5	total

Pattern B

Pattern A

4 inch Circle
for bean bag

Cut 2

ACTIVITY 4-4 (cont.)

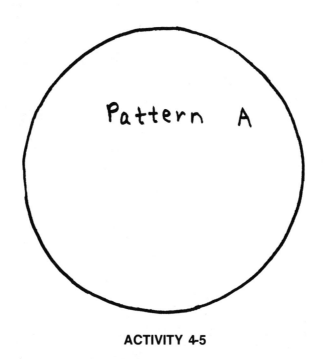

ACTIVITY 4-5

Fig. 4-6-D
5 X 5 inch
Square of
material

ACTIVITY 4-6

red

blue

Yellow

ACTIVITY 4-7

green

green

Pink

yellow

Fig. 4-8-A

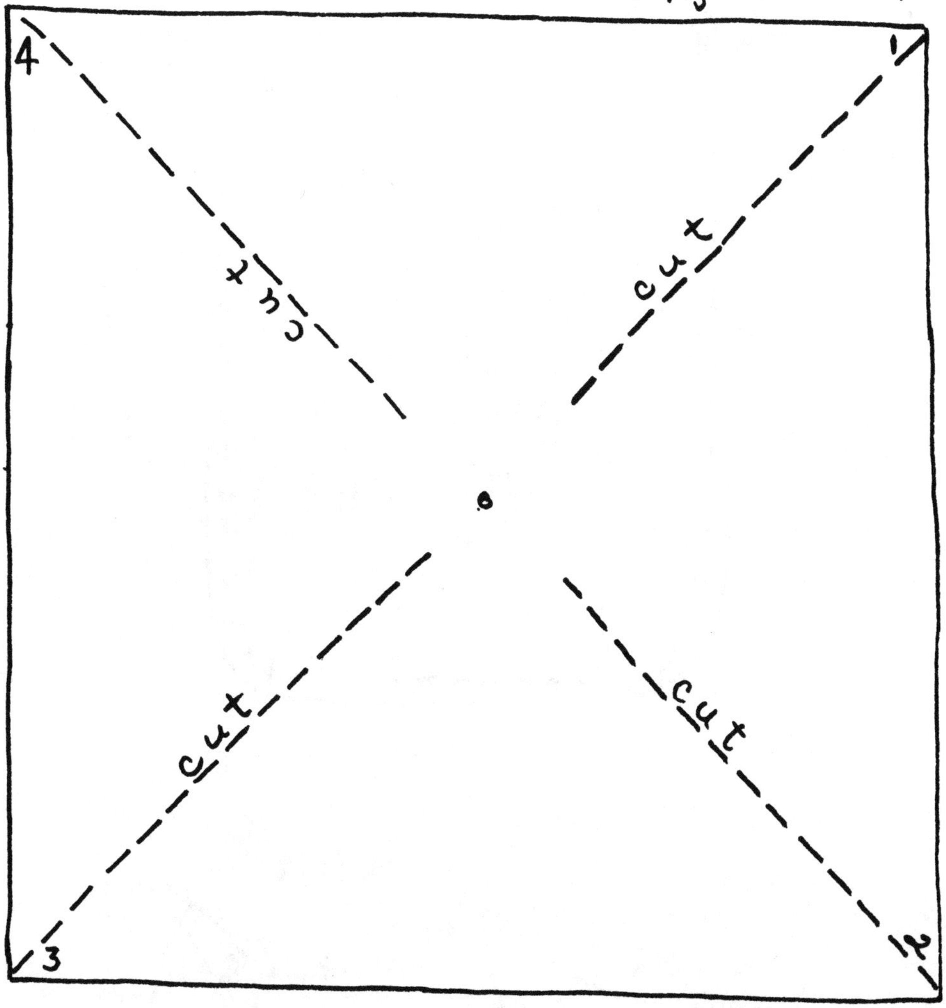

ACTIVITY 4-8

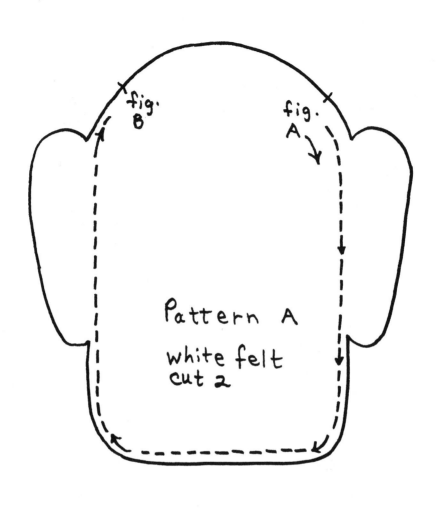

fig.
B

fig.
A

Pattern A

white felt
cut 2

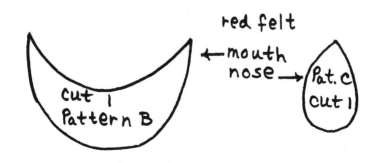

red felt
← mouth
nose →

cut 1
Pattern B

Pat. C
cut 1

ACTIVITY 4-9

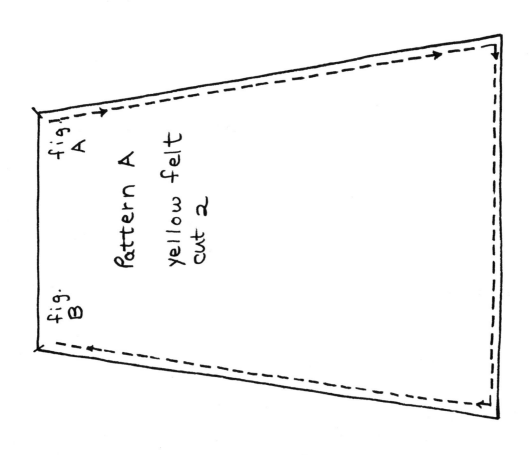

fig. A

fig. B

Pattern A

yellow felt

cut 2

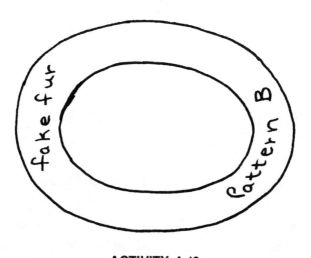

fake fur

Pattern B

ACTIVITY 4-10

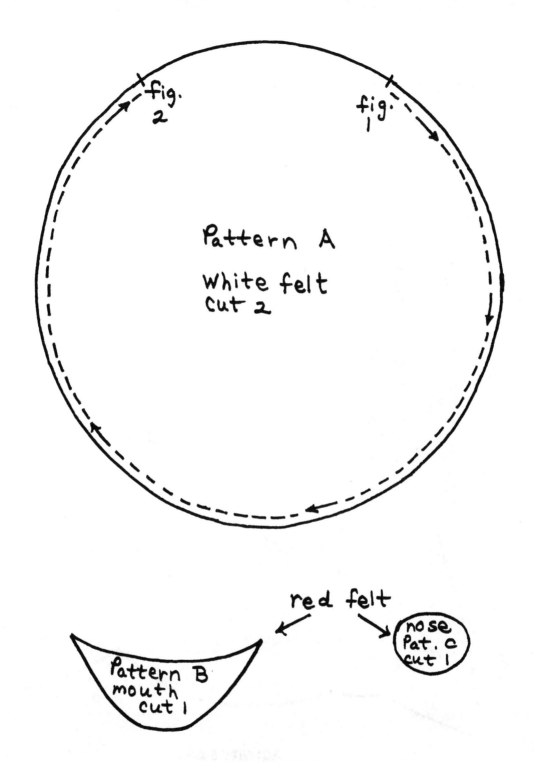

Pattern A

White felt
cut 2

fig. 2

fig. 1

red felt

Pattern B
mouth
cut 1

nose
Pat. C
cut 1

ACTIVITY 4-11

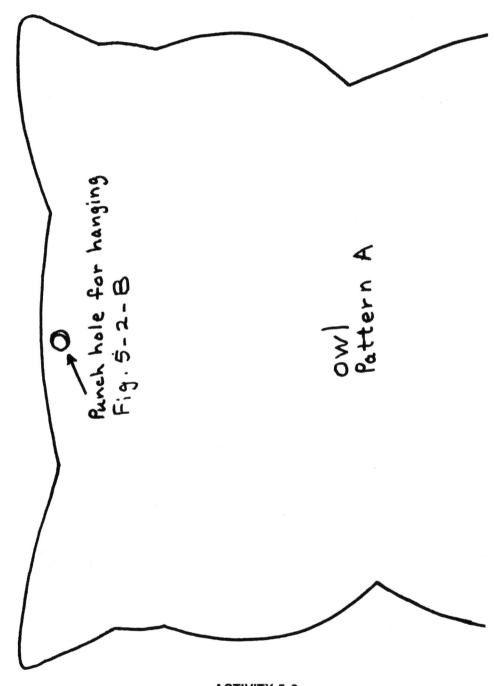

Punch hole for hanging
Fig. 5-2-B

Owl
Pattern A

ACTIVITY 5-2

ACTIVITY 5-2 (cont.)

Pattern B

4 X 5 inches

note book holder

contrasting material

Pattern C

2 x 4 inches

Pencil holder

eyes:
cut 2 _ green felt
cut 2 _ orange felt
use pinking shears

Pattern D
green

Pattern E
orange

Pattern F
cut 1
orange

Pattern G
1x2 inches

ACTIVITY 5-2

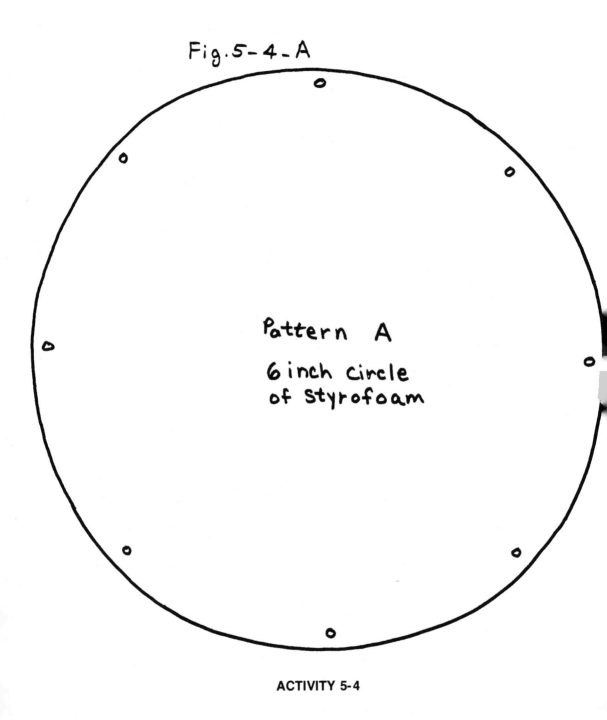

Fig. 5-4-A

Pattern A

6 inch circle
of styrofoam

ACTIVITY 5-4

window
Pattern A

ACTIVITY 5-6A

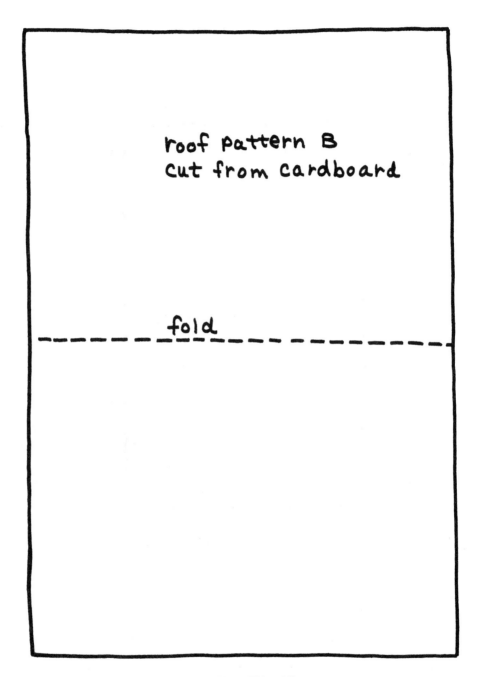

roof pattern B
cut from cardboard

fold

ACTIVITY 5-6B

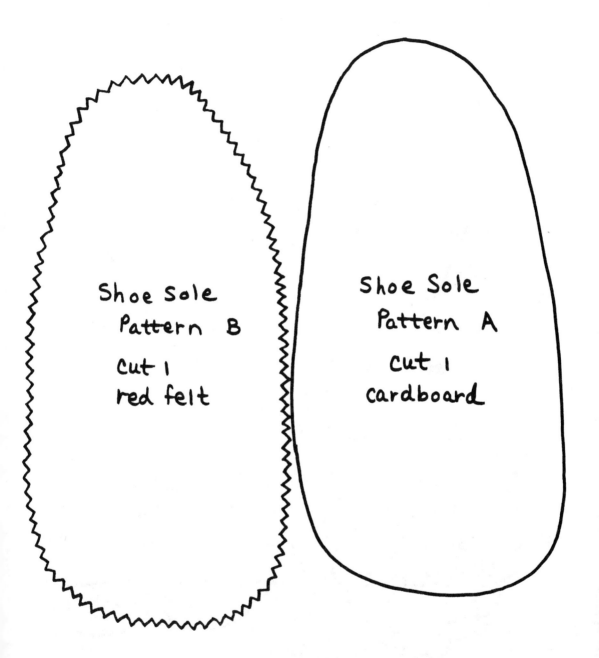

Shoe Sole
Pattern B

cut 1
red felt

Shoe Sole
Pattern A

cut 1
cardboard

ACTIVITY 6-10

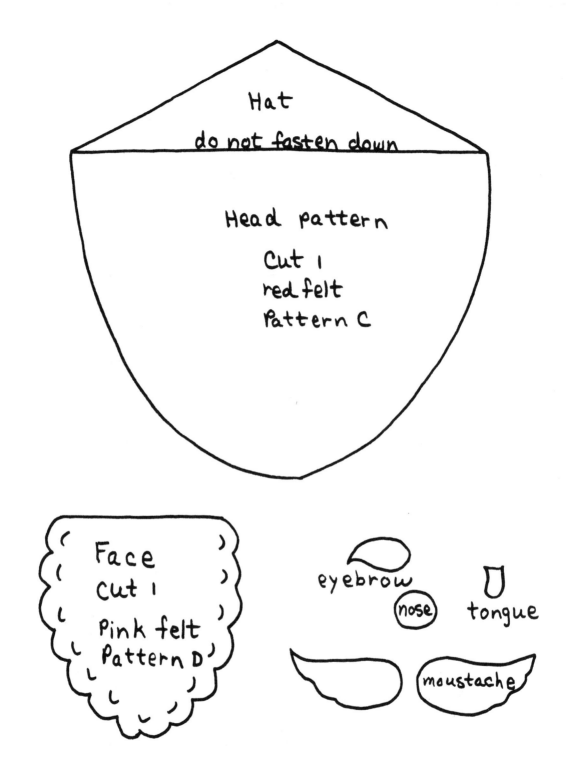

Hat

do not fasten down

Head pattern

Cut 1
red felt
Pattern C

Face
Cut 1

Pink felt
Pattern D

eyebrow

nose

tongue

moustache

ACTIVITY 6-10

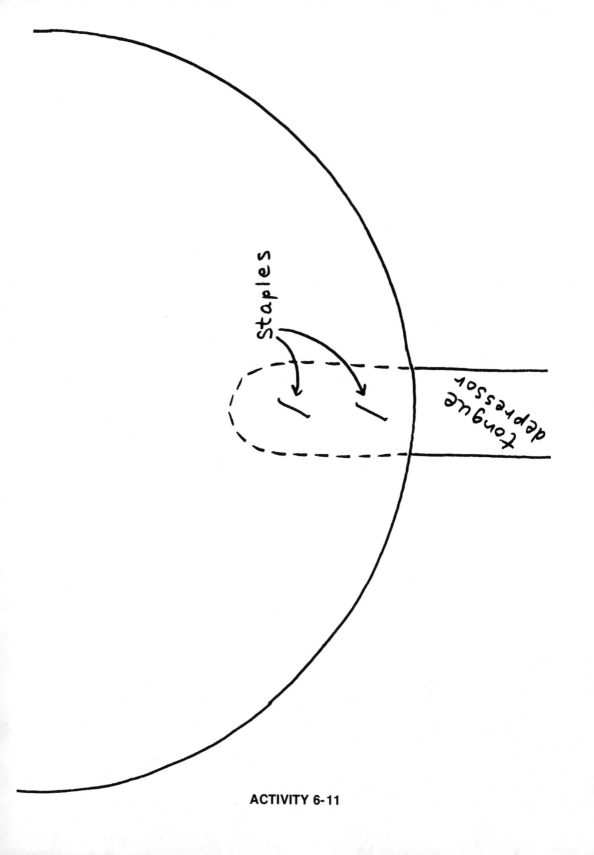

ACTIVITY 6-11

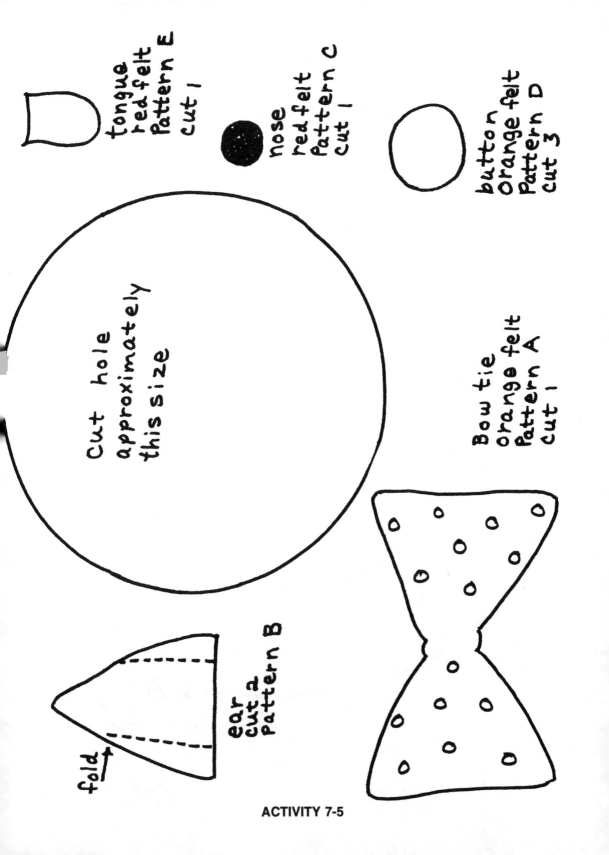

tongue
red felt
Pattern E
cut 1

nose
red felt
Pattern C
cut 1

button
Orange felt
Pattern D
cut 3

Cut hole
approximately
this size

Bow tie
orange felt
Pattern A
cut 1

ear
cut 2
Pattern B

fold

ACTIVITY 7-5

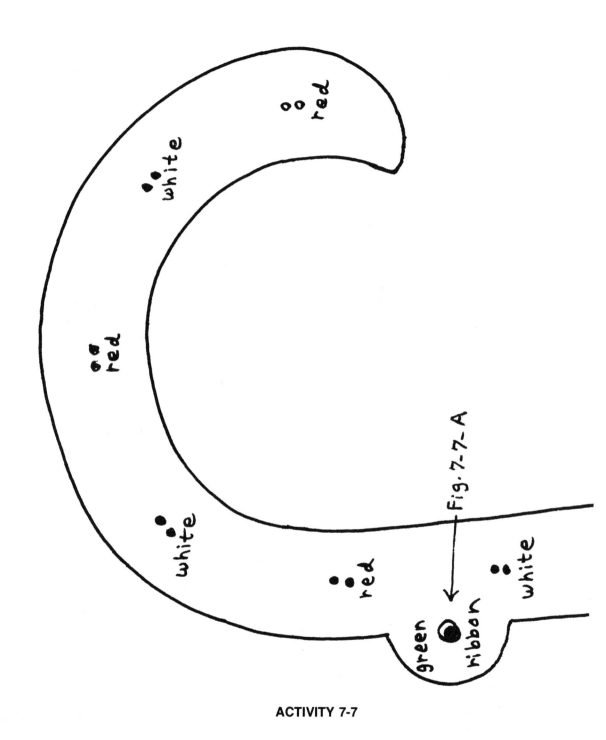

red

white

red

Fig. 7-7-A

white

red

green ribbon

white

ACTIVITY 7-7

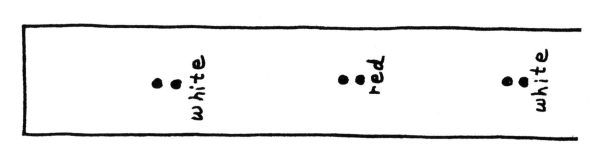

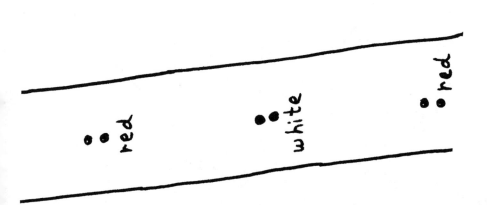

ACTIVITY 7-7

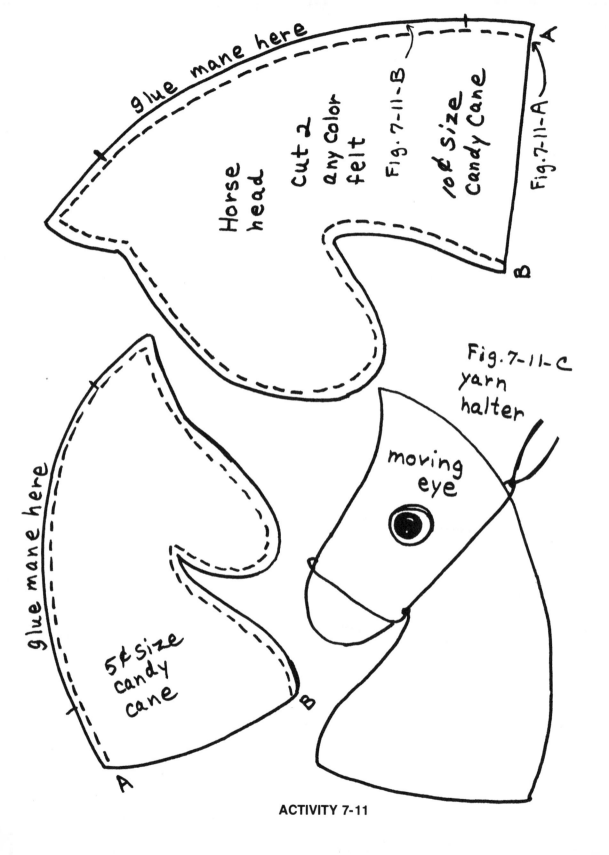

glue mane here

Horse head

Cut 2 Any Color felt

Fig. 7-11-B

10¢ size Candy Cane

Fig. 7-11-A

A

B

Fig. 7-11-C
yarn halter

moving eye

glue mane here

5¢ size candy cane

B

A

ACTIVITY 7-11

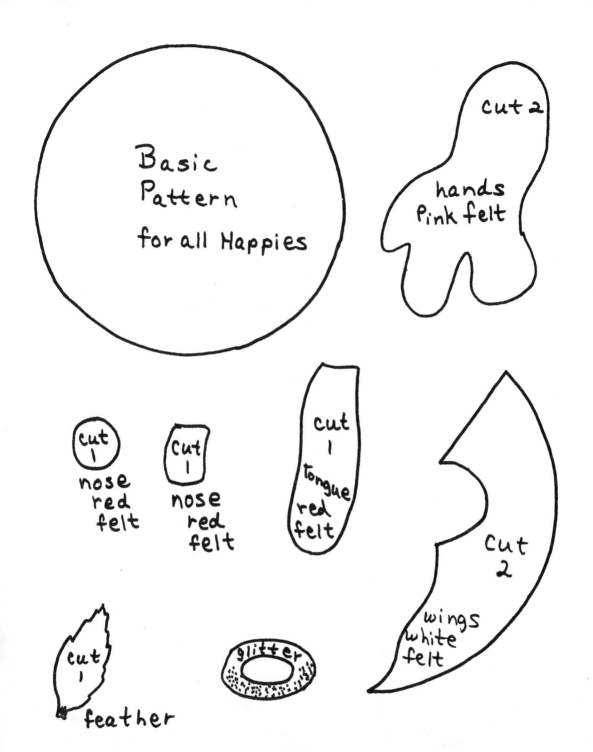

Basic Pattern for all Happies

cut 2
hands Pink felt

cut 1
nose red felt

Cut 1
nose red felt

cut 1
tongue red felt

Cut 2
wings white felt

cut 1
feather

glitter

ACTIVITY 8-4

Pattern A

ACTIVITY 7-9

The small hole is made as the Christmas balls are pushed into the egg cups.

ACTIVITY 8-5

Cut 1
Cardboard
Pattern A

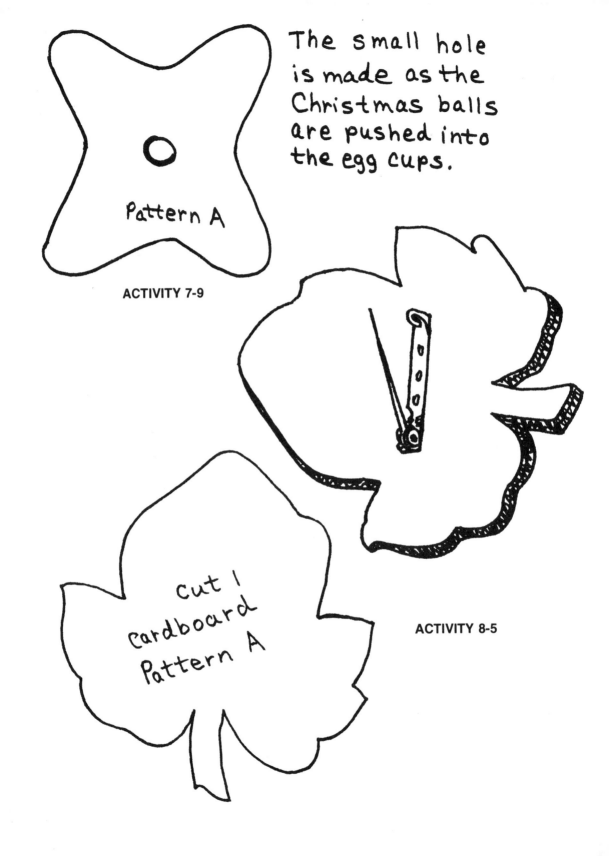

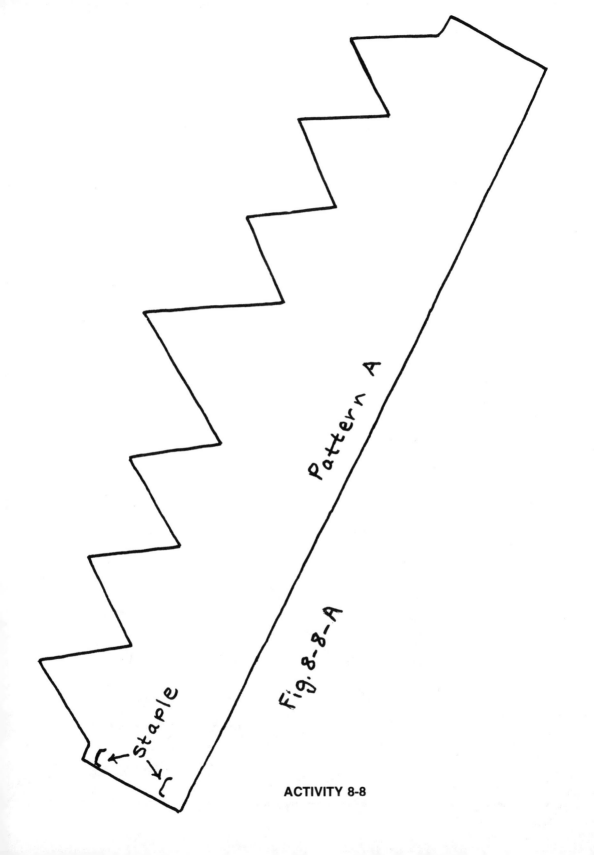

staple

Pattern A

Fig. 8-8-A

ACTIVITY 8-8

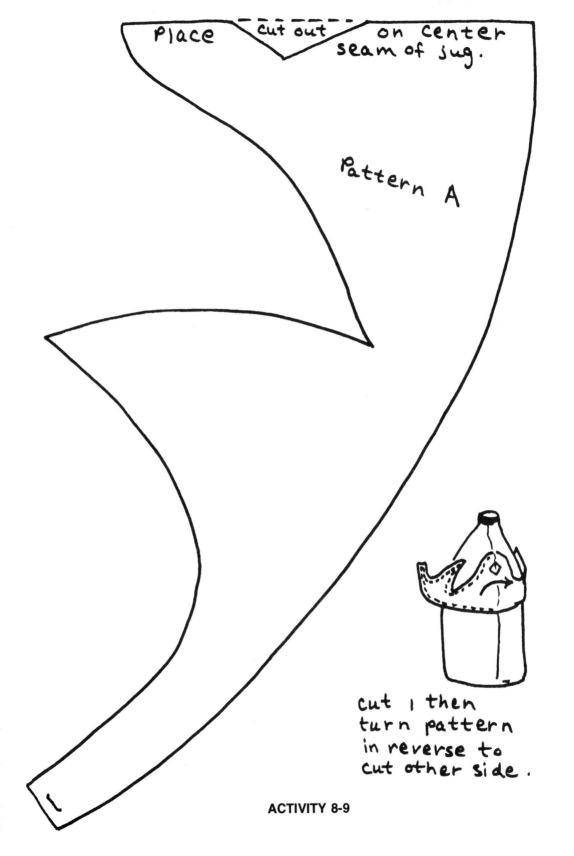

Place cut out on center seam of jug.

Pattern A

cut 1 then turn pattern in reverse to cut other side.

ACTIVITY 8-9

Bow tie
cut 1
Black felt

Pattern
A

Pattern
B

nose
cut 1
Pink felt

Pattern C
mouth
cut 1
Pink felt

ACTIVITY 9-4

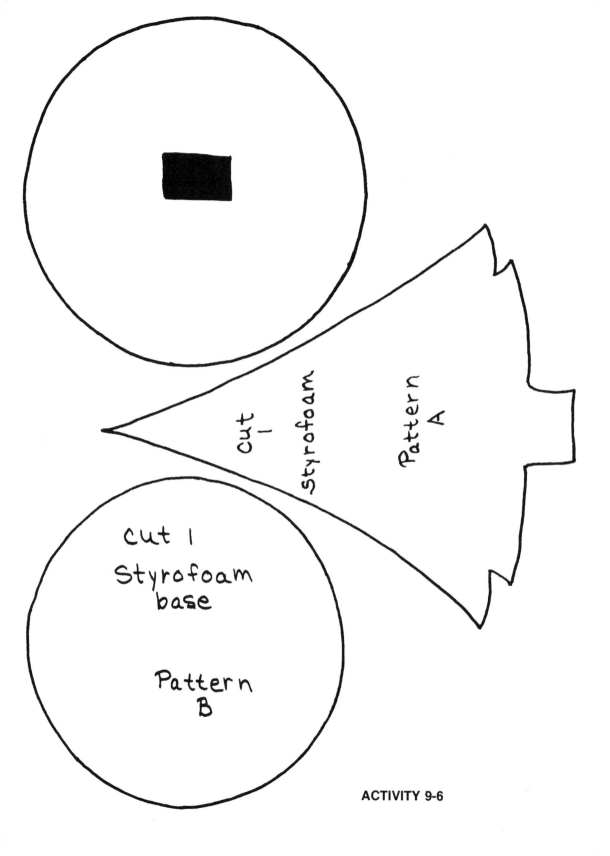

Cut 1 Styrofoam
Pattern A

cut 1
Styrofoam
base

Pattern
B

ACTIVITY 9-6

A

Hat
for Santa

Pattern C

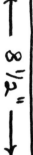

8½"

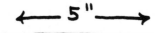

Mouth

Pattern B
cut 1
red felt

Pat. A
Nose

cut 1
red felt

ACTIVITY 9-7

← 5" →

B

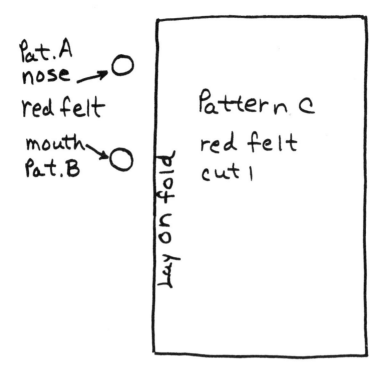

Pat. A
nose
red felt

mouth
Pat. B

Lay on fold

Pattern C
red felt
cut 1

ACTIVITY 9-8

felt flower

cut 2

ACTIVITY 9-13

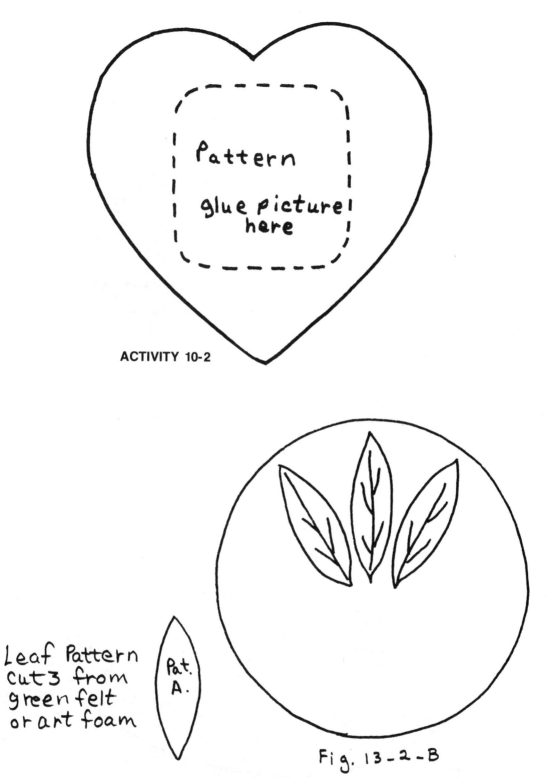

Pattern

glue picture here

ACTIVITY 10-2

Leaf Pattern Cut 3 from green felt or art foam

Pat. A.

Fig. 13-2-B

ACTIVITY 13-2

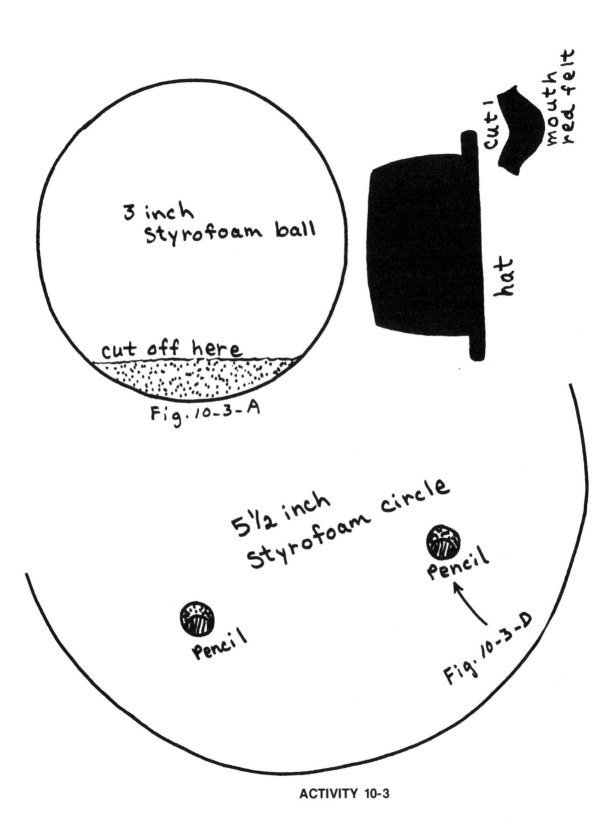

3 inch
Styrofoam ball

cut off here

Fig. 10-3-A

mouth
red felt

cut!

hat

5½ inch
Styrofoam circle

pencil

pencil

Fig. 10-3-D

ACTIVITY 10-3

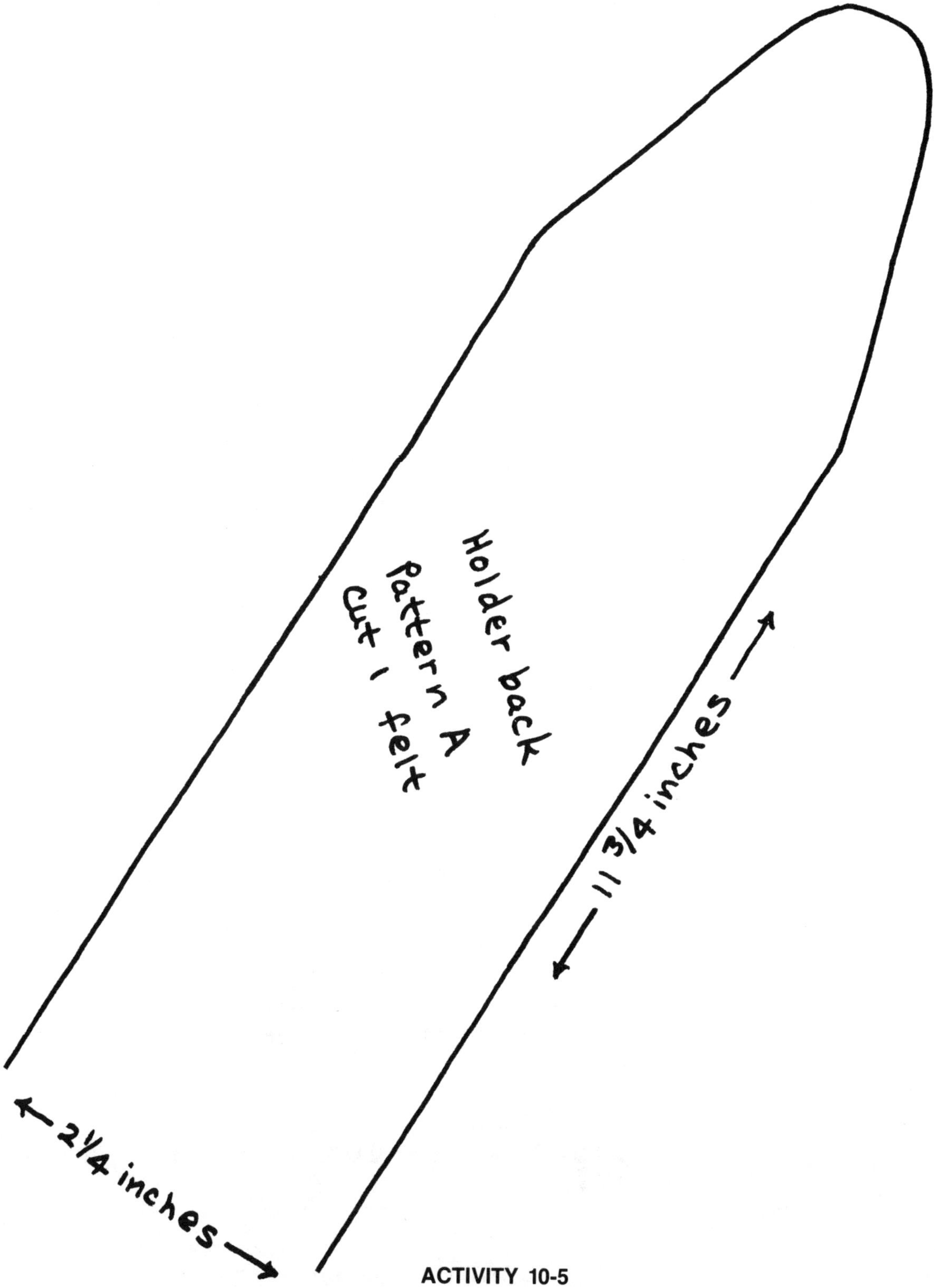

Holder back
Pattern A
Cut 1 felt

11 3/4 inches →

← 2 1/4 inches →

ACTIVITY 10-5

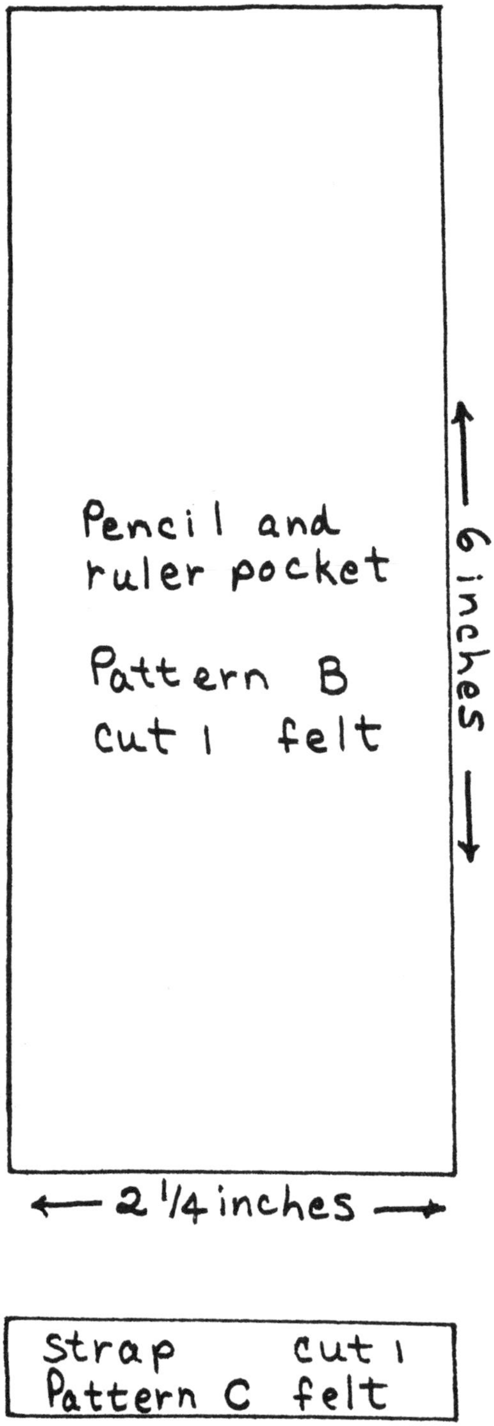

Pencil and
ruler pocket

Pattern B
cut 1 felt

6 inches

← 2 1/4 inches →

Strap   cut 1
Pattern C felt

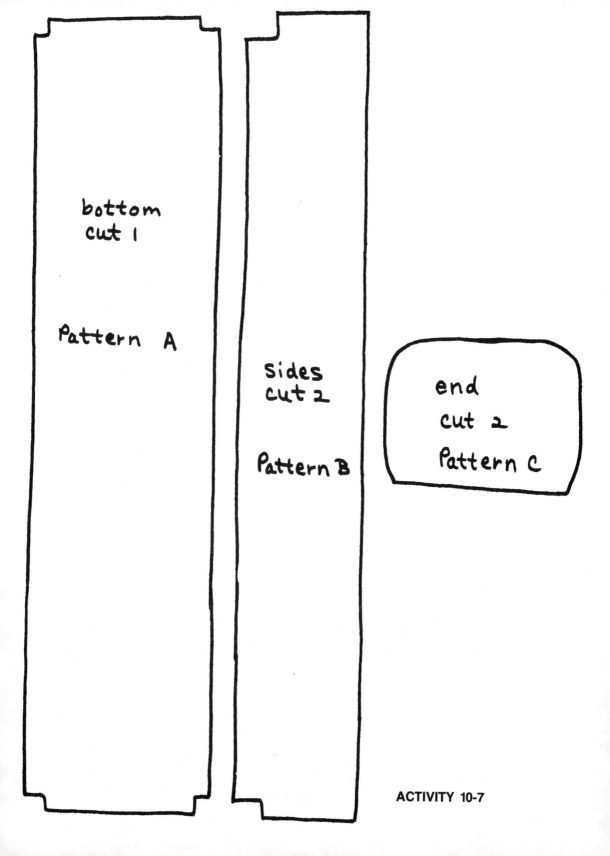

bottom
cut 1

Pattern A

sides
cut 2

Pattern B

end
cut 2
Pattern C

ACTIVITY 10-7

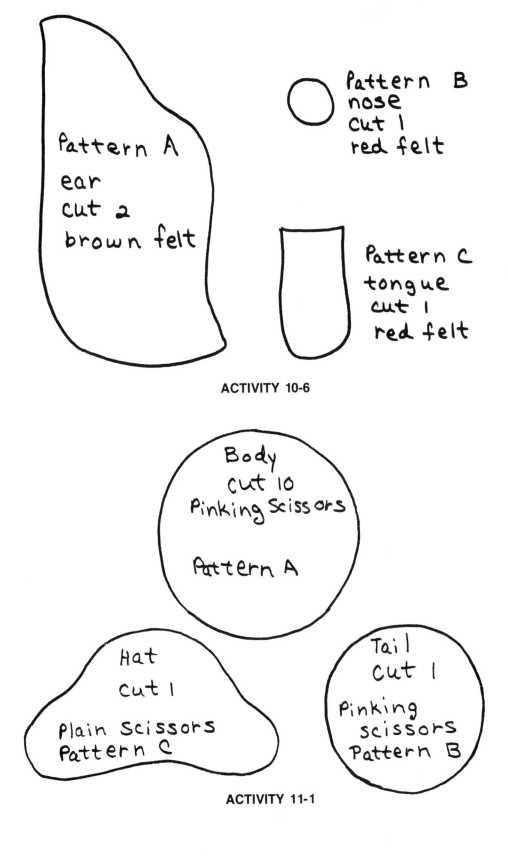

Pattern A
ear
cut 2
brown felt

Pattern B
nose
cut 1
red felt

Pattern C
tongue
cut 1
red felt

ACTIVITY 10-6

Body
cut 10
Pinking Scissors

Pattern A

Hat
cut 1

Plain Scissors
Pattern C

Tail
cut 1

Pinking
scissors
Pattern B

ACTIVITY 11-1

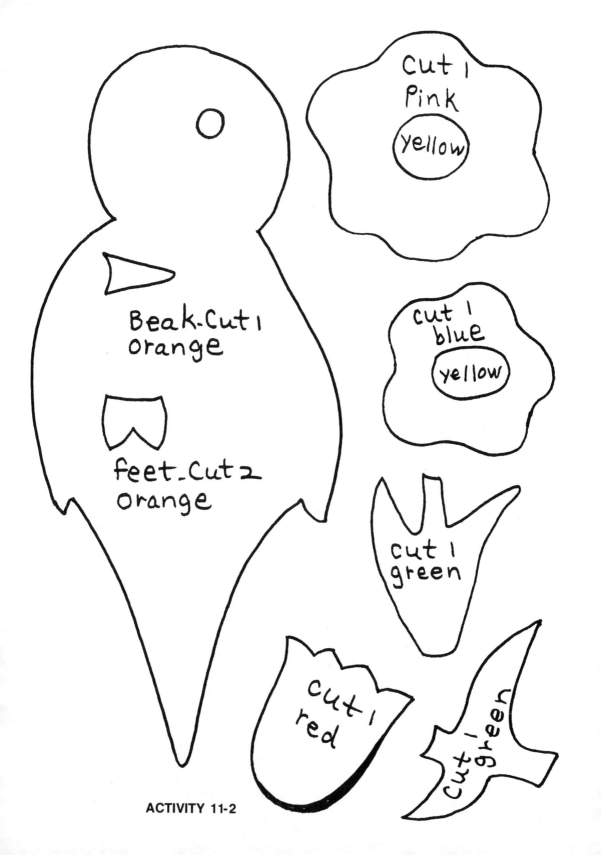

Cut 1
Pink

yellow

cut 1
blue

yellow

Beak. Cut 1
orange

feet. Cut 2
orange

cut 1
green

cut 1
red

Cut 1
green

ACTIVITY 11-2

ACTIVITY 11-3

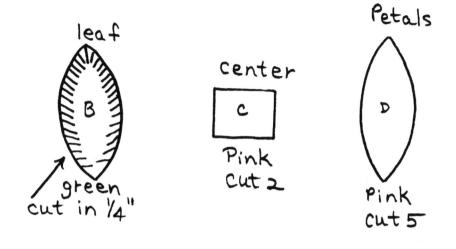

leaf

B

green
cut in ¼"

center

C

Pink
Cut 2

Petals

D

Pink
cut 5

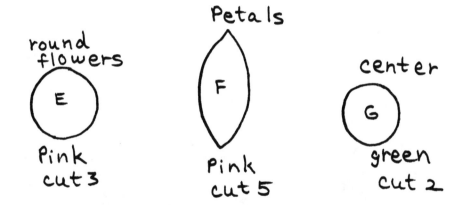

round
flowers

E

Pink
cut 3

Petals

F

Pink
cut 5

center

G

green
cut 2

ACTIVITY 11-3 (cont.)

A
Flower Pot
cut 1
green

Blue Bells

J

Blue
cut 3

Flower

H

Pink
cut 8

Flower

K

yellow
cut 4

Flower

I

Pink
cut 4

ACTIVITY 11-3

ACTIVITY 11-7

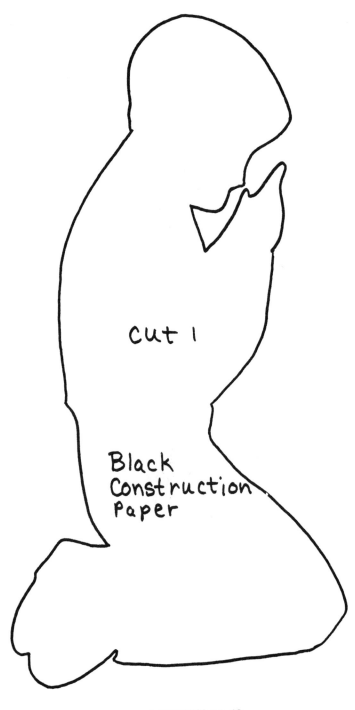

cut 1

Black
Construction
paper

ACTIVITY 11-10

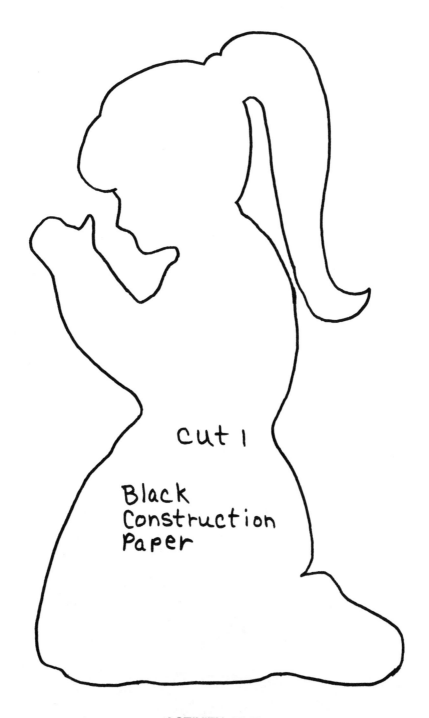

cut 1

Black
Construction
Paper

ACTIVITY 11-10

Fig. 11-11-A
Pattern A

Be Kind

Be Good

Please

Thank you

ACTIVITY 11-11

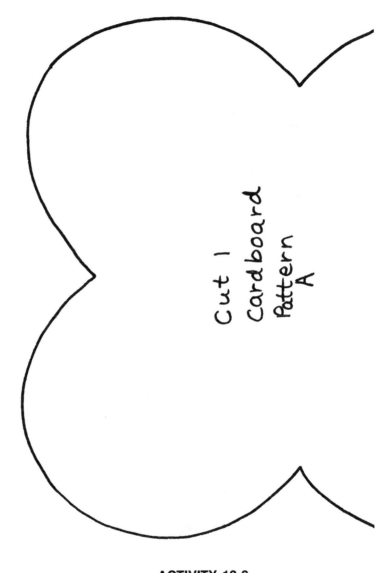

Cut 1
Cardboard
Pattern
A

ACTIVITY 12-2

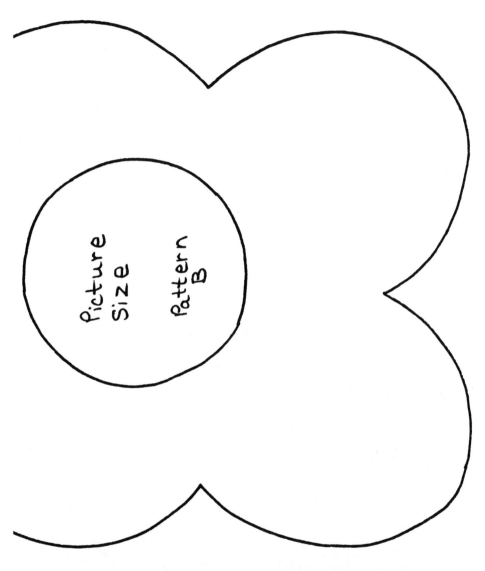

Picture
Size

Pattern
B

ACTIVITY 12-2 (cont.)

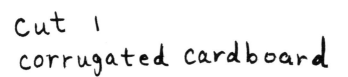

Cut 1
corrugated cardboard

Card Size
Circle

ACTIVITY 12-7

Spots from black felt

cut 1

cut 1

cut 1

cut 1

Fig. 13-4-A

Fig. 13-4-B

nose from black felt

Cut 1 each feet

ACTIVITY 13-4

feet
cut 1
of each
Pattern

cut 2
grey felt

Donkey body

← Fig. 13-5-A

ACTIVITY 13-5

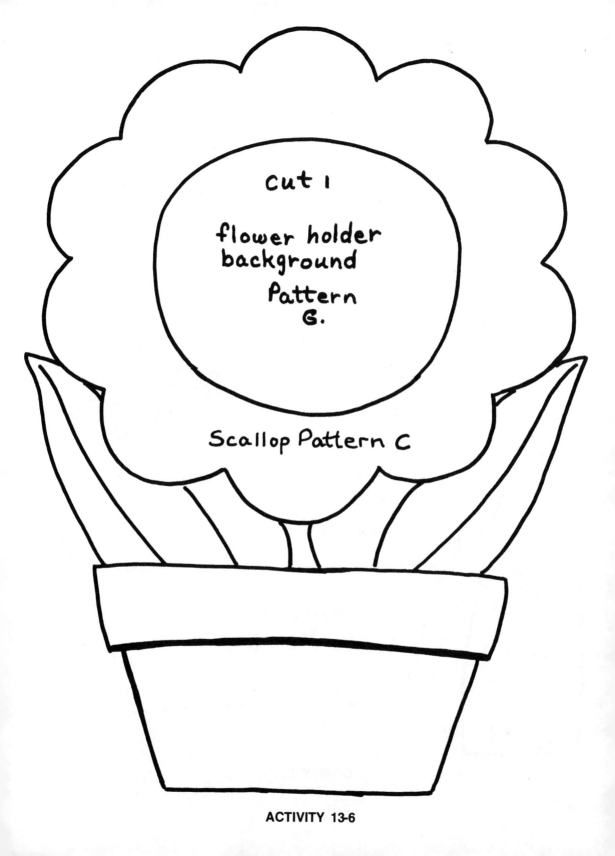

cut 1

flower holder
background
Pattern
G.

Scallop Pattern C

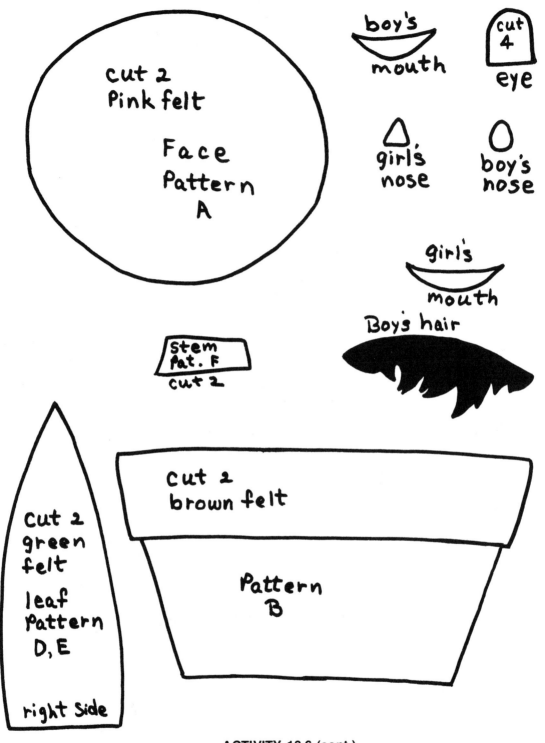

cut 2
Pink felt

Face
Pattern
A

boy's
mouth

cut
4
eye

girl's
nose

boy's
nose

girl's
mouth

Boy's hair

stem
Pat. F
cut 2

cut 2
green
felt

leaf
Pattern
D, E

right side

cut 2
brown felt

Pattern
B

ACTIVITY 13-6 (cont.)

Face
Pattern A
cut 2
white felt

Eye
Pattern D
cut 2 - pink felt

Fig. 13 - 7 - B

Fig. 13 - 7 - C

ACTIVITY 13-7

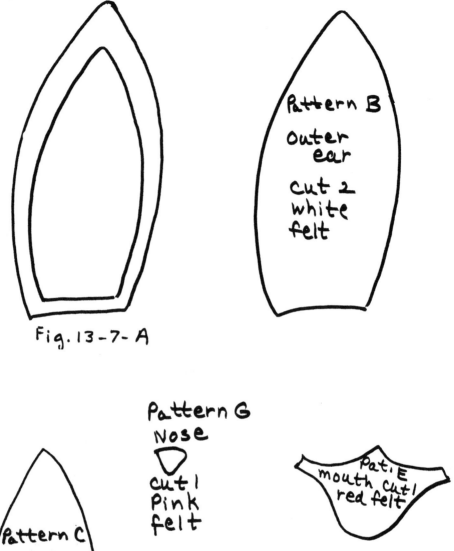

Fig. 13-7-A

Pattern B

Outer ear

cut 2 white felt

Pattern G
Nose

cut 1
Pink
felt

Pattern C
inner ear
cut 2
Pink felt

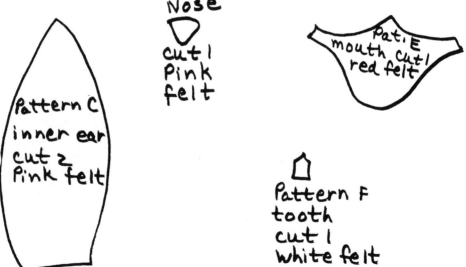

Pat. E
mouth cut 1
red felt

Pattern F
tooth
cut 1
white felt

ACTIVITY 13-7 (cont.)

ACTIVITY 13-7

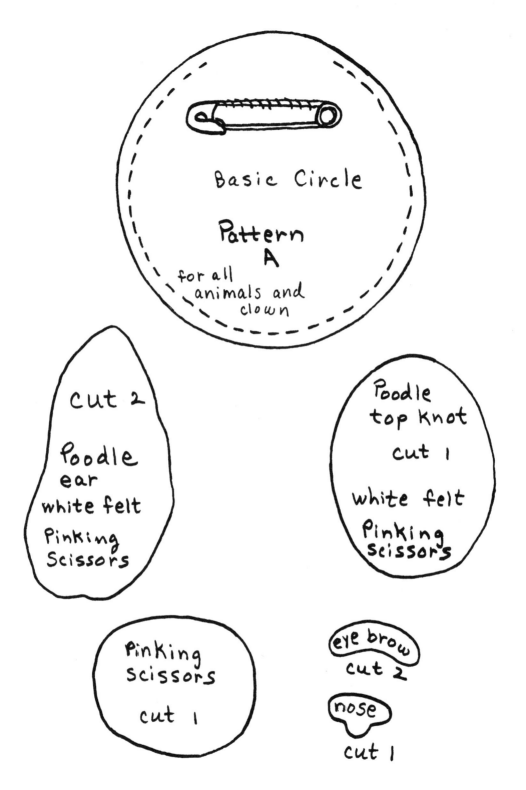

Basic Circle

Pattern
A

for all
animals and
clown

cut 2

Poodle
ear
white felt
Pinking
Scissors

Poodle
top knot

cut 1

white felt

Pinking
Scissors

Pinking
scissors

cut 1

eye brow
cut 2

nose

cut 1

ACTIVITY 14-1

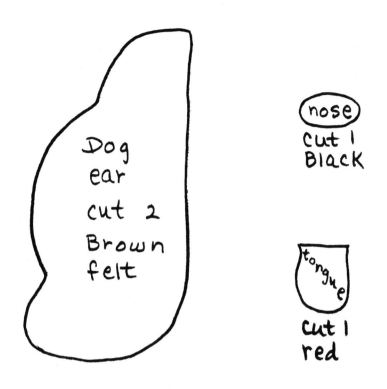

Dog ear cut 2 Brown felt

nose cut 1 Black

tongue cut 1 red

ACTIVITY 14-2

Turtle head cut 1 Pattern D

turtle foot cut 4 Pattern B

cut 1 tail Pat. C

ACTIVITY 14-3

ear
cut 2
white felt

mouth
cut 1
red felt

eye
cut 2
green felt

nose
cut 1
Pink
felt

mouth
cut 1
red felt

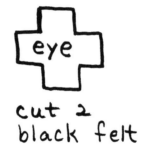

eye
cut 2
black felt

nose
cut 1
red felt

Lion
ear
cut 2
orange felt

tongue
red felt

ACTIVITY 14-4

Hot Pot Mat from beads

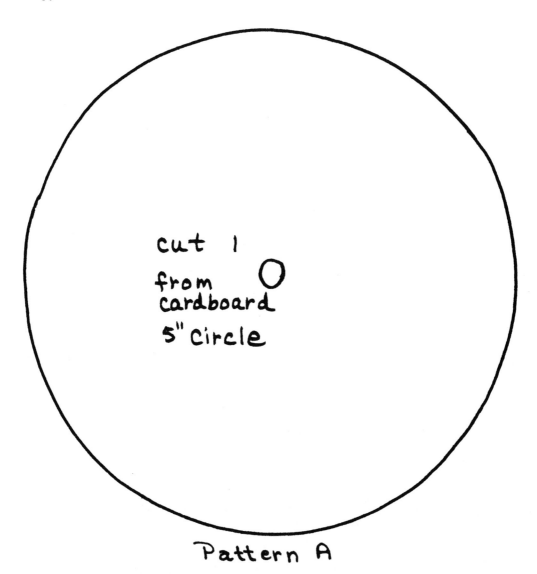

cut 1
from
cardboard
5" circle

Pattern A

ACTIVITY 15-2

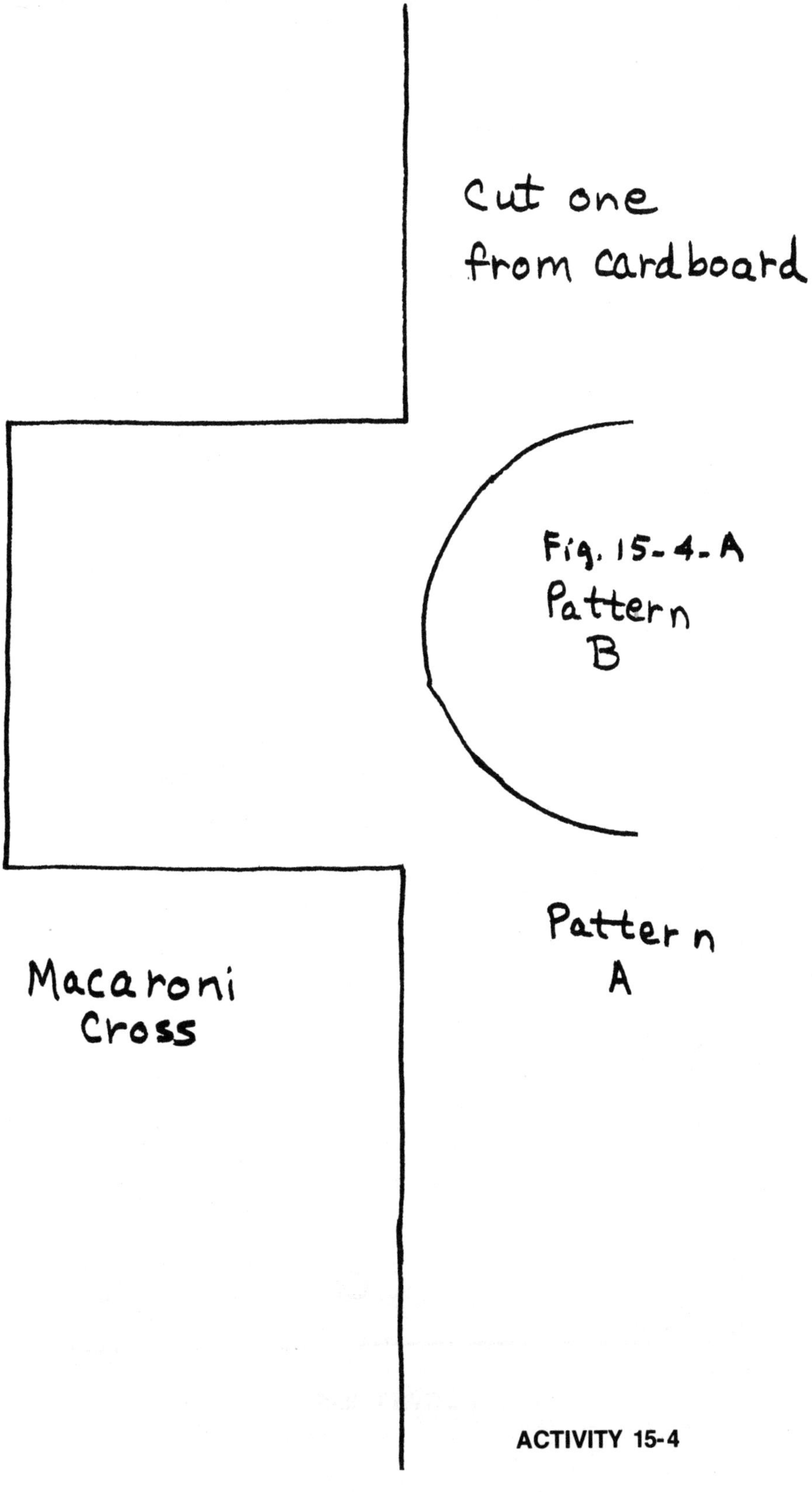

Cut one
from cardboard

Fig. 15-4-A
Pattern
B

Pattern
A

Macaroni
Cross

ACTIVITY 15-4

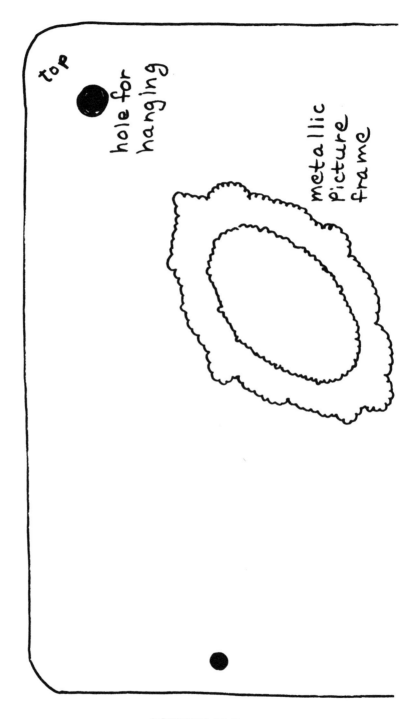

top

hole for hanging

metallic
picture
frame

ACTIVITY 15-5

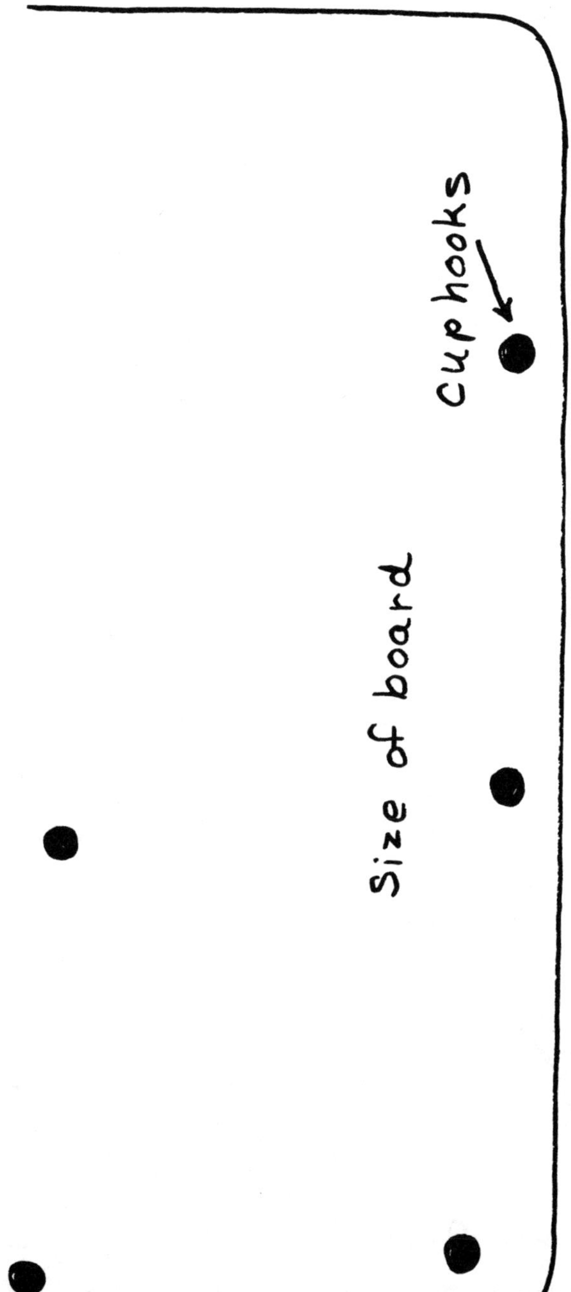

Cup hooks

Size of board

ACTIVITY 15-5 (cont.)

Hat no. 2
cut from
Plastic egg
carton

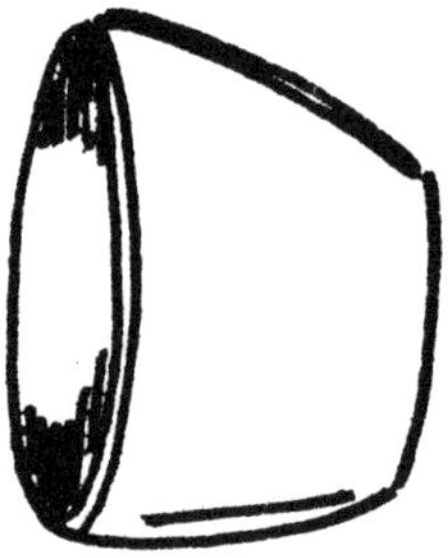

Fig. 15-6-A

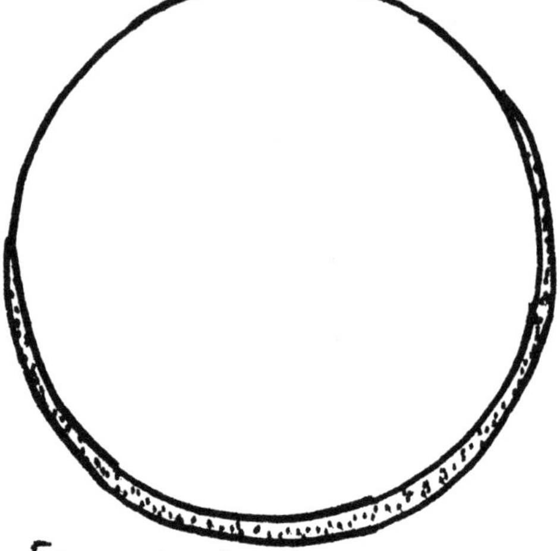

Fig. 15-6-B

Hat no. 3
cut from
Plastic meat
trays

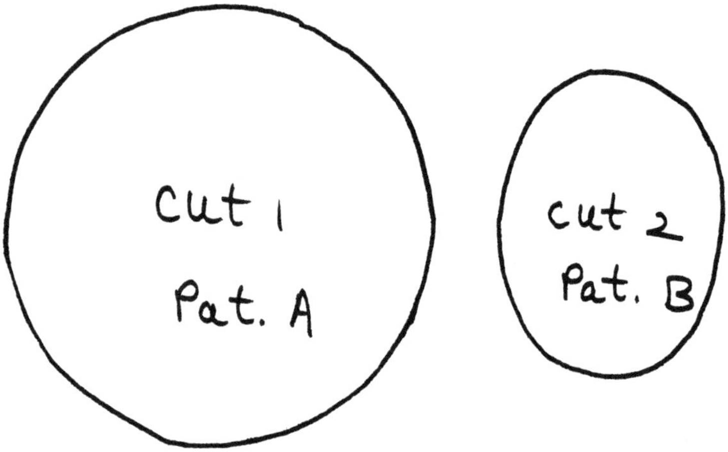

Fig. 15-6-C

Cut 1
Pat. A

cut 2
Pat. B

Hat no. 5
cut from indoor-
outdoor carpeting

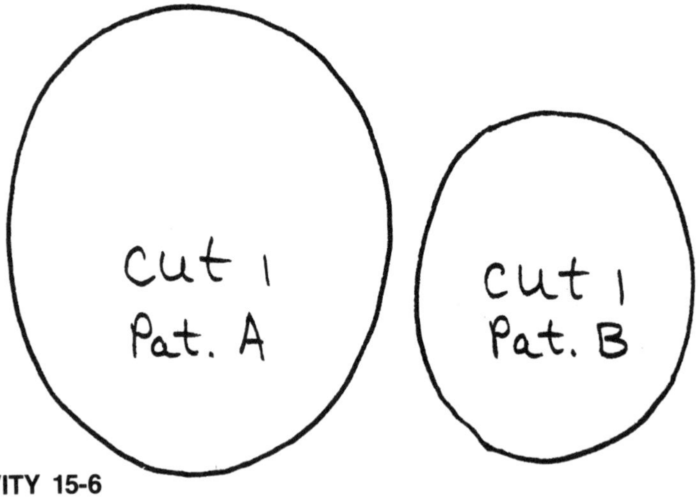

Fig. 15-6-D

Cut 1
Pat. A

cut 1
Pat. B

ACTIVITY 15-6

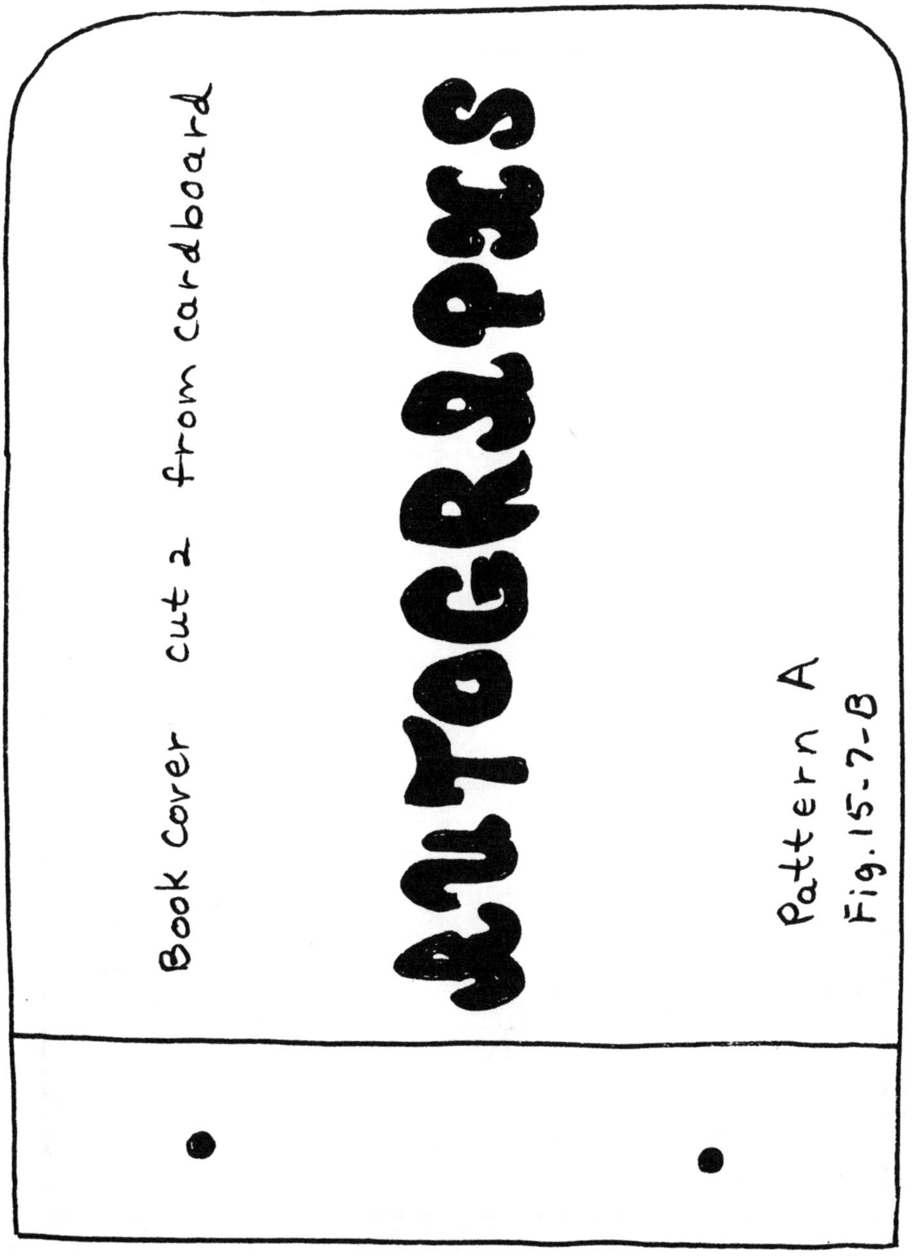

Book Cover   cut 2   from cardboard

AUTOGRAPHS

Pattern A
Fig. 15-7-B

ACTIVITY 15-7

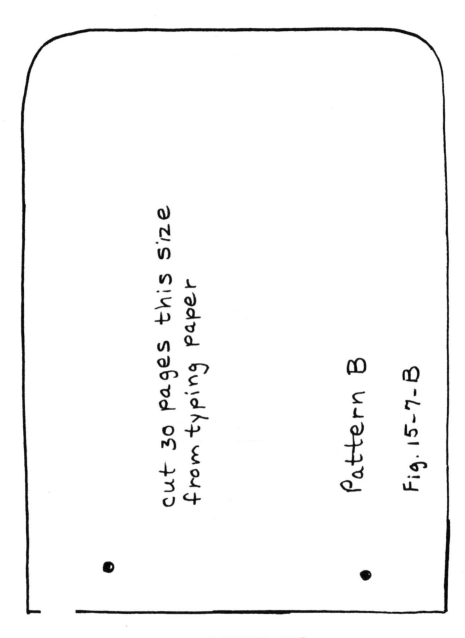

cut 30 pages this size
from typing paper

Pattern B

Fig. 15-7-B

ACTIVITY 15-7B

glue picture
here

←

_ _ _ _ _ _ fold line _ _ _ _ _ _ _

Pattern   A

_ _ _ _ _ _ fold line _ _ _ _ _ _ _

ACTIVITY 15-9

Index